Understanding Maoists

Notes of a Participant Observer from Andhra Pradesh

N. Venugopal

Setu Prakashani
Kolkata Delhi

Understanding Maoists

Notes of a Participant Observer from Andhra Pradesh

by N Venugopal

Cover Design : Ramanajeevi

Cover Page Photo by Sangeveni Ravindra

Many landlords in Telangana fled abandoning their forts as a result of the peasant movement. The picture shows greenplants bursting out of the deserted fort.

venugopalraon@yahoo.com

ISBN : 978-93-80677-42-2 (PB)
978-93-80677-43-9 (HB)

Rupees :Three Hundred and Seventy Five Only (PB)
Seven Hundred Only (HB)

Published by
Archana Das & Subrata Das
on behalf of Setu Prakashani,
12/A Shankar Ghosh Lane, Kolkatta-700 006, India
Ph : +91 33 2219 0704, +9194330 74548

Website : www.setuprakashani.com
e-mail : setuprakashani@gmail.com
setuprakashani@yahoo.co.in

Delhi Branch Office :
A-43, Mahendru Enclave, Galli No. 3
G.T. Karnal Road, Post Office : Azadpur, Delhi - 110 033

Page Layout : C. Rajashekar
Printed by : Sarada Printing Works
9C, Shibnarayan Das Lane, Kolkata - 700 006

In memory of Koti
My brother, comrade, and guide
Whom the world knew as Kishenji

As and When

Part fulfillment of 'Duty to Give'

A revolutionary character in The Wizard of the Crow, an epic novel by Kenyan writer Ngugi wa Thiongo, put it beautifully that everybody in this society has 'right to take and duty to give'. As a participant observer of the most historic and momentous revolutionary people's movement in my native land, Andhra Pradesh, for the last four decades I had exercised my right to take to a large extent and this part fulfillment of my duty to give is in a way a humble and modest repayment.

The Telugu-speaking part of south India, in its present form of Andhra Pradesh or even in its earlier forms, has been a hotbed of alternative thought and practice. The legacy can be traced back to hundreds of years of people's struggles which lingers on as collective memory of defiance, but it would be suffice to say that the influence of communist ideals has been prevalent here since the late thirties of the last century. This land has witnessed the famous Telangana Peasant Armed Struggle (1946-51), the first of its kind in the sub-continent and ever since the fire of people's movements under the influence of Marxism never ceased. Sixteen years after the official withdrawal of the Telangana armed struggle in 1951, it was Srikakulam which responded immediately to the call given by Naxalbari in 1967. Even when the Naxalite upsurge was suppressed at its origin as well as in Srikakulam, it was again Telangana which rekindled the spirit within no time. Not only keeping the fire alive, the revolutionary activists from Andhra Pradesh also spread across the country in the last three decades like seeds in a fertile soil. That's why now invariably the names of Telugu activists come up in any event related to the Maoist movement anywhere in the country. On the other hand, it is the police from Andhra Pradesh with their experience of decades, who go out circumventing administrative borders to collect and supply intelligence to and help in killings and arrests by the police and paramilitary forces in other states. Thus there is always a felt need to understand the events and processes that made this formidable and continuing revolutionary base in the region. Indeed, the story of the Naxalite/Maoist movement in Andhra Pradesh needs to be told in detail to understand this all pervasive importance.

Unfortunately, even as there is an immense felt need, there is also a dearth of commensurate literature on the subject, particularly in English. A comprehensive history of the four-decade old Maoist movement in Andhra Pradesh is yet to be written. The literature available on the subject in English, besides the ill-informed journalistic quick cookies and occasional references in much larger accounts with a different focus, is restricted to one or two academic works and one police version. An activist's insider account or a sympathetic observer's narration from outside is conspicuously absent.

This book, however, cannot make a claim to fill the void. Despite a strong desire to take up that stupendous task, postponing it for future, I wanted to collect some of my earlier published and unpublished notes and articles into this volume. I have been a close observer of the movement since my childhood and came of age with it, had also tried to publish most of my observations as and when possible. Besides being an observer, I had an opportunity of being a participant in students', literary and general social movements for over three decades. Though ceased to be a participant (rather thrown out of Revolutionary Writers' Association in 2009 for a political blunder I committed), I continue to be a keen observer of, as well as a strong believer in, the movement.

Throughout I have been taking notes and at least since the early 1980s I have been publishing them, both in Telugu and English. These notes evolved out of my moral responsibility, philosophical perspective, and political conviction and found expression by the times I lived in. As successive steps in social history they are as much collective as mine. My role as a chronicler might have added, subtracted, ignored, suppressed, distorted, threw a new light on the various obtaining aspects of the times, but nevertheless, those were the 'times'a changing' and I was a miniscule part of that cauldron. In these notes, written as and when the social current flowed, I tried to capture the ebb and tide of the current, but I am sure there might have been some transmission and distribution losses in my comprehension, capturing and presenting the current to larger audience. Since there are not many accounts of the movement in Andhra Pradesh, I am humbly presenting this collection, despite its possible inadequacies.

In all these activities – participation, observation, understanding, taking notes and publishing them – I was helped and encouraged by hundreds of friends, some of them brutally killed by State in the course of time and some had to remain nameless or under different acquired identities in order to postpone the immanent untimely death. That's why these notes, in the first place, belong to all those who laid down their invaluable life in the cause of people. I happened to closely know hundreds of them. I was an admirer, perhaps a messenger and a friend and a follower, of them. When I say that these are result of my moral responsibility, I mean I owe that responsibility to the departed friends. We cherished the same dream and their dream was cut short by the State's brutal bullets. I think it is my duty to letter their unfulfilled dream. My moral responsibility also extends to all those acquainted and unacquainted friends who continue the struggle in the face of death. And of course, the moral responsibility is more towards the exploited and oppressed masses of this country struggling for liberation.

Apart from the moral responsibility, my philosophical perspective and political conviction also form basis to this effort. The philosophical perspective is an unabashed, unrepentant and firm belief in Marxism-Leninism-Maoism and my political conviction is that Naxalbari, with all its difficulties and ups and downs, had shown the real way for the liberation of oppressed and exploited Indian masses.

The first essay in chronological order 'Tendu Leaf Labourers of Telangana' was written in a hot summer in 1984 and its story needs to be recollected here. Reading several inspiring reports on the ongoing struggles of tendu leaf pickers in Karimnagar forests appearing regularly in *Kranti*, the then fortnightly organ of the CPI (ML) (Peoples' War), AP State Committee, I asked Mallojula Koteswara Rao (the then Secretary of the AP State Committee under the name Prahlad) whether I could use those reports and write a piece to *Economic and Political Weekly*. He asked me to meet the person in charge of the struggle and get the first hand facts, rather than depending on published reports and arranged my meeting with Muppala Lakshman Rao (perhaps, the then secretary of Karimnagar district committee). I spent a whole day with him, who after two decades would become Ganapathy, the general secretary of the CPI (Maoist) and the *bête noire* of Indian State, collected a lot of data and filed the report to the EPW. As a first year student of M.A. (Economics), I was not only diffident in my English, but also unsure of my position of whether I was a participant or a reporter. Krishna Raj, editor, EPW allayed my fears of diffidence by publishing it immediately and the friendship with him continued till his death. I fondly cherish the memories of Koteswara Rao (who later became Kishenji), Lakshman Rao and Krishna Raj.

Subsequently, different occasions and demands, events and processes inspired and forced me to write the other notes and rereading each of them makes me relive that past filled with tears and blood, perhaps a few smiles, and excitement. But that past does not remain there static and is ever moving dynamically in a continuous search for newer alternatives for a wider present and bright future. The idea of collecting these articles of/on the past into a single volume would be fulfilled if it helps in a better understanding of the present and the future.

- N V

Hyderabad,

October 9, 2012

❖ ❖ ❖

Acknowledgements

Because of its sheer enormity, acknowledging the help and cooperation of friends towards this work that spread over thirty years, and sufficiently thanking them is highly difficult. Every expression – facts, figures, details, explanations, anecdotes, analyses, arguments – and the thought process itself could well be linked to a friend or a group of friends or a book or a point in time. And to the people's movements in myriad ways. Simply put one has to record immense gratitude to all those who directly or indirectly shaped and determined one's social being and consciousness.

Being an infinitesimal part of the gigantic powerhouse of social movements, I came into contact with thousands of people and learnt something or other from each of them. While the force and course of history pushed some of those friends away from me, their memories come back quite often in unfathomable ways. The same history brought some friends nearer to heart even when they are far away. There are yet other friends with whom I continue to walk, think, write and act. It is my duty to remember and thank some of them.

First of all, I have to acknowledge hundreds of martyrs who laid down their precious lives untimely in the course of Indian revolution. Without their work and sacrifice this book could not have been written. They are too many to name here but each name is chiseled in blood and tears on my heart. Surapaneni Janardhan, Jannu Chinnalu, Saini Prabhakar, Gopagani Ilaiah, Puli Anjaiah, Chintala Venkataswami, A Santosh Reddy, Nalla Adi Reddy, G Lingamurthy, Diwakar, E Veeraswami, Sakhamuri Appa Rao, Patel Sudhakar Reddy, Azad and Kishenji are only a few names in that long list I fondly remember.

Then I have to acknowledge hundreds of friends who are in the process of building Indian revolution braving death almost every second. Wherever they are spread across the hills and forests and villages and towns and jails of this country, they have a special warm place in my heart.

During the time I was writing these notes I was helped by several members of Radical Students Union, Radical Youth League, Raithu Cooli Sangham, Singareni Karmika Samakhya, Andhra Pradesh Civil Liberties Committee, Chaitanya Mahila Samakhya, All India League for Revolutionary Culture, All India Peoples' Resistance Forum, Revolutionary Democratic Front, Andhra Pradesh Teachers Federation, Democratic Teachers Federation and other mass organisations. I gratefully acknowledge the time I spent and the discussions I had with all the known and unknown friends from the organisations.

My thinking, writing and entire practice evolved out of *Sahiti Mitrulu,* the group that ran *Srjana*, my second nature. Of the three decades I wrote these notes, twenty seven years I was a member of Revolutionary Writers' Association and I owe a lot to that organisation. Though I am not a part of it right now, my gratitude to the organisation is immeasurable and inerasable.

Of course, I cannot leave all the people helped me faceless and nameless. C V Subba Rao, RS Rao, K G Kannabiran, K V Ramana Reddy, Cherabanda Raju, T Madhusudan Rao, K Balagopal, G Haragopal, C Prasad, Gaddar, G Kalyan Rao, T Krishnabai, CSR Prasad, G Prasadam, V Chenchaiah, G Pinakapani, S Ravikumar, V V Narayana Swamy, Sudhakiran, G Srinivasulu, Arun, S Seshaiah, V Mohan Prasad, Ashok Kumbam, Alpa Shah, B Anuradha, K Anuradha, K Sudha, V Vasantalakshmi, A Annapurna, G Udaya, K Dileep Reddy, Shivasundar, N Babaiah, M Bharathi, K R Chowdry, B S Raju, V Hanumantha Rao, P Aravinda, K Bal Reddy are among the many whom I thank for their contributions in their own different ways to my thought and expression.

I am grateful to the editors of Economic and Political Weekly, Frontier, Tehelka, The Economic Times, Deccan Chronicle, Andhra Pradesh Times, Mean Time, MRZine, Comprehensive History of Andhra Pradesh, and Fifty Years of Andhra Pradesh who published these notes earlier. I would also like to thank the organisers of various seminars where some of these papers were presented.

The team at Veekshanam, Telugu monthly that I currently edit - Y Ramachandram, D V Ramakrishna Rao, S Venkatesh - have been part of me and my work for the last ten years and thanking them would be superfluous. C Rajasekhar of Veekshanam team also helped me in page layout and presentation.

My immediate family and extended families have been a source of strength to keep my spirits alive in my bad times and without their support I could not have written these notes. Varavara Rao is not only a family member, but also a hero and a model for me and gratitude would be a gross inadequate word. Similarly, I cannot thank my companion C Vanaja and our son Vibhaatha since they occupy my entire world – both physical and mental space and time.

Even though there were different plans for a long time to write fictional or non-fictional narratives on the Naxalite movement in Andhra Pradesh or at least to bring all the published articles together, this plan would not have seen the light of the day if Ajay Dandekar and Amit Bhattacharyya have not encouraged me to do that. Bhattacharyya had also taken pains to propose it to Subrata Das of Setu Prakashani who accepted it at once. I cannot fully express my gratitude to Subrata Das.

I

Context

This section, consisting of five pieces written or published between 1999 and 2007, attempts to provide a picture of social, political, economic and cultural state of Andhra Pradesh in order to locate the people's consciousness and struggles in a proper perspective. Even as a lot being written about the influence of Maoists on Telugu society, there do not seem to be sufficient studies to understand what elements of that society had provided a fertile base for the spread of the influence. Usual police accounts, picked up by journalists quite often, would like to think and make the readers believe that it is with gun and coercion the Maoists are holding their power on the minds of Telugu people. As a person deeply involved in social movements, obaserved thousands of people influenced by Maoists and intimately knew several Maoists themselves, I think it is not the Maoists that influence Telugu society, but the influence is mutual and dynamic. A number of historians have shown that the Telugu society has been very vibrant, progressive and defiant for quite a few centuries, thanks to a number of geographic, social, economic and political factors. The five essays included here do not go back that far into history, but try to capture what has been happening in the last five decades since the state was formed. At times, the narration goes back in history till the early part of the last century.

The first three essays were part of 'Fifty Years of Andhra Pradesh 1956 – 2006', co-edited by me along with Prof R S Rao and V Hanumantha Rao. Conceived and published by Centre for Documentation, Research and Communications (CDRC), Hyderabad, this huge volume quite ambitiously wanted to be a comprehensive reference tome on the state and the first article here was an introductory piece that tried to put the development of Andhra Pradesh in a perspective. Studying the state through the lense of light and shade of social phenomena, this article portrayed both the 'developments' and 'deprivations' that occurred in the state from a people's point of view.

As a corollary to this introductory piece, I also wrote the second piece as an exploration of social history and tried to study the fifty years of history as a train of social movements. This essay looked at the society as a continuous interaction of people's movements and concluded that social movements, rather than any thing else, were the motive force of Telugu society.

Post-globalisation, and particularly after Chandrababu Naidu became the chief minister, the governance of the state had directly come under the tutelage of the World Bank and the role of external funding had multiplied. The third essay tried to capture the influence of external capital on not only the governance but also the entire value system of society going back to the beginnings and extending far beyond till 2006.

The other two essays in this section dealt with specific aspects of Chandrababu Naidu's rule as well as cotton farmers' suicides.

❖ ❖ ❖

1

Fifty Years of Development Light and Shadow

The concept of development is both complex and simple to understand, at the same time. It could be understood simply because of its strong visibility. It is complex and difficult to understand since we will not be able to comprehend the dark patches it creates as easily as we do the brightness it generates.

—R S Rao

Andhra Pradesh celebrates fifty years of its existence in 2006. The state had a number of unique and special features at its formation on November 1, 1956 because of its specificity as the first linguistic state to be formed in the country, a result of unity aspirations of a nationality that existed two centuries separately, a unity that tried to push the differences of opinion under the carpet and as an administrative unit that evolved out of a Gentlemen's Agreement. Again its history of 50 years is full of several qualitative changes, momentous and sensational developments, great people's movements and a number of social, economic and political events that deeply stirred social life of people.

In fact, fifty years time span in the life of any nationality can not be uneventful. In the history of Telugu nationality it is much more so. A single essay or even a book would not be sufficient to review this unusual history in detail. The task of explaining the events in almost all fields and trying to abstract the essential elements and content of those processes needs a meticulous and painstaking study. This essay would

Published in Fifty Years of Andhra Pradesh 1956-2006, Edited by R S Rao, V Hanumantha Rao and N Venugopal, Published by Centre for Documentation, Research and Communication, Hyderabad, 2007

like to bring into relief the premises for undertaking that research. Even these grounds are neither complete nor comprehensive. One has to add more arguments to make them comprehensive. Moreover, even to the premises suggested here there may be more and different angles than referred here. This essay aims to be a first step to that broader attempt to comprehend the scenario of light and shade of Andhra Pradesh development between 1956 and 2006.

Any reading of the history of five decades of Andhra Pradesh can have some grounds in philosophical perspectives, movement of political economy, internal and external stimulations and dynamics.

When one looks at the fifty years of Andhra Pradesh history, the most striking aspect is the fact that it contains parallel and simultaneous elements of progress and reaction, and development and decline. The analysis of D.D. Kosambi about the peaceful co-existence of most modern means of production and primitive relations of production in Indian society reflects much more visibly and in a complex manner in Andhra Pradesh. Thus the statement that Andhra Pradesh progressed a lot is as truer as the assessment that the state has not progressed or remained under-developed. One can supply as many statistics to prove the first statement as one could to substantiate the second statement.

This is not just a class perspective that looks at each and everything from the viewpoint of the oppressed and exploited or otherwise. It is not a relativist attitude that says each phenomenon would have a positive and a negative aspect. It is not even taking a particular stand and finding fault with the other stance. The various definitions of development, different perspectives, the attitudes chosen by the commentators, the philosophical and ideological positions of the analysts and the tools used by them – all of them influence their assessment of reality. Indeed the reality itself has multifarious, multilayered, complex and complicated existence rather than having a single, absolute and simple identity. For example, the total length of roads in the state in 1956 was 26,762 km. According to the latest available statistics, by 2003, this road length has gone up to 2,01,203 km. On the whole, the state appears to have achieved commendable progress with seven and half times (751 per cent) growth in road length.

But which section of the population was benefited by these roads? Whose interests did the traffic and cargo that moved on these roads serve? From which areas to which areas the raw materials moved on these roads? From which areas to which areas commodities were moved in search of markets? From which areas to which areas these roads encourage migrations? What happened to those societies or communities as a result of these migrations? If one goes deep into the analysis of these questions, the overall growth scenario of road length turns out to be a picture of complicated and mixed reality. Not only that, while the growth of roads on the whole for the state seems to be in the order of a high magnitude, if one delves deeper into region-wise, districtwise and mandal-wise break-up, one could easily realise that down the line the growth may not be much more than double or triple.

If we take another example, in 1956 there used to be 1,626 tractors in agriculture. According to the latest available figures, the number of tractors in agriculture has grown to 90,333 in 1999. Those who believe that the level of mechanisation in agriculture is a symbol of growth that follows the path of agricultural development in the US and Europe might feel elated at this growth rate of 500 times achieved by the state. They might assess that agriculture in Andhra Pradesh is moving ahead in big leaps. There may be some truth in this. But at the same time, one has to look at the other side of the coin: one has to keep in mind the fact that this growth in the number of tractors was achieved by some districts only. Another more important aspect is that not only there is no significant growth in the net area sown but also an actual decrease over the last fifty years. The net area sown used to be 112.91 lakh hectares in 1955-56 and it came down to 104.31 lakh hectares in 2004-05. The highest point it reached was in 1970-71 with 117.34 lakh hectares and the lowest point was 97.30 lakh hectares in 2002- 03. That means the net area sown in the state hovers around 2.4 to 2.8 crore acres, out of the total geographical area of 6.8 crore acres. Even if one discounts forest, barren and uncultivable lands, land put to non agricultural uses and permanent pastures and grazing lands, the area available for cultivation would be much more than this 2.8 crore acres. The area of cultivable land but not available for cultivation remains static at least around one crore acres. Here we need not go into that for the present. The point one has to take note of is that 88,000 new tractors have entered into the land where the net area sown has not increased. What does that mean? Even at a modest calculation each tractor might have replaced at least 10 agricultural labourers and what could have been the fate of those labourers? With this rise in unemployment what could have happened to the existing wage rates? With the loss of livelihood to such an extent what could have happened to the families of those labourers? What happened to the education of their children? What happened to their healthcare? The phenomenal increase in the number of tractors might be very illuminating, but that hides a stark darkness that anyway is not visible.

Let us take another example: it is almost conventional wisdom to identify usage of machines and modern personal automobiles as a symbol of development. Some even brandish those numbers as if social development lies in the growth of personal vehicles. Undeniably Andhra Pradesh, in comparison between 1956 and now, is fast moving ahead in the use of automobiles. The number of registered motor vehicles in the state in 1956 was 26,559. According to the latest available statistics, by 2004-05, the number of motor vehicles in the state has gone up to 57,97,012. There is an obvious 218 times growth, but if one goes deep into the complexity of this extraordinary figure and the need to disaggregated analysis, the symbol of development turns out to be too difficult a proposition to define as development.

To accept an indicator as an index of development, one has to make it comprehensive by taking into consideration its scope, limitations, mutually contradictory standards, interests, and specificities of space and time. An element that comes as development of a particular region might drive another region into backwardness. An element that significantly benefits the living standards of a particular class of people might have destroyed the life of another section of population. More over, even in the comprehension of a society what was seen as unquestionable development yesterday, might turn into lopsided, problematic, underdevelopment and unequal today, thanks to the growing awareness of environment and the society's own requirements and resources.

Looking from this backdrop, a macro development indicator like growth in the modern transport facilities would become problematic at micro level. If one disaggregates the number of vehicles at the state level to regional, district and further local level, the result would be quite astonishing. If one divides the number of public transport vehicles and private and individual transport vehicles, the results would be different. If one compares the number of people who do not have any transport facilities and the population who have all the transport facilities, the results would be different. Similarly, what is the quantum of fuel that is consumed with the hundreds of times of growth in the number of vehicles? What is the share of that fuel in the economy? What is the percentage of people that use these vehicles and is there a correlation between their share in population and the share of their fuel consumption in the economy? If one attempts to answer these questions, the results would be shocking. This analysis takes cognisance of the state of affairs as on today, but if one goes on to think about the future results and the fate of future generations, in terms of pollution, depletion of natural resources and fall in the human lifespan, it is impossible to assess the predicament.

Here one can cite a small example to buttress the point. Perhaps there was no entry called Rigs (a machine that drills into the earth and digs borewells) in the list of registered vehicles in 1956. But by March 2003, there were 1,491 Rigs in the state. One can interpret this as an unmistakable growth. But if one goes deep into this figure, Karimnagar district seems to top the list with 251 Rigs followed by Nalgonda district with 240 Rigs and Rangareddy district with 205 Rigs. But the other side of the coin is that these three districts present a scenario of depleting underground water, receding water table, abandoning of traditional wells, loss of livelihood of carpenters, blacksmiths and leather workers who used to help with instruments for drawing water from open wells, and fall in the cattle population because of their non-use in water drawing. Thus one would not be in a position to give a straight forward answer to the question whether the entry of a modern instrument of production called Rig into a remote Telugu village was a development or not? At the same time Rig as a modern industrial product becomes a symbol of modernity and development, as well as a symbol of anti-development as a driver of depletion of underground water. It can also be seen as a deliberate conspiracy when it is seen as a destroyer of a collective livelihood dependent on traditional wells without showing any alternative. Karamchedu in Prakasam district was seen as a model of development by several observers before 1985. That village earned a name of its own in commercial crops and market-oriented farming for about half a century before that. There was considerable surplus in agriculture and that flowed into contracts, fertiliser and pesticide business, tobacco and cotton trading, and film making and distribution.

The village attracted modern facilities and gadgets. Considerable number of people from that village came into regular contact not only with cities like Madras and Hyderabad but also with foreign countries. All this development and forward-looking scenario received a big jolt with the massacre of Dalits in the village on July 17, 1985. It came to the knowledge of the public at large that despite all the so-called development in the village, untouchability was very much in practice in the village, there was caste discrimination and there were obstacles to the self respect of Dalits. The same castes and individuals who until then were looked at as the channels of modern development, turned out to kill fellow human beings with primitive and obscurantist beliefs.

If this line of argument is extended, every development indicator appears to have another, may be contrasting, angle. Irrigation canals certainly resulted in increase in agricultural output. But at the same time they displaced lakhs of people from their lands. Entry of tractors in agriculture made farming in vast fields easier, but destroyed the lifestyle of lakhs of agricultural labour. Rigs have drawn water from the depths of the earth, but remained an example of ecological crisis. Modern means like roads, transport, communications, and modern administrative practices that aimed to modernise and bring people together do not appear to fulfil their aims. The modern communications not only could not remove the primitive feelings of caste and religion and spread modern community living, but also acted as channels of reactionary and obscurantist ideas.

Taking all this process into consideration is a necessary precondition to attempt writing of modern Andhra Pradesh history. Definitely one cannot dare say in a single word that there was development *per se* or otherwise during the last fifty years. There is light, but there is also darkness along with the light. Again, some brighter spots brought darker marks along with them inadvertently. Some other brighter spots led to blemishes, due to deliberate aims. Yet other darker spots were created because the managers of social, economic and political institutions for the last five decades thought there was no need to focus light on some areas. Some other dark spots are continuing in history and social system for centuries and decades. All these complex issues have to be coordinated and recognised as inherent parts of five decades of development process. Only then an authentic and credible history of Andhra Pradesh can be written.

This light and dark shade is a philosophical issue and along with that we have the problem of assessing the political, economic and cultural angles of the real developments during the last fifty years. In assessing the actually occurred developments, a major issue would be identifying the real twists and turns in the last fifty years journey. Can one find out a particular method in the way Andhra Pradesh society moved during the last half a century? Indeed, the movement of Andhra Pradesh that began its journey on November 1, 1956 till now has not been a straight line. This journey had witnessed upward movement in some years and downward movement in other years in a zigzag fashion. Economists have been discussing whether this journey can be neatly compartmentalised into some phases based on these upward or downward movements. There have been some arguments about a phase till 1970s, another phase between 1970s and 1980s, and yet another phase after 1990s. On the whole this fifty year developments have been categorised into three or four periods.

However, it remains to be seen whether this periodisation applies only to economy and fiscal affairs or could it be extended to all the social spheres. It would have been possible to have a clear-cut periodisation if there were any qualitative changes and perceptible trends in social and economic spheres. But what we have now are only some indicators that talk about changes independently and sporadically in political arena or fiscal policies or industrialisation or changes in agricultural system or political administration. We do not have indicators that apply to all the spheres equally and uniformly. That means the entire evolution of Telugu society for the last fifty years cannot be explained through a single periodisation scheme. This is a sign to conclude that there has been a deep-rooted unevenness in the development process of Telugu society.

Similarly, another major issue that has to be addressed in the study of the history of the last fifty years is the changes that occurred in the class composition and caste composition. These changes are neither simple nor clearly marked. The tenancy reforms promulgated in both the areas even before the state formation, the land ceiling legislations brought in after 1956, and land transfer regulations in agency areas – even as all these legislations have been implemented in haphazard manner, they have to some extent brought in changes in the land ownership in the rural areas. The moot question is whether these changes resulted in the desired transformation. Have they achieved the aims like equity in rural land relations, social prosperity and increase in productivity? In the same way one can discuss whether the rural agrarian surplus flowed into extended reproduction and paved the way for industrial development. Has an indigenous and independent industrial capitalist class grown out of this surplus? On the other hand it has to be analysed how the agricultural surplus from the coastal districts entered unproductive service and trading sectors like real estate, film production and distribution, finance, liquor, mafia, transport, etc. and led to the evolution of a new class composition.

Then coming to the caste composition, the obtaining bitter truth is that contrary to the ideals set in the 1950s, Telugu society has become a society that is more dominated by reference to caste. The analysis of Dr Ram Manohar Lohia in the 1950s that Telugu society would travel from the then existing political predominance of Brahmins, Kshatriyas, Reddys and Kammas to the ascendancy of backward castes, became reality in a crude fashion. Telugu society could not disprove the analyses of the US social scientists Selig Harrison and Caroline M Elliott in 1950s and 1960s that caste is a dominant factor in Telugu society and it was the basis of the strength of all the political parties. The same kind of castes and caste compositions that had supremacy in the state's political, economic, social and cultural fields, are in power even after 50 years. Of course, the scenario now is more undemocratic, more brazen and more reactionary.

Thus while assessing the development process of fifty years of Andhra Pradesh, one has to take into consideration this relative strengths and weaknesses of different castes, classes and class-caste compositions. More over, the collective consciousness and sense of self-respect that grew among Dalits, Bahujans and *Adivasis* in the last two decades and unity among the oppressed castes have thrown light on the political and social history of Andhra Pradesh. One has to understand these developments also from their roots.

Another important aspect that has to be recognised in the study of the last fifty years history is the growth of infrastructure. In this sector, it is conventional to identify power, roads, railways, communications, irrigation, canals, etc. as economic infrastructure and education, healthcare and social welfare facilities as social infrastructure. Out of these two, the state has witnessed the growth of the former a little more than the latter. However, even here all the questions about the light and shade apply. In each of these infrastructural facilities, there appears significant growth between 1956 and today. But the same thing is not as visible in the impact on the amelioration in people's lives. That means even the apparent development does not seem to have percolated down and spread across evenly. Here it appears that both the Nehruvian 'trickle down model' and the 'increasing the cake model' followed by Chandrababu Naidu have failed in reaching the fruits of development to the poorest of the poor in the state.

One can cite some contrasts to portray this point: Hyderabad has earned an unenviable place as the corporate health capital of the country attracting patients from across the globe and at the same time, within a thousand miles to that capital, thousands of helpless Adivasis had to die with ordinary fevers and malaria. Under the very nose of the hi-tech city where ultra modern science and technology including nano technology prosper, primitive human sacrifices and witchcraft go unchecked. Solemn proclamations on sophisticated rule of law on one hand and series of extrajudicial murders on the other go hand in hand. This contradiction symbolises the unevenness, ups and downs and anarchy in the life of Andhra Pradesh social life and all this gets cultural expression.

Indeed, all the changes listed above have found expression in cultural field. These cultural changes have resulted in the evolution of a widespread middle class in Telugu society. Not only the number of industrial workers and employees grew, but also the class division in the society became more pronounced and complex by the day. In fact, Andhra Pradesh is one of the states where urbanisation took place on a very large scale. At the time of formation of the state in 1956, the urban population was 17.4 per cent and by 2001 Census, this has gone up to 27.3 per cent, making 10 per cent more urban population in fifty years. But if this is set in a perspective, the growth in the number of industrial workers and employees is not commensurate. Thus one might conclude that even the urbanisation process happened in a highly skewed manner.

Urbanisation has not happened as per the requirements of the society and happened in an uneven fashion, leading to unwarranted pressure on urban and civic amenities. Another corollary of this process is that in almost all the urban centres in the state, real estate trade boomed not on realistic basis but as a bubble. Thanks to this nature, mafia entered real estate and politics followed mafia. Thus if one were to study a cultural phenomenon like urbanisation in the social evolution of Andhra Pradesh, one also has to deal with an economic phenomenon like real estate business and a political, legal and administrative phenomenon like politician-underworld nexus.

There are peculiar changes in the relative share of primary (agriculture, forestry, fishing and mining), secondary (manufacturing, construction, power, gas and water supply) and tertiary (trade, hotels, restaurants, transport, financing, services, etc) in Andhra Pradesh gross domestic product. Maybe this peculiarity gave rise to the specificity of fifty years of Andhra Pradesh development. The share of primary sector was 51.85 per cent in 1955-56 and fell down to 26.6 per cent in 2005-06. During the same timeframe the secondary sector share has grown from 14.7 per cent to 22.7 per cent and the share of tertiary sector grew from 32.74 per cent to 50.7 per cent. Again in this, if one disaggregates the share of trade, hotels and restaurants it increased from Rs 528.06 crore in 1961-62 (1980-81 prices) to Rs 14996 crore (1993-94 prices) registering 28 times growth. The share of banking, insurance and financial services rose from 0.81 per cent in 1956 to 5.88 per cent in 2005 and sale and purchase of real estate, dwelling houses and allied activities increased from 2.3 per cent to 6.88 per cent during the same time period.

Another important aspect of the fifty years of evolution of Andhra Pradesh is the history of people's movements. In the evolution of a society, the driving forces would be the aspirations of different groups for their rightful share in the social product, and the efforts they make to realise their share, as well as their demands. These aspirations, demands and struggles form the motive force and add colour, flesh and blood to that society. They inform the basis of quantitative and qualitative changes. Telugu social history is replete with such social movements. The movements might have taken the form of open and dynamic manifestation at times and continued as underlying burning discontent at other times. Whatever may be their form, each of the struggles will be reflecting and symbolising various social, economic, political and cultural aspirations and discontents. Thus the systematic explanation of all these struggles experienced by Telugu society would become the social history of Andhra Pradesh of the last fifty years.

Even before the formation of Andhra Pradesh, Telugu society under two different administrative regimes conducted great social movements. While, Telangana part of the then Hyderabad State had Telangana Peasant Armed Struggle (1946-51) against the Nizam and the British in the first phase and against the Union Government in the next phase. Andhra - Rayalaseema parts of the then Madras state had movement for a separate Andhra State, which was realised in 1953 after the death of Potti Sri Ramulu after 58 days of fasting in 1952. Even the demand for a united state – *Visalandhra* – was the demand of a mass movement. The apprehension of a region about the probable difficulties in the united state also took the shape of a mass movement. Even in the first decade of the formation of Andhra Pradesh, small and sporadic demands for change in the existing agrarian relations manifested in various struggles. As a solution to the growing unemployment problem in Telugu society, youth movement erupted with the slogan 'Visakha steel, right of Andhras' in 1966. With the realisation of violations of the Gentlemen's Agreement and injustices to Telangana region, a movement demanding separate statehood for Telangana began in 1969. By the same time Naxalite movement demanding land, livelihood and liberation spread its roots in Andhra Pradesh. That movement is not only going on unending in the state, but also resulted in great impact on social and political life. In the following three decades there have been a number of movements on various demands. *Jai Andhra*, struggle against rising prices, struggle for self respect of Dalits, movements of various castes, women's movement, anti-liquor movement, struggles to protect Regulation1/70, struggles for protecting Adivasi rights, struggles against World Bank dictated policies, struggles demanding irrigation projects, struggles to resolve the problems of project oustees, struggles against state repression, protests against farmers' and weavers' suicides, movement against power tariff hike, agitations against local and small problems, are some of the movements during the last three decades. A movement demanding separate statehood for Telangana has been raging since 1996. If one counts all the people participated in these movements, it is not an exaggeration to say that there is not a single section in Telugu society that has not taken the path of agitation.

Keeping in view all these aspects are essential to understand the process of evolution of society in Andhra Pradesh during the last fifty years.

❖ ❖ ❖

2

Social Movements as Motive Force

History is about the sequence of events that led to the lives we lead today. It is the story of how we came to be ourselves. Understanding it is the key to finding out if and how we can further change the world in which we live....Such changes do not, however, occur in a mechanical way. At each point human beings make choices whether to proceed along one path or another, and fight out these choices in great social conflicts. Beyond a certain point in history, how people make their choices is connected to their class position....The great struggles over the future of humanity have involved an element of class struggle. The sequence of these great struggles provides the skeleton round which the rest of history grows.

- Chris Harman,
A People's History of the World

If one were to pick out the single most influential motive force of the development of Telugu society it would be none other than innumerable small and big social contradictions that manifested and culminated in social movements on various issues. That Telugu society in general and Andhra Pradesh in particular has been very dynamic and always in the forefront of all kinds of social movements is a historical fact that goes without saying. One can go as far back as possible in history to show that Telugu society as a whole at times and at least some sections at other times have waged courageous battles with the

Published in Fifty Years of Andhra Pradesh 1956-2006, Edited by R S Rao, V Hanumantha Rao and N Venugopal, Published by Centre for Documentation, Research and Communication, Hyderabad, 2007

powers that be and attempted to change the existing modes of survival and thought. At this juncture one need not go into that hoary past but restrain to the last fifty years and a little earlier to recognise that various social movements played a great role in the making of modern Andhra Pradesh and transformation of social values in all the spheres.

The characteristic fighting spirit of the Telugus had acquired comprehensive social and philosophical viewpoints during the later part of the nineteenth century with the influence of British education on one hand and the emergence of civil society and new ideas thanks to the surplus generated by tamed mighty rivers and consequent modern agriculture on the other. Telugus were living under two different regimes at that time and the development in social consciousness and its expression represent some unavoidable unevenness. Andhra Pradesh was formed in 1956 by merging these two distinct political and regional entities and both the areas separately had glorious histories of social movements during the early part of that century. The social movements of the first part of the 20th century were waged on the issues of social and religious reform, language and cultural identity, gender equality, caste oppression, political and social assertion, amelioration of agrarian situation, egalitarian ideas, trade union rights and democratic rights and in the process raised several radical questions. The questions were radical not only in the sense that they were unconventional, original and much-ahead of their times, but also for the fact that their solutions, if the movements continued until reasonable solutions, would have brought about a radical rupture with the existing norms. This contention can be proved by taking each and every social stirring in coastal Andhra starting with social reform activities of Samineni Muddu Narasimham (1800-1858) and Kandukuri Veeresalingam (1848-1919) and in Telangana with Library Movement (beginning 1901) and Andhra Jana Sangham (beginning 1921) activities. These movements were followed by *Raithu Rakshana Yatra* of 1937- 38, anti-*zamindari* struggles, particularly in Mandasa, Challapalli, Munagala, Venkatagiri, and Kalipatnam *zamindari*s during the 1930s and 40s, anti-Brahmin movement of 1930s, as well as national movement in coastal Andhra and the movements led by Andhra Mahasabha, State Congress, Communist Party of India in Telangana in 1930s and 1940s.

It is also true that most of these social campaigns, spread over seven decades in coastal Andhra and five decades in Telangana before the formation of Andhra Pradesh, were sectional and limited to a minority in society in terms of participation and influence and were essentially middle class in nature. There were, of course, militant and non-militant actions from the lower strata also during this period, but a consistent and reliable history of those movements is yet to be explored.

However, it is an undeniable fact that a single and continuous thread of dynamic social movements that brought radical questions on to the social agenda time and again, informs the history of Telugus in the modern period.

The immediate precursors of the formation of Andhra Pradesh were three most important movements: Telangana Peasant Armed Struggle (1946-51), agitations for separation of Telugu-speaking areas from Madras and formation of *Visalandhra* in coastal Andhra and Rayalaseema areas (1948-53), and Mulki Agitation (1952) in the then Hyderabad state. All these social movements had raised radical questions in their own way and enriched the consciousness of people and acted as motive forces for the social development.

Telangana Peasant Armed Struggle began as a movement against feudal practices including predominant extra-economic coercion like *vetti* and highly inequitable agrarian relations and developed into an armed struggle aiming state power, with significant mass base. It was radical not only in its basic questions, but also in terms of its pioneering spirit that stands as a beacon for all militant peasant movements in the sub-continent even today. Telangana Peasant Armed Struggle was a natural outcome of the movement led by Andhra Mahasabha (1931-46) which began as an effort for the protection of language and culture culminating in basic struggle for land, livelihood and liberation.

Visalandhra movement was led by the Communist Party of India and joined by other forces. This movement had its roots, among others, in a pamphlet written by P Sundarayya in 1946 titled *Visalandhralo Prajarajyam*. When the peasant movements in both Hyderabad state and coastal Andhra were on the rise, this pamphlet visualised a people's state in a united land of Telugus. One need not attribute any motive to this now, as is usually done anachronistically, but nonetheless, the slogan and consequent demand for *Visalandhra* were problematic, then in a small measure and later much more. One must concede that the ideas behind this movement were radical, at least in the 1950s, if not now, for the simple fact that the ideas were informed by nationality question based on language and culture and rejection of the rule by others, which was also unconventional at that time.

The third movement, in 1952, was for safeguarding the Mulki Rules which were in operation in Hyderabad State since 1919. The movement, basically led by students, had seen a lot of wrath from the state, including police firing on agitating students. The Mulki Agitation, on which unfortunately sufficient studies have not been done, can also be described as a social movement that raised radical questions since it was almost the first stirring that asserted the rights of the sons of soil in post-1947 India.

Looking at these movements from a different angle, the forms of struggle taken up by these movements and participation also help in describing them as radical. All of them opted for mass mobilisation, fasting unto death, taking up awareness campaigns through publications, holding public meetings and seminars, picketing and obstructing government work, harvesting the crops claimed by landlords, occupation of lands under the illegal possession of landlords, spreading education, according due respect to the people's oral traditions, spreading the ideas of equality between castes and religious harmony, using indigenous and modern weapons and attacking symbols of power and wealth – all signs of exceptional social movements.

Thus Andhra Pradesh inherited a rich legacy of social movements with radical questions and solutions and the following five decades also witnessed a number of social movements, on almost all social issues, with similar disposition. Almost all social sections either participated or supported these movements. While some of these movements were spontaneous, sectional and local, yet others were organised, comprehensive and regional, if not state-wide. There are some overlapping issues as well as separate, particular, local or regional issues. One important factor of all these movements is that, either at the time of conception or during the course, they raised radical questions in every walk of life and attempted to offer meaningful solutions.

After the formation of Andhra Pradesh, the first major social struggle seems to be the peasant struggle led by the then undivided Communist Party of India during 1962-64. There are a couple of cursory mentions of this struggle in the available literature through which it can be concluded that this agitation was basically against the increase in land revenue and water cess. However, some authors described it as land occupation struggle also. It appears that this agitation was primarily in the areas where the Communists were strong and going by the accounts, it is not clear whether this was essentially an agitation of land-owning farming community or a struggle of landless for land.

The agitation demanding setting up steel plant in Visakhapatnam might be another major and state-wide agitation in Andhra Pradesh in its early days. When the Central government announced its intention of establishing a steel plant in the public sector in mid-1960s, people in Andhra Pradesh, basically students, unemployed youth and middle classes came into the streets with the slogan *Visakha ukku Andhrula hakku* (Visakha steel is Andhras' right) and this agitation witnessed massive participation. Ultimately the Centre had to concede the demand of people and set up Visakha Steel Plant. It is another matter that even after forty years, the problem of displaced due to the steel plant is not solved.

It is also interesting to note that the same society which demanded a major industrial project in 1960s, refused to accept major projects in 1990s and 2000s. The movement of 1960s has to be seen in the context of rising unemployment and aspirations of employment in public sector as well as ideas of national development through major projects. The idea of social costs of industrialisation did not yet dawn on the minds of people at that time. Looking at this movement from another angle, the Telugu society was not as fragmented as it is forty years later and almost all sections of society demanded for the steel plant in a united voice.

Another major social movement that challenged the basic existence of a single Telugu society and the linguistic state of Andhra Pradesh was the struggle on the demand of a separate statehood for Telangana. This struggle, as mentioned earlier, has its roots in separate existence of Hyderabad State, away from other Telugu-speaking areas for at least two hundred years. In the fifty years history of Andhra Pradesh the struggle for Telangana is most significant and even by sheer occurrence it is the most recurring and consistent struggle. The agitation began as a demand for respecting the safeguards to Telangana accepted in the Gentelmen's Agreement of February 20, 1956. Andhra Pradesh was specifically formed based on this agreement that promised a number of safeguards to Telangana region in return to the merger.

The Gentlemen's Agreement came in the wake of the report of States' Reorganisation Commission (1953-55) headed by Syed Fazl Ali, which recommended separate existence of Telugu-speaking districts of Hyderabad state, at least till the next general election. The Central government was not in favour of this recommendation and was willing to go by the demand of the then Congress leaders from coastal Andhra, which was also supported by Communists. Government of India made the leaders of both the regions sit and come to the agreement. Even as the agreement provided for a number of safeguards in terms of education, employment, budgetary allocations and administrative berths, the promises were observed more in violation. The movement for separate Telangana statehood was a reaction to these violations and the discontent was simmering since the early 1960s to erupt in 1968. In the last forty years the movement for separate statehood for Telangana broke out at least thrice with a combined duration of over fifteen years. When it appeared for the first time in 1968-69, it was basically a movement of students and employees, particularly non-gazetted officers, against discrimination in education and employment. The movement was crushed by the government by killing 370 people in police firing. The movement went on for about one year intermittently with loss of an academic year and closure of government offices. The Central government also tried to address the issues raised by this movement through the announcement of eight-point formula (1969) and five-point formula (1971). In the meanwhile, as a reflection of the movement, Telangana Praja Samithi, a loose amalgamation of separatists won 11 out of 14 seats in mid-term parliamentary elections in 1971, but the organisation joined Congress later.

When the Supreme Court of India upheld the Mulki Rules in 1972, some political leaders in coastal Andhra aroused passions of people there saying that the court verdict would prevent them from seeking employment in their own capital and the sentiment led to an agitation under the banner of *Jai Andhra*. The *Jai Andhra* movement demanded the formation of a separate Andhra state if Telangana did not merge with coastal Andhra unconditionally and without any safeguards. At the same time, people of Telangana also started another agitation repeating their demand for separation. However, Government of India rejected both the demands and announced a six-point formula (1973) which resulted in an amendment to Constitution of India and Presidential Order. Even the Presidential Order was not implemented in its letter and spirit and the consequent dissent among the people of Telangana resulted in another phase of the movement in mid-1990s and found its political expression in the formation of Telangana Rashtra Samithi in 2001. The movement, both under the leadership of TRS and otherwise, is going on consistently.

Andhra Pradesh was also an important centre for students' movements and from its inception to until 1990s student movements were very strong in the state. Particularly students associations affiliated to the left political formations were very active during the 1970s and 1980s. The students' movements not only fought for their own demands but also were instrumental in development of social consciousness. Several students' organisations took up a number of social and political issues and waged heroic struggles. Thanks to the idealism and enthusiasm at that age students played significant role in almost all the issues on social agenda. Political activity at student level contributed a lot to the making of future politicians. However, this dynamism in student world was scuttled by forbidding student union elections in educational institutions in the late 1980s and banning of a student organisation in 1992.

The history of movements among writers and consequent blossoming of ideas in Andhra Pradesh is too large to present here and needs a separate study. While there was a great polarisation between writers just before the formation of Andhra Pradesh during the 1955 mid-term election in Andhra state, the Telugu writing community has witnessed polarisation and organisation on ideological basis a number of times. This contention of ideas and practice led to widespread influence of writers and Telugu society has seen a rare combination of active and militant participation of writers in social movements.

Andhra Pradesh has also witnessed a number of agitations against price rise and most significant of these struggles was in the mid-1970s. The movement was almost parallel to the similar movements in Gujarat and Bihar. Discontent against rising prices and falling standards of life have been a constant source of struggle, small or big.

Though the state was under uninterrupted Congress rule till 1983, it also had a strong presence of anti-Congress sentiments and thus when

Emergency was imposed on June 26, 1975, it was Andhra Pradesh that witnessed a great deal of repression of political dissent and press censorship. Hundreds of political activists and intellectuals were arrested and incarcerated for months. Thousands of political dissenters were subjected to torture in illegal custody for days together. There was a widespread resentment against these Emergency measures and slowly a silent movement against Emergency atrocities gathered momentum. This resulted in large scale struggles of students, youth, peasants and workers in the post-Emergency period. The situation was so inflammable that a single small incident of a death and rape in police custody led to a great mass movement and complete standstill for days together in 1978. When a hapless couple Ahmed Hussain and Rameejaa Bee were taken into illegal custody by policemen of Nallakunta Police Station in Hyderabad, and the policemen killed the husband and raped the wife, the entire state erupted in violence against powers that be. The simmering discontent amongst the people against the government and the way things were going got a powerful expression in the movement. Similarly, when Nadendla Bhaskara Rao, a cabinet colleague of the then Chief Minister N T Rama Rao organised a coup and tried to dethrone the chief minister with the support of the then governor Ramlal, the entire state stood solidly behind the wronged chief minister and helped him regain power. Both these incidents show that Telugu society is eternally vigilant in fighting for a right cause.

The evolution of modern Andhra Pradesh has also witnessed quite a bit of caste oppression and the first recorded sign of such brutal practices was in the killing of Koteshu in Kanchikacherla of Krishna district. Arguably this might not be the first case of caste oppression, but this incident in 1968 received the attention of society and there was considerable opposition. This kind of brutality against Dalits and downtrodden continued and in another two decades got its response in a great upsurge in the form of Dalit movement. It was after a carnage in which six Dalits were killed in Karamchedu in Prakasam district on July 17, 1985. The ghastly incident was followed by several other cold-blooded incidents in Neerukonda, Chunduru, Timmasamudram, Chalkurthi, Vempenta, etc. These incidents forced the Dalits to get organised and wage consistent struggles against all forms of oppression.

However, over the time the Dalit movement has seen some fissures in it and some sub-castes, including Madiga, started questioning the hegemony of Malas in usurping all the benefits of reservation. Madiga Hakkula Parirakshana Samithi holding the banner of *Madiga Dandora* demanded further classification of the Scheduled Castes and provide reservation according to the relative backwardness. Though the demand was democratic and seeking redress of piled up discontent, nonetheless the movement resulted in fragmentation of Dalit movement.

Though women's struggles in Telugu society have a long history beginning from the late nineteenth century, after the formation of Andhra Pradesh the struggles started taking shape in the early 1970s and the International Woman's Decade gave a fillip to the women's consciousness and organisation. During the post-Emergency period there appeared a number of women's organisations and groups that propagated the consciousness of challenging the existing patriarchal order. One of the offshoots of the women's consciousness was the massive anti-liquor agitation that began from Nellore and forced the government change its excise policy and introduce prohibition policy.

While the landless and small peasants waged struggles for land and better wages, land-owning farmers in Andhra Pradesh are engaged in a number of struggles on a wide variety of concerned issues. Struggles for proper seed supply and against spurious seeds, struggles for quality and reliable power supply, struggles for irrigation water, struggles for better fertilisers, pesticides and extension services, struggles for better warehousing and marketing facilities, and struggles for remunerative prices include these farmers' efforts to get what is due for them. Of late the farmers have realised that the faulty and pro- MNC government policies are behind their tribulations and have been turning their ire against the government and traders. Despite the fact that the farming community inherits fighting spirit and solidarity, the farmers of Andhra Pradesh are also committing suicides, unable to overcome the difficulties.

Tribals of Andhra Pradesh have been at the receiving end for decades without realising their proper share in social development. But they are the most valiant fighters for their cause for over a century starting from Rampa rebellion of the late 19th century. Post-Andhra Pradesh formation they were subjected to untold suffering and it was the Naxalite movement that came to their rescue. The Naxalites organised the tribals, gave them leadership and made them take up struggles against the traders, landlords, forest officials and police.

Repression on Savaras and Jatapus in Srikakulam, Koyas and Kondareddis in the agency spread over Visakhapatnam to Khammam, and Gonds and Kolams in Adilabad for the last four decades is horrible and needs a separate study. Killing of more than 13 Gond tribals in police firing at Indravelli of Adilabad district when the tribals came to hold a conference of their association is a blot on the history of modern Andhra. The incident showed the cruelty of the powers that be when it came to the assertion of tribal rights and in fact the incident led to more militancy of tribal struggles. There have been a number of struggles by different tribal groups under the leadership of various political and nonpolitical formations.

Despite the fact that Andhra Pradesh, without a substantial industrial base was never a hub of working class struggles, Andhra Pradesh had recorded some heroic outbursts of workers' struggles. Andhra Pradesh has a large miners' community with its stretch of coal mines covering four districts. The Singareni coal miners had a history of dynamic struggles even before the formation of the state and the same legacy continued in Andhra Pradesh. Similarly, Andhra Pradesh had a large public sector base, with state transport segment and power utilities occupying a majority portion, and all the staff of these units played important role in workers' struggles. The state government employees also waged a number of struggles not only on their economic demands but also on some social and political demands.

Post-1995, Andhra Pradesh is one of the key states that implemented globalisation policies heavily. In fact, Andhra Pradesh came under direct tutelage of the World Bank and began implementing privatisation policies. People of Andhra Pradesh started waging struggles against these policies and at least one of them, the agitation against power-tariff hike has to be mentioned. Following the World Bank's diktats, the state government trifurcated the then profit making Andhra Pradesh State Electricity Board and abrogated its social responsibility by handing over the decision making power to a so-called independent regulatory commission. Apparently on the orders of the commission, but really at the instance of the World Bank the power tariff was hiked and the people's sentiments against the globalisation policies found expression in a widespread mass movement against this hike. The movement forced all the political parties except the ruling TDP and its ally BJP to extend support. The government tried to crush the movement by opening fire and killing three agitators, but in the end, it had to restrain from hiking the tariff. In the same vein as anti-globalisation movements, one could add the struggles against displacement due to major "development" projects as well as struggles with environmental concerns. While Telugu society demanded Nandikonda (current Nagarjuna Sagar) project in the mid-1950s, fifty years later the same society is looking at projects like Polavaram, Atomic Power Plant, Uranium refinery, Pulichintala, Fab City and Outer Ring Road with a lot of suspicion. The society at large feels that the so-called development projects would only result in displacement, poverty, unemployment and environmental degradation. Some of these apprehensions are culminating in widespread protests and movements.

Then one has to examine the Naxalite movement which has been consistent in Andhra Pradesh for the last forty years. Andhra Pradesh sheltered the movement and held forte even when the movement suffered major setbacks in other areas. The present spread of the Naxalite movement across the country is generally explained as an extension from Andhra Pradesh. A comprehensive history of the Naxalite movement in Andhra Pradesh is yet to be written, but here we attempt to outline its broad contours.

The Naxalite movement in the state could be traced to two major streams: the first one developing from the tribal struggle under the Communists in Srikakulam which began in late 1950s and accepted the ideological leadership of Naxalbari line in the late 1960s and the second one emerging out of debates within the Communist Party of India (Marxist) in 1967-68 and consequent split. When the Communist Party of India (Marxist-Leninist) was formed on April 22, 1969, Srikakulam struggle and its followers formed a part of it and the deserters of the CPI (M) formed themselves into AP Coordination Committee of Communist Revolutionaries. Over the next forty years, broadly, inheritors of the first line changed themselves into the CPI (Maoist) and those of the second line are in various Marxist- Leninist formations. On the whole Andhra Pradesh now has at least six parties or groups that adhere to the Marxist-Leninist line of thought in organising people's struggles. The influence of this line of thought is much larger than their organisational strength.

First of all, the movement has to be put in its proper perspective, refuting some popular misconceptions. That the Naxalite movement recognises itself as an agrarian revolution is common knowledge but it has to be recognised that the movement is much more than a set of ideas regarding agrarian relations and if one reduced the movement to land question alone, one would tend to believe naively that a successful land reform programme would see the end of the Naxalite movement. This is far from truth, for neither a successful land reform programme is possible under the given state of relations of production, nor is it the sole agenda of the Naxalite movement. The second popular misconception, propagated by the state and media, is that the Naxalite movement is basically a movement that preaches and practises violence. Though it is true that counter-violence has a major role in the ideology and practice of the Naxalite movement, reducing it to that single factor would tantamount to denying the radical questions it raises and the social transformation it envisages.

Here it would not be possible to examine all the radical questions the movement raised since they are too numerous, but five basic aspects of the movement have to be understood to understand its radical nature. These five aspects are land, livelihood, liberation, organisation and forms of struggle and in each of these the Naxalite movement brought forth new questions, new modes of thinking and new solutions. The history of four decades of the Naxalite movement in Andhra Pradesh vouches for this novel thinking and it could be substantiated by several examples.

Even as the land question occupies a place of prime importance in the left political practice ever since the Telangana Peasant Armed Struggle, the attention it drew over the following decades is quite uneven, both in ruling parties and the parliamentary left. After the formation of Andhra Pradesh, it was only during the late 1960s land reform measures were initiated by the state, thanks to the Naxalite movement.

The struggles for land led by the Naxalites began in the late 1960s and witnessed massive participation during 1977 to 1992, with a respite from 1985 to 1989. These land struggles were so widespread that they covered the entire state from Adilabad to Chittoor to Srikakulam, including the unlikely places of Krishna and West Godavari. Here it would not be out of place to mention that the government's attempts to legislate in favour of protection of tribals from land alienation (1970), prescribing land ceiling (1973), distribution of government land to landless, particularly Dalits (1977) and getting the lands occupied by landless poor registered (1990), were in direct response to the questions raised by the Naxalite movement.

But, post-new economic policies, the land reform ideas have received a short shrift in the corridors of power. Post 1992, there was not even a mention of land reform in official documents, even as the Naxalite movement was going ahead with land occupations and land struggles.

Again, during a brief respite when the government and two Naxalite parties wanted to hold talks on various issues of social concern, the land question occupied centre stage. The paper 'Land Distribution – Development of Agriculture: Our Perspective' submitted by the two Naxalite parties during the talks was radical in more than one way, but it would suffice to refer to the specific proposals where for the first time in the country's history of land reforms the Naxalites argued to eliminate all the absentee landlords if they had any other source of income. The paper also suggested identification of surplus lands in villages rather than through an all pervasive legislation and in revenue offices. The paper also suggested to begin the distribution of land from Dalits and registration of distributed land on the names of women. Though the talks failed, the subsequent land distribution by the government included these two suggestions.

The issues of livelihood cover a wide range of hundreds of small and big and widespread and sporadic issues from domestic violence to state violence. The Naxalite movement has enlarged the scope of the struggles for livelihood in terms of aspirations of better life, whether it is freedom from oppression, gender equality, fight against all forms of subjugation. They are radical in redefining the scope as well as their spread across all sections of society. Whether it was the struggle against rape of Rameeja Bee by police in Hyderabad or the rape of a servant maid by the son of a mining officer in Bellampalli or a struggle for raising the wages of tendu-leaf pickers in the forests of north Telangana, or a struggle for the self-respect of Dalits, or a struggle for better wages for agricultural labourers or a students' struggle for better hostels and improved living conditions or a struggle for house sites for poor or a struggle against price rise or or a struggle against liquor or a struggle for improving the working conditions of coal miners, or a struggle against the ill-effects of globalisation and privatisation or a struggle for remunerative prices for farmers – name any struggle, the influence of the Naxalite movement is there and similar movements in other states can be compared to identify the radical nature of these struggles in Andhra Pradesh.

While the struggles on land and livelihood are described as "economic struggles" in the Naxalites' parlance, the movement is marked by its "political struggles". These are struggles for liberation. The Naxalites treat all their economic struggles as consciousness raising exercises on the way to achieve this liberation. The Naxalites think that the current political expression is democratic only in form and not in essence and thus they think it is not a people's state. In this sense, this is the most radical question that is posed to the current state and thanks to the influence of the Naxalite movement in Andhra Pradesh for the last forty years, each and every subsequent movement even if it says it opposed the Naxalites, has included the nature of the state in its discourse. Thus the Naxalite movement not only raised a fundamental radical question but also made all the other movements follow on the same lines. One could argue that the Naxalite movement's single most contribution to all the social movements in Andhra Pradesh is its idea of questioning the character of the representation of the state in a radical way.

In terms of organisation and forms of struggle also the Naxalite movement has added new elements in the tradition of social movements in the state. Until the Naxalite movement came on to the scene in Andhra Pradesh, the political parties did not know that there was scope for non-parliamentary political processes and in itself the idea was a radical posture. Brutal state repression, unmindful of fundamental rights and directive principles of Constitution, was successful in terrorising people from joining or supporting this alternative political process openly. Gradually space for this political process was shrunk and the Naxalite movement and the people who subscribed to the ideology and practice had to search for alternative routes for this process, giving scope to much more illegal and clandestine activity instead of open, legal, democratic and constitutional activity. In the process, this gave rise to violence and counter violence spiral killing thousands of people.

Besides its social, political and economic questions, the significance of the Naxalite movement lies in its radical cultural paradigm, where self-less sacrifice is juxtaposed to the all pervasive selfishness, acquisition, consumerism and careerism. In fact, this idea of sacrifice has become a radical touchstone for all social movements.

To conclude this never-ending story of constant eruption of social contradictions, one could draw that Andhra Pradesh society has not only enriched itself with all these struggles but also presented a picture of dynamism to the world outside. It may also be true that handling these contradictions was not proper and led to unnecessary fragmentation and violence at times, but one has to accept that without these movements various sections of this society would not have been where they are now. There is not a single section of society that doesn't demand its due share, that doesn't participate in the social discourse, and that doesn't have a dream of its own. Providing each and every section of society with its due share is the fundamental nature of egalitarian social order. Allowing every member of the society in the ongoing debate is the quintessence democracy. Offering space to every segment of society to have its own dream is the soul of social development. Andhra Pradesh society is thus moving ahead with these social movements as its motive force.

❖ ❖ ❖

3

Impact of External Funding

A society that suffers from shortage of funds required for development of infrastructure as well as for fulfilment of people's needs and aspirations might have to seek the necessary funds from external sources, in case it doesn't generate sufficient resources internally. It is a moot question whether Andhra Pradesh, as a state richly endowed with natural resources, wealth accumulated over centuries and a vast pool of human resources, needed in the first place to go out seeking external funding. Even as there are considerable expert opinions which argue against external funding and favour exploration of internal resource options, the state governments, at least for the last three decades, have been advocating that there was an inexorable need for going out for external funding. This craving for external funding has been frenetic during the last ten years, leading to a number of significant changes in public policy, government performance and social responses.

At the outset, the expression 'external funding' itself is ambiguous and could offer different meanings to different people depending on their respective perspectives. However, in the present context, 'external funding' is used to mean the kind of funding that comes from those sources which are beyond national or federal boundaries. In fact, at various points of time, Government of Andhra Pradesh or Telugu society might have found themselves in need of funds and got the same from various state and national financial agencies, other state governments, Union government, and commercial banks or public at large. This scenario of seeking funds from an external agency, in the sense of the government getting resources other than taxation, and entrepreneurs getting loans

Published in Fifty Years of Andhra Pradesh 1956 - 2006, Edited by R S Rao, V Hanumantha Rao and N Venugopal, Published by Centre for Documentation, Research and Communication, Hyderabad, 2007

from financial or government agencies, can be seen ever since the state was formed. For the purposes of this paper, all these state and national sources are not considered as external and only those sources which are located outside India – whether they are international financial agencies, governments of other countries or international charity organisations – are considered as external agencies.

Another word of caution with regard to the usage of the term 'external funding' would be in order. Though there are a number of external agencies including the World Bank, Overseas Economic Cooperation Fund of Japan (OECF), Organisation for Economic Co-operation and Development (OECD), Overseas Development Administration (ODA), Department for International Development (DFID), International Development Association (IDA), International Finance Corporation (IFC), Asian Development Bank (ADB), European Economic Commission (EEC), International Fund for Agricultural Development (IFAD), various UN organisations, governments of erstwhile USSR camp, European and US aid organisations, and international commercial banks extending loans and grants to the Government of Andhra Pradesh and local entrepreneurs, accurate information on all the funding operations is not forthcoming except in the case of the World Bank and hence this paper would like to concentrate on the World Bank alone.

In modern Indian history, there has been a school of thought which considers these external sources, however philanthropic and benevolent they may be, with a pinch of suspicion, and rightly so, in the context of colonial rule and drain of wealth for about three centuries. This school of thought dominated Indian freedom struggle[1] and thus even in the post-1947 developments, the external funding has been looked at with apprehension.[2]

These apprehensions formed the backdrop for various political and social movements during the last two decades in the state and hence it would be worthwhile to trace the history of external funding in the state and its impacts, both positive and negative.

Beginnings

As already mentioned, external funding and external influences in India have a long and complex history. The present day Andhra

Pradesh was under two distinct political regimes till 1956 (more so till 1948 and a little lesser later) and the external influences were also to varying degree.

The current coastal Andhra and Rayalaseema districts were part of the then Madras Presidency and directly under the rule of the British crown. Thus the areas did have the influence of English culture and ethos in almost all spheres of life, besides the British influence on political economy. Several infrastructure projects like irrigation systems, transport and communication systems, banking and insurance sectors and early industrialisation projects were funded directly or indirectly by external agencies. The external influence, both in cultural and financial spheres, had percolated down to the lower rungs of society also.

The present-day Telangana districts were part of the then Hyderabad state under an autocratic and feudal kingdom. This area had the influence of the English on one hand and the French on the other but the influence was limited to the upper rungs of the society, mainly the ruling elite, in terms of culture while in the matters of political economy, spread of the influence was significant. The ruler depended on external funding for the development of modern infrastructure. The history of the region during the later half of the nineteenth and early twentieth centuries provides several instances of external financial and cultural influences and resulting controversies.[3]

The areas under Madras Presidency witnessed a strong national movement, including civil disobedience, non-cooperation and burning of foreign goods, and were against the external influence, while the Telangana districts witnessed an anti-feudal struggle, which was also considered to be anti-colonial, under the leadership of the Communists, and thus were against external financial and political influences.

Thus when Andhra Pradesh was formed in 1956, the society by and large had strong sentiments against external influences. It was not that the new-born state did not have any requirement for external funding but the dominant political and social ideas were precluding external funding based on the experiences of colonialism for over three centuries.

However, as the Constitution of India listed external affairs and financial transactions under the Union List, the states did not have any independent role and had to abide by whatever the Union government does in that regard. Government of India did negotiate with external financial agencies during the early decades on behalf of the states and passed on the funds to the respective states with or without the latter's participation in the negotiations. Thus Andhra Pradesh also received some external funding during the late 1950s and 1960s without any active participation from the state government.

As far as the information is available, it seems the first externally funded – the World Bank funded – project in Andhra Pradesh was Kothagudem Power Project. The project's Phase I was funded by the World Bank's arm IDA in May 1963 to an extent of $24.13 million and the Phase II was funded by IBRD in June 1965 to an extent of $14 million. A comprehensive history of relations between the international financial agencies and the Government of Andhra Pradesh is yet to be written but in the absence of such a detailed account what one gets is quite a bit of anecdotal information. This information includes an account by a bureaucrat who was at the helm of the affairs, particularly in finance, during the mid-1970s[4]. In that account he narrates the series of events that led to acceptance of a conditional loan from the World Bank in 1976. He must be referring to any one of the three projects of that period – Pochampad Irrigation (July 1971 – IDA - $40.60 million), the Godavari River Barrage (February 1975 – IDA - $45 million), and AP Irrigation Project (May 1976 – IBRD - $145 million).

The other projects, which received external funding, particularly the World Bank funding during the earlier period include:

- AP Agricultural Credit (December 1970 – IDA - $25.53 million),
- Andhra Fisheries (May 1978 – IDA - $17.50 million),
- Ramagundam Thermal Power Phase I (January 1979 - IDA - $200 million and IBRD - $50 million),
- Ramagundam Thermal Power Phase II (December 1981 – IBRD - $300 million),
- AP Extension (March 1982 – IDA - $6 million),
- Krishna-Godavari Petroleum (October 1982 – IBRD - $165.50 million),
- II AP Irrigation (March 1986 – IDA - $140 million and IBRD - $ 131 million),

- Hyderabad Water Supply (March 1990 – IBRD - $10 million and IDA $79.90 million), and
- AP Cyclone Emergency Reconstruction (October 1990 - IBRD/ IDA - $ 271 million)
- NTPC Power Generation (June 1993 - IBRD/IDA - $ 400 million)
- AP Forestry (February 1994 – IDA - $77.40 million).

The projects designed and proposed by the Union government and part of whose funds were allocated to the state are not included here.

Similarly, the World Bank's private investment arm International Finance Corporation had also funded some projects in the state, which include Republic Forge Company Ltd (1959 - $1.50 million), Nagarjuna Coated Tubes Ltd (1981-82 - $1.74 million), Nagarjuna Steels Ltd (1981-82 - $3.12 million), Nagarjuna Signode Ltd (1982- 91 - $0.41 million), ITW Signode (1982-93 - $4.00 million), Switching Technologies Guntur Ltd (1987 - $1 million), and Global Trust Bank (1994 - $3.2 million).

There is another important piece of information in the available anecdotal record: Speaking at the foundation stone laying ceremony of the now famous HITEC City structure in 1998, the then Chief Secretary of Government of Andhra Pradesh K Madhava Rao said that he used to be against the World Bank policies in his early service days but his views changed after he attended a World Bank - sponsored reorientation programme in 1983. He also mentioned that the reorientation programme was one of the first initiatives of the World Bank in imparting training to the bureaucrats in the state. Thus it may be recognised that the World Bank and other international financial institutions began the process of changing the mindset of the influential bureaucrats and political leaders during the early 1980s. Here it would not be out of place to recollect that N Chandrababu Naidu, who a decade later became the champion of the World Bank-dictated economic reforms in the state was elected as the general secretary of the Telugu Desam Party in 1983 and the party was one of the first few political parties to make use of computers in public opinion monitoring and shaping, again a tool promoted by the World Bank elsewhere.

Out of the 548 projects funded by the World Bank in India between 1949 and 2006, about 35 were in Andhra Pradesh and out of this, 16 were prior to Chandrababu Naidu's regime, 11 were during Naidu's rule and

Table 1

IBRD/IDA funding to Andhra Pradesh prior to Chandrababu Naidu

S.No.	Project	Date of Approval	Amount ($million)
1.	Kothagudem Power Project I	May 1963	20
2.	Kothagudem Power Project II	June 1965	14
3.	AP Agricultural Credit Project	December 1970	24.4
4.	Pochampad Irrigation Project	July 1971	39
5.	Godavari Barrage Project	February 1975	45
6.	AP Irrigation Project	May 1976	145
7.	AP Fisheries Project	May 1978	17.5
8.	Ramagundam Power Project	January 1979	250
9.	Ramagundam Power Project II	December 1981	300
10.	AP Agricultural Extension Project	March 1982	6
11.	Krishna – Godavari Exploration Project	October 1982	165.5
12.	AP Composite Irrigation Development Project	March 1986	271
13.	Hyderabad Water Supply and Sanitation Project	March 1990	89.9
14.	AP Cyclone Emergency Reconstruction Project	October 1990	210
15.	NTPC Power Generation Project	June 1993	400
16.	AP Forestry Project	February 1994	77.4

the rest are after 2004. However, the dates of approval in the corresponding tables may be misleading since there will be elaborate and time-consuming discussions in the project cycles.

There is a marked difference between the external funding that entered the state during the first and the second halves of this half century. For, in the meanwhile, the World Bank and IMF have also initiated their Structural Adjustment Loan programmes in the late 1970s and Government of India had availed its first SAL from the IMF in 1981. Thus post-1983 relations between the World Bank and the Government of Andhra Pradesh are to be seen in a different light. However, Andhra Pradesh had witnessed a lot of uncertainty in political climate during 1983- 1994 with four governments formed by three different parties (1983-84 – Telugu Desam under N T Rama Rao, 1984 – splintered Telugu Desam under N Bhaskara Rao, 1984-89 – Telugu Desam under N T Rama Rao, 1989- 94 – Congress under M Channa Reddy and N Janardhan Reddy) coming to rule. Thus the reorientation to bureaucrats and influencing politicians had only played a ground clearing role during this decade and the actual onslaught of the external funding began from the mid-1990s.

Of course, this post-1994 external funding was not smooth and it had its own political ups and downs. N T Rama Rao's Telugu Desam Party achieved victory at the 1994 general elections basically on two popular slogans – implementation of prohibition policy as well as provision of subsidised rice to the poor at Rs 2 a kg. Though ridiculed as populist measures, both these acts had a sound basis in the political economy. The prohibition policy was a response to a massively popular political and economic movement led by women all over the state against liquor consumption of their men as well as the government's policies that were destabilising their lives. The subsidised rice scheme was a response to the widespread poverty in the state recognised by almost every data collection agency. However, the international financial agencies and the multi national corporations were ideologically opposed to both these pro-people, welfare measures. Even as the external agencies were stronger in influencing the powers that be by then, the then chief minister was a kind of a maverick and he would not listen to anybody, particularly on those two issues, which were supposed to be close to his heart.

The external funding agencies then wanted a young, brash, not-so-popular and amenable person (in other words a likely puppet) to be at the helm of the affairs and the then finance minister N Chandrababu Naidu's revolt within the ruling party gave them an opportunity they were eagerly looking for. With Naidu in power from September 1995, the external funding agencies started enjoying a heyday in the corridors of power in the state. That rule continues till now, even though Naidu's TDP was defeated by Dr. Y S Rajasekhara Reddy's Congress at the May 2004 elections specifically on the strident criticism of the former's allegiance to the external funding agencies. The tables show that the pace was slower during 1956-94 timeframe with 16 projects in 38 years and became forceful during 1994-2004 with 11 projects in less than 10 years. Though the subsequent government initially appeared to be critical of the World Bank policies, the pace of dependence became much more feverish with 6 projects in less than three years. In fact, all the projects were negotiated or approved in the last one year of the three years.

1990s – Direct rule of the World Bank

Coming back to the earlier phase, the World Bank almost began its direct rule in Andhra Pradesh with N Chandrababu Naidu as chief minister. Several MNCs and international financial institutions started describing him as CEO of Andhra Pradesh rather than as chief minister.[5]

During the less than ten years period between September 1995 and May 2004, the state witnessed unbelievable changes in policies, implementation, power structures and administration. In contrast the state also witnessed tremendous negative responses to the World Bank-dictated economic reforms.

The responses range from more than a hundred small and big publications against the reforms to the famous agitation against power tariff rise that led to police firing killing three persons and finally to the debacle of Chandrababu Naidu at the 2004 May polls. It needs a full-length monograph to elaborate on all the changes but this paper would like to outline briefly what happened during that time.

High Level Committees

As it is in vogue, the World Bank's operations in any country do not begin on a particular date since they are a gradual process. And hence much before Chandrababu Naidu assumed office, the World Bank sought to introduce the policies that would pave the way for its entry in the state. Appointment of four high level committees by the Telugu Desam government to look into the performance of power sector, state level public enterprises (SLPEs), government departments and higher education sector respectively was an attempt in this direction. An incredible thing about these four committees headed by different people was that they were all in one voice in their major suggestions in tune with the World Bank-dictated reforms.

The High Level Committee headed by Hiten Bhaiya that studied power sector performance and suggested measures to restructure it, primarily advised the government to unbundle power sector, to privatise distribution, and to reduce agricultural subsidies among other recommendations. The committee that looked into SLPEs headed by K Subrahmanyam concluded that not more than half a dozen out of 49 SLPEs were fit to be maintained and suggested closure, reduction of workers, privatisation, and disinvestment with regard to the others. Staff Review Committee under the chairmanship of Gangopadhyay studied the government departments and concluded that there was redundancy in staffing and some of the departments could be disbanded and staff strength could be reduced. Koneru Ramakrishna Rao Committee studied education sector and concluded that higher education should be privatised. In one word, all these committees were advising the government to follow the globalisation agenda of privatisation and liberalisation.

These recommendations, Chandrababu Naidu's assumption of power and favourable mention of Andhra Pradesh as a "progressive" state by the World Bank's Country Report 1995 should be seen in consonance.

White Papers

Within a short time of Naidu coming to power, in June 1996, the government of AP tabled a set of seven White Papers on the floor of the state legislature. The White Papers were concerned with State Finances, Irrigation, Power, Public Enterprises, Public Distribution System, Public Employment and Welfare. These papers were ostensibly aimed at educating people at large on the dire economic condition of the state.

Table2

IBRD/IDA funding to Andhra Pradesh during Chandrababu Naidu's regime

S.No.	Project	Date of Approval	Amount ($million)
1.	AP First Referral Health System Project	December 1994	133
2.	AP Hazard Mitigation and Emergency Cyclone Recovery Project	May 1997	150
3.	AP Irrigation Project III	May 1997	325
4.	AP State Highway Project	June 1997	350
5.	AP Economic Restructuring Project	June 1998	543.2
6.	AP Power Sector Restructuring Project	February 1999	210
7.	AP District Poverty Initiatives Project	April 2000	111
8.	AP Economic Reform Loan/Credit	March 2002	250
9.	AP Community Forest Management Project	July 2002	108
10.	AP Rural Poverty Reduction Project	February 2003	150.03
11.	AP Economic Reform Programme II	February 2004	220

The White Papers repeated the recommendations of the high level committees and carried forward the ideological direction of the reports. In fact, the White Papers were an attempt to whitewash the obtaining situation and force the people to believe that there was no alternative[6] than going in for external funding.

Agenda for Economic Reforms

These developments prepared a conducive atmosphere for the World Bank to occupy the centre-stage. Within three months of the White Papers, the World Bank published an important document with far-reaching consequences on Andhra Pradesh economy and society. Titled 'India-Andhra Pradesh: Agenda for Economic Reforms', the report of the World Bank (Report No. 15901-IN) was initially circulated as a confidential document and after a little controversy in the media, it was made public in January 1997.

Appreciation of the earlier committee reports as well as White Papers by Agenda for Economic Reforms clearly shows that all of them were singing the same tune. For example, Agenda says, "the measures proposed by the Committee constitute a sound starting point for designing a power sector reform in AP". It was also observed that the language and expressions in the reports of high level committees, White Papers, and Agenda for Economic Reforms were unmistakably similar and several sentences and passages were simple reproductions from one to the other.

Agenda for Economic Reforms attempted to provide a list of dos and don'ts to the state government in a manner that was very humiliating for a government with over forty years experience. Starting from suggesting macro political economy policies down to minute details on what seminar to be conducted where were also dictated by the Agenda. Time tables and milestones were drawn with regard to retrenchment of staff, closure, disinvestment and privatisation of SLPEs. The measures to be adopted, as dictated by Agenda for Economic Reforms were wide ranging from taxation to power tariff, transport charges, water taxes, subsidies, expenditure restructuring, rationalisation of staff, cutting down welfare schemes and infrastructure and reforms in public enterprises - in other words, encompassing all economic, social and political matters in the state.

Andhra Pradesh Economic Restructuring Project, the largest ever external funding to the state with over $540 million was concluded following Agenda for Economic Reforms. In fact, the Agenda and the APERP documents read similar. The documents and the discussions between the World Bank officials and the state bureaucrats clearly show the hegemony of the international moneylender and the subservience of a so-called independent legislature and executive.

Vision 2020

Following the general direction given in Agenda for Economic Reforms, the state government got McKinsey & Co to prepare a long-term policy paper called Vision 2020. Released on January 26, 1999 the document was scheduled to be implemented from April 1999, giving people hardly two months time to discuss such an important document that would have a bearing on their future. This voluminous document, which was neither written nor completely translated into the language of the people whose future it was supposed to change, selected 14 key areas of state future and made recommendations in line with the World Bank policies of helping MNCs exploit natural resources and spread their market.

The document set most laudable and altruist goals before society: "By 2020, every individual in Andhra Pradesh will be able to lead a comfortable life, filled with opportunities to learn, develop skills, and earn a livelihood. Poverty will have been eradicated and current inequalities will have disappeared. Disadvantaged groups – scheduled castes, scheduled tribes, backward classes, and minorities – as well as other groups in need of special attention, such as women and children, will be empowered and provided with opportunities they need to achieve their full potential…"

However, all these high sounding phrases are a veneer to the real intentions. Vision 2020 was so transparent and within a few pages came out saying, "to achieve the growth levels targeted, the government will have to seek transformation on many dimensions: at least Rs 16,00,000 crore will have to be invested in building infrastructure in the state….This calls for investment on a scale far beyond the resources of the government, pointing to the need to attract large-scale private investment."

Overwhelming influence

Thus Vision 2020 prepared the ground for the government to go in for external funding and within the next couple of months a number of economic hitmen from the US and the UK have become the permanent fixtures in the state Secretariat. Several loan agreements, memoranda of understanding, letters of intent were signed and a number of deals were struck. Each of these agreements prescribed dos and don'ts to the government and each of them reflected in the public policy. At least six

Table 3
IBRD/IDA funding to Andhra Pradesh after Chandrababu Naidu

S.No.	Project	Date of Approval	Amount ($million)
1.	Third AP Economic Reform Loan/Credit	January 2007	225
2.	Hyderabad Urban Water Project II		180
3.	AP Water Sector Improvement Project		435
4.	AP Road Sector Project		320
5.	AP Community-based Tank Management Project		200
6.	AP Urban Reform & Municipal Services Project		233

new loan agreements with far reaching consequences were signed during this less than five-year period. The state's debt has gone up to over Rs 57,000 crore during this period. Power sector restructuring programme was one among the new loan agreements and it dictated that power tariff should be consistently increased and the sector should be allowed to the free play of private operators.

Again in 2002 the government released another set of White Papers to take the reforms ahead. A new Implementation Secretariat was created under the diktats of DFID to oversee closure and sell-off of SLPEs. Single window mechanisms were created to provide hassle-free environment to MNCs that wanted to exploit natural resources and expand market in the state. New infrastructure projects like airports, ports, fly-overs, four-lane and six-lane roads, cold storage warehousing, markets, computerisation and special zones for IT, biotechnology and service operations were conceived in a frenzy for the benefit of international business houses and their Indian junior partners. If at all people, particularly middle classes, benefitted by these new infrastructure facilities, it was only a byproduct but not an intended goal.

Post-Chandrababu Naidu

The Indian National Congress was in opposition all through and went to the extent of saying it would review and repeal the conditionalities of the World Bank if it comes to power in the next general elections. Suffering under the heavy burden of Chandrababu Naidu's World Bank-dictated policies, people also believed the promises of the Congress, despite the fact that it was the Congress which brought in globalisation policies into the country.

The Congress government could not dare to strike new deals with the World Bank in the first two years of its rule but all the same it was implementing the earlier policies as well as negotiating with the World Bank for new loans on new conditionalities. The new loan agreements started materialising by the end of 2006 and Dr Y S Rajasekhara Reddy's government concluded its first ever agreement in January 2007, followed by five more loans in quick succession.

Impacts

The external funding, particularly the World Bank funding, was categorical in prescribing political and economic policies to the government. Each and every such condition was directly or indirectly helpful to one or other MNC or its junior partner here. If there was not direct or indirect beneficiary, the policy prescriptions would in general promote a way of life that would help grow capitalist enterprise, at least in ideological sense. On the whole the ten years of direct rule by the World Bank in the state resulted in significant changes in social, political and cultural life of Telugu people.

A meticulous record of the external funding conditionalities and their influences can be seen in Foreign Funding in Andhra Pradesh, published by Centre for Environment Concerns, Hyderabad in 1995. The record shows that the conditionalities, even before 1995, led to deep rooted changes in polity and economy. The observations of that study have to be taken further in the post-1995 period as the latter period provided scope to much more significant changes.

Politically, the impact of external funding resulted in most undemocratic and autocratic behaviour on the part of the decision making authorities. As already mentioned even the most important documents like Vision 2020 were not placed before the people or legislature for proper discussion. Even as there were hundreds of policy changes during 1994-2006 period, none of them was scrutinised by legislature. Some times even the state cabinet did not discuss and approve key policy changes. Chandrababu Naidu was on record saying that power tariff reduction was not in his hands and the World Bank would not approve.[7] Thus the political class in the state lost all its authority and completely surrendered its powers to the external agency, which in turn ruled the state through some bureaucrats.

Financially, people of the state had to bear the brunt of these developments with a major chunk of state domestic product being spent on debt servicing. The state, with an external debt of about Rs 60,000 crore, was pushed into a debt trap where one had to take new loans to pay off the old loans and interest payments.

Culturally, the people were forced to believe in consumerism, selfishness, acquisition and money-mindedness, thanks to the influence of the all-pervading value system created by the World Bank-dictated reforms. A small minority of middle classes and upper classes reaped the benefits of the new economy and they became the role models for the rest of the society, while those who did not get the fruits of these changes started feeling about either worthlessness of their living or attempting to imitate the upper classes in acquiring money by hook or crook.

Reduced investments in agriculture on one hand and promotion of commercial crops and over dependence on international market on the other led to increasing pauperisation of farmers and as a consequence more and more number of farmers started committing suicide.

A number of public sector industrial and business units were closed down or downsized and the new industrial or service units did not provide employment sufficiently. Thus there was an enlarging unemployed pool with growing number of educated youth seeking employment on one hand and former employees pushed into the army of unemployed on the other.

Due to cut in welfare spending, education, health, and social welfare sectors suffered a lot leading to a lot of deprivation. Increasing corporatisation of education and health added fuel to this fire.

While poverty, unemployment, deprivation and illiteracy were growing at a high speed, urbanisation, access to modern gadgets and garish lifestyles, astronomical salaries, and ultramodern service sector began growing in a couple of cities providing access to a miniscule portion of the population. At a rough estimate, one could conclude that the ratio of people who benefited from the influence of external funding to those who suffered might be anywhere in the range of 10:90.

Obviously this kind of social rupture would lead to violence and hence creating peace zones was part of the World Bank package. In the name of creating peace zones the rulers that be indulged in suppression of basic democratic rights and the consequent repression on people and their expression of dissent was enormous.

To sum up, external funding, a supposed to be benevolent monetary help ultimately led to social tensions, political bankruptcy, cultural uncertainty and administrative repression.

Bibliography

ABK Prasad (2000) – *Runaandhra Pradesh – Prapancha Bank Taakattulo Telugu Prajalu*, Hyderabad.

B V Raghavulu (2004) – *Prapancha Bank Firmanalu – Prajaakantaka Vidhanalu*, Hyderabad.

Centre for Environment Concerns (1995) – Foreign Funding in Andhra Pradesh, Hyderabad.

Communist Party of India (Marxist) (1998) – World Bank Loan – Boon or Bane?, Hyderabad.

D Narasimha Reddy (ed) (1998) – *Andhra Pradesh Arthika Samskaranalu – Prapancha Bank Agenda*, Hyderabad.

Government of Andhra Pradesh (1996) – White Papers, Hyderabad.

Government of Andhra Pradesh (1999) – Vision 2020, Hyderabad.

Government of Andhra Pradesh (2002) – White Papers, Hyderabad.

Government of AP (2000) – Visit of James D Wolfensohn

High Level Committee (1995) - Report of the High Level Committee – Guidelines on Restructuring and Privatisation of Power Sector and Power Tariff, Hyderabad.

http://www.globalpolicy.org/socecon/bwi-wto/wbank/2004/0203indialoan.htm (2004), World Bank Loans to Andhra Pradesh: Financing Bloodshed and Impunity?

K Ramachandra Murthy (2001) – *Vidyut Valayam – Samskaranala Visleshana,* Hyderabad.

N Venugopal (1999) – *Ammakaaniki Andhra Pradesh*, Hyderabad.

Public Interest Research Group (1995) – The World Bank and India, Delhi.

Vemulapalli Venakataramaiah (2003) – *Prapancha Bank Vishavalayamlo Andhra Pradesh,* Hyderabad.

Working Group on Restructuring of Public Sector Undertakings and Cooperative Enterprises (1995) – Report on Restructuring of State Level Public Sector Undertakings, Hyderabad.

World Bank (1996) - Background Paper on Irrigation – The Andhra Pradesh Study, Prepared by Engineering Staff College of India.

World Bank (1997) – India Andhra Pradesh: Agenda for Economic Reforms

World Bank (1998) – Letter to Chief Secretary, Government of Andhra Pradesh, February 2, 1998.

World Bank (1998) – Project Appraisal Document – APERP

World Bank (1999) – Loan Agreement – AP Power Sector Restructuring Project

World Bank (1999) – Project Appraisal Document – AP Power Sector Restructuring Program

World Bank (1999) – Transferring Irrigation Management to Farmers in Andhra Pradesh

World Bank (2003) – India: Power Sector Reform in Andhra Pradesh (Participation in Macroeconomic Policies Case Studies), www.worldbak.org/participation/web/webfiles/indiapower.htm

End notes

1. See the famous treatise of Dadabhai Naoroji (1901), Poverty and Un-British Rule in India, London. (Indian edition published by Publications Division, Government of India, under Classics of Indian History and Economics series in 1962).
2. There is a large body of analytical literature in this regard and most probably the earliest of these expressions appeared in Natarajan L (1952), American Shadow Over India, with a foreword by Gandhian economist J C Kumarappa.
3. The famous controversies being Palmer & Co and Chanda Railway scandals involving British officials and businessmen in the late 19th century.
4. This account forms part of B P R Vithal's overview published in the same volume.
5. Two analogies could be cited here: Mir Osman Ali Khan, the seventh and last Nizam of the erstwhile Hyderabad state was also accorded the title of "faithful ally" by the British queen. A chief minister is bound by an electoral mandate and answerable to a house of people's representatives, at least in theory whereas a CEO is neither bound nor answerable to people, he would only be accountable to his paymasters.
6. Chandrababu Naidu was a key votary of TINA (There Is No Alternative) philosophy and in fact his image builders attempted to bracket him along with Bill Clinton and Tony Blair.
7. This was before 1999 General Elections and even before his government came to power for the second time, Chandrababu Naidu, in a public meeting said policy making with regard to power was not in his hands.

❖ ❖ ❖

4

Chandrababu Naidu's Myths and Reality

With a huge propaganda machine at work and a "managed media", the Chief Minister of Andhra Pradesh, N Chandrababu Naidu is always presented as the hope of India's future and a politician with a difference and vision. From global media organisations to vernacular newspapers, from the likes of Bill Gates and Bill Clinton to the trade bodies like CII and MNCs and local industrialists have been showering accolades on him. No need to mention the compliments paid by the World Bank, global investors, national big business houses, foreign dignitaries and leader writers in the Indian English press. These newspaper writings have been giving an impression that he is doing a lot of development work in the state and he has all the people of Andhra Pradesh behind him.

However, nothing could be farther from truth. Chandrababu Naidu's seven-year rule has systematically pushed every section of society into crisis. The Telugu Desam Party's regime is nothing but following the diktats of the World Bank, Multi National Corporations and big business houses. The government has been giving away the rich resources available in the state to all the rich and powerful from within and outside the country. Every possible opportunity is being created to pave the way for the MNCs and their operatives to enter the vast market in the state. Under the mask of "development" and "welfare" Chandrababu Naidu has been practising a policy of development and

Published in MeanTime, Fortnightly, March 21 – April 3, 2003.

welfare of the rich and powerful, including national and international business interests, only. While doing all this, he has been managing the media to get favourable write-ups. In fact, "managing media" has been his favourite phrase and he has been asking all his party functionaries to "manage the media" which only means bribing or bullying the media to get sycophancy reports.

It is a well known fact that Naidu is in the forefront of implementing the policies of Globalisation, Liberalisation and Privatisation. The implementation of the policies in the state is result of the directions from the World Bank. Naidu does not exhibit even a modicum of self-respect and shame in obeying his imperialist masters, manifested in the World Bank directions and enters the modern Indian history as the key back-stabber of whatever little sovereignty we had earlier. Indeed, he was so audacious to accept that he "could not take a particular policy since the World Bank does not accept it" thereby admitting his servitude to the international financial agency and the MNCs behind it.

The late N T Rama Rao came to power in 1994 routing the Congress with a thumping majority of more than two-thirds in the state assembly. N Chandrababu Naidu became the minister for finance in the NTR's cabinet and his evil designs of mortgaging and selling off the state to the MNCs and the World Bank started then and there. In fact, by that time itself, the World Bank was heavily advising the state and it wanted its 'yes-man' as the finance minister.

The early directions by the World Bank resulted in formation of four committees: Hiten Bhaiya Committee "to study the performance of the state electricity board (SEB) and suggest remedial measures", Subrahmanyam Committee "to study and suggest measures to improve the performance of state level public enterprises", Gangopadhyay Committee "to study the staff position within the government and suggest optimal utilisation of human resources", and K Ramakrishna Rao Committee "to study higher education and suggest improvements".

All these committees clearly violated their terms of references and suggested only one thing, privatisation, instead of recommending measures for improvement. None of the improvement options were considered and privatisation, liberalisation, closures, lay-offs, voluntary retirement schemes and retrenchments were the only suggestions given by these committees. These recommendations amply show that the panels were only voicing the concerns and interests of the imperialist agencies.

In the name of suggesting improvement in the performance of the state electricity board, Hiten Bhaiya Committee asked the state government to trifurcate the functions of the APSEB into generation, transmission and distribution. It asked to privatise distribution and transmission in the first phase and generation in the next phase. It asked the government to give up the subsidies given to the agricultural sector. The whole exercise was aimed at offering the Rs 50,000 crore worth assets of APSEB to the private parties for a meagre Rs 6,000 crore on a silver platter. In the process, thousands of the APSEB employees were left in the lurch without any job guarantee or security.

In view of Subrahmanyam Committee, the improvement of state level public enterprises (SLPEs) only meant sabotaging and closing down the 'loss-making' enterprises with throwing thousands of employees and their families on to the streets. When the SLPE is a profit making one, Subrahmanyam Committee asked the government to sell it off at a throwaway price to the private parties. The committee studied 49 SLPEs and some other units in the co-operative sector and came to a conclusion that except five or six units, all others could be closed down. Reducing the staff, offering the units to private parties, and reducing government stake in some of the units were the other recommendations of the panel.

Gangopadhyay Committee came to a conclusion that most of the government departments have more staff than required and asked the government to reduce the staff. It also suggested that some of the departments could be closed down. It identified "excess staff" and redundant staff and asked the government to redeploy or retrench them. In order to reduce the government expenditure, the panel suggested that welfare departments could be closed.

K Ramakrishna Rao Committee, which was to study higher education segment only, went beyond its brief and gave suggestions for overall privatisation of all the segments of education, including primary and secondary segments. The committee subverted the social goals of education and said it should be based on the market principle of "user paying the cost". The panel succeeded in putting the education field on the cost-benefit principle rather than on social purpose.

While the guiding principles of state policy were being changed into such an unrecognisable shape, there has been a significant political change. Making use of disgruntlement amongst the TDP legislators against the autocratic behaviour of NTR and unconstitutional power being enjoyed by his wife Lakshmi Parvati, Naidu organised a palace coup. He back-stabbed his own father-in-law and party leader NTR and replaced him as chief minister. The role of media in positioning him and getting support is everybody's knowledge.

After becoming chief minister, Naidu's servitude to the World Bank, MNCs and the rich and powerful has come into open. Within six months of coming to power, he released seven 'White Papers' on the state economy to pave the way for the reform package given by the World Bank. The White Papers of Naidu were nothing more than white lies, pure and simple. All the lies were compiled to arrive at the anti-people remedies given by the World Bank and the White Papers offered those measures as inevitable.

The "White Papers" were on the state economy, state government's finances, state electricity board, state level public enterprises, welfare schemes in the state, state government employees and irrigation. In the "White Papers" there was not a single word on the existing poverty and the need for welfare measures in the state. All the "White Papers" tried to argue how the government was spending unnecessarily on welfare schemes and how the state government employees were a drain on the state revenues. Though the state government tabled these "White Papers" on the floor of the state assembly and claimed that they were prepared by the government itself, the Americanised language and expressions and the set goals clearly show that they were written by the World Bank consultants.

While the White Papers were released in June 1996, within three months the World Bank has entered the scene directly. In September 1996, the World Bank has prepared a "confidential" document – *Andhra Pradesh: Agenda for Economic Reforms*. In fact, this is for the first time the international agency has interfered in the economic affairs of a state government and started advising.

The document consists of a number of policy prescriptions starting from macro level like overall fiscal discipline to the lowest level like organising a two-day seminar in Hyderabad on value added taxation policy. In the name of people's participation, the World Bank report directed the state government to withdraw from a number of sectors and constitute "users' organisations." Following this direction, the state government has started Vana Samrakshana Samitis, Water Users' Associations, Village Education Committees, Mothers' Committees, etc and rejuvenated the existing self help groups. These bodies, under the garb of an acceptable principle of people's participation, were aimed at taking away the government's role in financing these activities. The existing employment in all these areas was sought to be removed or redeployed.

The "confidential" document was made public in January 1997 and became the guiding principle for state policy ever since. The state ruling classes have become so audacious that the document was not even put for public discussion through press or tabled on the floor of the assembly before finalising it. Of course, the final version did not have any significant changes.

As if the World Bank's Agenda for Economic Reforms was not sufficient, the state government, the MNCs and the World Bank wanted to have a long term plan for perpetrating exploitation of the resource-rich Andhra Pradesh. As a result, the state government was asked to appoint McKinsey and Co, a consulting MNC close to the World Bank and other imperialist interests, to prepare the Vision 2020 document. The document is nothing but an offering of the valuable natural and human resources in the state to the MNCs and an open invitation to them to exploit the resources. Couched in attractive and bombastic wording, the document listed all the available resources in the state and lured the international business community to descend on the people of the state. The document guaranteed peace, law and order to ensure smoother oppression and exploitation. It cited unrealistic and unsubstantiated figures of Rs 30,00,000 crore for the total project and Rs 16,00,000 crore for infrastructure building over twenty years, only to say that "the government would not be able to generate such huge investments and hence it is imperative to approach international private capital."

Each of the sections of the document – dealing with education, agriculture, industry, services, irrigation, power, roads, ports, airports, cold storage plants, etc. – went on and on heaping praise on private capital and privatisation of hitherto existing public facilities. The basic ideology behind the document is promoting privatisation and withdrawing government and public accountability from all walks of life. The document clearly denounced the idea of all round development and propagated the concept of development in specific selected fields, described as "Growth Engines".

Chandrababu Naidu has been friendly with press and media ever since he entered active politics in the late 1970s. He is very shrewd in realising the importance of media in modern-day world and he has been using the media for his own selfish motives. During the palace coup in 1995, when he started keeping some MLAs as hostages in Hotel Viceroy, a leading Telugu daily exaggerated the number of hostages so as to influence the then neutral MLAs. It is rumoured that a couple of chief reporters and editors supported the back-stabbing received huge sums of money and flats and plots in posh Jubilee Hills area.

Later, Naidu cultivated a host of media personalities with various gifts and alms and the information and public relations department spent more than Rs 400 crore on promoting Naidu as a brand. This media management spread its tentacles to international media also with employing global PR agencies and giving liberal advertisements in international newspapers. Almost every significant newspaper and magazine has been made to write a pro-Naidu piece in the last seven years. Most of the reporters and feature writers have enjoyed the state government's hospitality and had conducted tours by the government and wrote eulogies. A top-ranking media personality is believed to have got a luxury flat in Jubilee Hills for writing a book on Naidu for an international publisher.

The anti-people policies contemplated and implemented by Naidu are, in fact, a legion. His policies have hit almost all sections of population, except a few local rich and powerful and all imperialist forces. The anti-people policies of the state government include hike in charges of government road transport buses, hike in power tariff, removal of power subsidy for agriculture, removal of rice subsidy, hike in educational and hospital charges, hike in motor vehicle taxes, hike in water cess, throwing roads and bridges open to private contractors and leaving people at the mercy of their exorbitant toll taxes, forcing more than 400 cotton farmers to commit suicide with its pro-market policies, throwing thousands of workers' families by closure of Republic Forge Company, Azam Jahi Textile Mills, Allwyn Watch Division and a number of spinning and sugar mills in co-operative sector, removing all NMR, contingency and casual staff from various state government departments, speaking openly against land reforms, etc.

Not a single day passes in Hyderabad without some or other white skin holding a press conference and heaping praise on Naidu. What must be the reason behind this kind of exaggerated praise by the colonial masters? Just because Naidu has become a faithful 'His Master's Voice' and openly said, "we must be thankful to the British for ruling us for three hundred years," he has been getting hefty kickbacks in all the deals, overboard and underhand. In turn, he is offering a lot of tax concessions, exemption from stamp duty and land registration fee, free land, concessions in municipal, water and power tariffs, etc. While denying concessions to the poor and the under privileged, in the name of critical state of the economy, he has been offering thousands of crores of rupees worth concessions to international and national business interests. Andhra Pradesh is a resource-rich state with more than 2.5 crore acres of arable land, about 1.5 crore acres of forest, 1000-km coast line, large reserves of minerals, central location in the country and valuable human resources. The state also offers a large market of about 7 crore population for the imperialist goods and services.

Helping the US information technology industry with captive market and resource base in the state, Naidu has been using the IT tools for mystifying and hoodwinking people. Information Technology has become an incomprehensible *mantra* for him where he chants the *mantra* day in and day out to deceive people. Since half of the state population is illiterate and less than 10 per cent understand English amongst the literate, Naidu has been using the high-tech language to make people feel terrorised, mystified and looked down.

To sum it up, Chandrababu Naidu is ruling Andhra Pradesh as a prince under the crown of the World Bank and the MNCs. Though P V Narasimha Rao and Dr. Manmohan Singh have started the new economic policies, Naidu has proved himself to be the most loyal servant of the MNCs and the most active perpetrator of the conspiracy of selling Indian people off to the MNCs. The only difference between him and the earlier imperialist agents is his knack of shrouding his deceptive anti-people policies in most attractive language. He kills people with an impressive speech that he was actually helping them. From increased "encounter killing" of Naxalites to police firing on the protesters against power tariff hike, brutal lathi-charge on *anganwadi* women workers to preventing all opposition parties from protesting, he is trying to crush the entire social dissent and aspirations for a better life free from imperialist exploitation through "iron heel" giving free hand to police force.

❖ ❖ ❖

5

Pests on a Farmer's Life: Suicides of Cotton Growers

In a society that is becoming insensitive to the sufferings of farmers under a "hi-tech", "development-oriented" and "media-savvy" regime in Andhra Pradesh, at least the sheer volume of unnatural deaths, more than 250 suicides in three months, should be a sufficient reason to wake up. Yet, the administration, political class – both the rulers and the opposition – and commentators and observers do not show enough signs of rising to the occasion. Instead, there have been a number of lopsided responses, right from blaming the victims to blaming the nature, both of whom certainly will not be able to set the record straight.

For the media the story is sensational and starts from immediate past, may be from the first suicide or a little earlier. For the government and the scientist the starting point is either the farmer's improper pest management or excessive spending on pesticides. For the opposition the issue comes as a blessing in disguise just in time for the elections and for them the history of suicides starts on the day the present ruling party has taken over. What is obtaining is a surreal drama with arbitrary selection of facts! Of course, even in a surreal drama, one needs to sift through the facts and try to find the patterns and tie the loose ends and put the facts in a perspective. Here is also an attempt to explore how cotton entered the life of an ordinary peasant in Warangal, Karimnagar and Medak, the water-scarce Telangana districts and how the Telangana small peasant was drawn into this *padmavyuha* of international cotton market.

Written in 1999. Unpublished.

In relation to cotton, Andhra Pradesh ranks third in area (14.1 lakh hectares) and fourth in production (16.26 lakh bales) in 1995-96 accounting for 15.5 per cent in all India area and 12.4 per cent in all India production. Between 1970-73 and 1990-93, Andhra Pradesh witnessed the highest ever growth of 220 per cent in per centage share in cropped area compared to all the other states. Similarly, the state has seen the growth of average yield from 40 kg/ha in 1970-71 to 260 kg/ha in 1995-96.

Traditionally, cotton was used to be grown in black cotton soils of Adilabad, Kurnool and Anantapur districts. Even then it was the local variety of short staple. But by the late 1960s, medium and long staple varieties have entered the scene and slowly Varalakshmi, a HYV, made its appearance in the early 1970s with a host of other HYVs following suit.

The hybrid varieties were introduced in the Guntur district in 1971 and now the district ranks fifth in all India production and first in AP. Even as Adilabad followed with second rank, Warangal made it to fourth position increasing its area from 3,666 ha in 1981-84 to 54,433 ha in 1988-91 with a production of 5,000 bales and 71,833 bales respectively. The Warangal district's share in state production during this period has gone up from 0.7 per cent to 8.3 per cent.

It is interesting to find out the factors that helped this phenomenal growth. Though short staple cotton was known to Warangal farmers earlier, particularly those cultivating black cotton soil, the present HYVs came here through migrant farmers from coastal Andhra.

The migrations took place at least in four different periods over the last seventy years. The erstwhile Nizam government invited enterprising farmers from outside, by publishing "lists of areas available for colonisation" in 1922 and 1923. Much of this cultivable land was in Warangal and Nizamabad districts. By then Warangal and Nizamabad had considerable irrigated areas under the large tanks of the Kakatiya regime of 12th century and the newly constructed Nizamsagar respectively. Thus the first wave of migrants settled in these areas during 1920s.

The colonisation scheme was again initiated in 1941 and according to an estimate, 2,714 peasant families were settled in Nizamabad district with an allotment of 23,319 acres. During the 1950s there was a large influx due to several factors. Since the state was formed in1956 and due to the lack of eligible local candidates (literacy rate was less than 10 per cent in the erstwhile Nizam's Hyderabad state), several coastal people were given government jobs in Telangana and a majority of them purchased lands locally.

After the withdrawal of the Telangana Peasant Armed Struggle by the Communist Party of India in 1951, many of the erstwhile CPI cadre settled as farmers in their earlier struggle areas.

The latest migration was after 1972. Several farmers' families came to Telangana after the failure of the separate Telangana movement of 1969 and 1972. The failure of the movement encouraged the apprehending migrants to settle down in Telangana. In fact, the farmers from Krishna and Guntur districts have not only migrated to Telangana but also to all the irrigated areas in Karnataka on the banks of the Tungabhadra.

It was these latest migrants who brought in HYVs and introduced latest farm techniques in Telangana while the earlier settlers were instrumental in general commercialisation of agriculture. All these migrants have settled in Telangana wherever there was black cotton soil and irrigation facilities. That is why, one finds "Andhra camps", colonies, and "Guntur *palle*"s under the command areas of several large, medium and minor irrigation projects like Nagarjunasagar, Sriramsagar, Nizamsagar, Kadem, Wyra, Pakhal and Laknavaram.

Coming back to cotton, it used to be grown basically in black cotton soils of Guntur and Prakasam districts earlier. The districts also had assured water supply from the Krishna canals. The enterprising migrants from these districts introduced commercial crops like sugarcane, chillies and cotton in Telangana replacing rainfed foodgrains, oilseeds and pulses and coarse millets like jowar and bajra. Their prosperity and entrepreneurial abilities had great demonstrative effect and slowly local farmers started to cultivate marketable crops. (As a side effect, the settlers shifted to market committees and trading to sell seeds, fertilisers and pesticide where profits are assured).

The strong peasant movement in the area saw many large landholders leave their agriculture and settle in urban centres. Thus, the potential commercial farmers leaving the scene, it fell on the shoulders of the new, first generation landholders or tenants who managed to own or lease in a couple of acres. The small holdings forced them to take up high-value crops like cotton. If one browses through the list of the victims, a majority of them are in their twenties and come from 'lower' castes. Many of them are either small farmers owning less than two acres or leased in a piece of land. This indicates that a new breed of farmer is trying to emerge in the Telangana countryside. The fact that out of 1,100 acres of cultivated land in Ogulapuram in Warangal district about 800 acres is under cotton shows the thirst for the cash crop amongst Warangal farmers. Similarly, out of the 250 victims, more than 180 are from Warangal district alone.

However, this farmer, as he is from 'lower' caste and ignorant of manipulative practices associated with commercial agriculture, was unable to mobilise the required funds, generally high volume, for the commercial crops. He does not even know that these crops get crop loans from banks. He relinquished the cultivation of his customary foodgrains but has not learnt the art of influencing bankers and winning friends in the market. Thus he became a natural prey for moneylenders. The institutional credit facilities, from nationalised, private and co-operative banks, if any, have been cornered by the rich and powerful. It is estimated that the entire institutional credit in Warangal district did not exceed Rs 10 crore where there was a requirement for Rs 120 crore. Even the state government admits that the institutional credit serviced only 15 per cent of the requirement. So much for the priority sector lending!

This credit scenario forced the farmers enter the vicious circle of moneylending and usury. The prevailing rates of interest are anywhere between 36 per cent to 84 per cent per annum. In fact, in most of the cases money lender is none other than our own seed-fertiliser-pesticide dealer in the neighbourhood. He provides seed, fertiliser and pesticide on credit and free advice to boot!

Especially in case of commercial agriculture in new areas one needs to be advised on a regular basis. The agriculture department appoints extension workers to help farmers in this regard. But, as an extension worker is in charge of more than 20 villages, he is as good as not there and the farmers have to depend on the pesticide dealer for advice by compulsion. The trader advises to his benefit!

This forced the farmers to spend more than needed on the crops. It is reported that while the cost of cultivation accounts to Rs 7,000 per acre for cotton, the farmers have spent about Rs 12,000. It should be remembered that this cost does not include labour charges (mostly family) and interest on loans. Even by moderate estimates the cost of cotton cultivation might go up to Rs 15,000 per acre. It is estimated that in chemical farming of cotton, pesticides account for 58 per cent of the cultivation costs.

Generally cotton yield is estimated at 10-12 quintals per acre (over 4-5 pickings) and the price has been around Rs 1,600 to Rs 2,000 per quintal. If the latter figure prevails, that leaves a marginal surplus for a small farmer which does not even account for his family labour charges.

For the last couple of years, the yield has been going down due to various reasons. One, scientists say that cotton should not be cultivated continuously on any piece of land as it depletes the required minerals and nutrients and continuous farming diminishes yield. Two, there have been untimely rains coupled with drought conditions in the area. Three, there has been a sort of dumping of adulterated and sub-standard seed on the farmers. Four, generally, the market is being dumped with spurious and adulterated pesticides. Five, there has been a widespread attack of a range of pests over the years. Six, the cotton prices in the market are widely fluctuating. All these reasons aggravated the situation this year. As the scenario persisted for four years in succession, farmers ended up in a morass of indebtedness.

The cotton seed market is dominated by MNCs' high yielding varieties. Since the branded seed is expensive, spurious seed suppliers, who pack sub-standard seed collected from ginning mills with fake certification and sell it at a lower price, are making fast buck. It is also understood that there is no proper planning as to what kind of seed is suited to the available soil. RCH 2, a variety much used in Warangal seems to be popularised by seed suppliers alone without any recommendation from agricultural scientists. Long duration varieties suitable to areas with assured irrigation are introduced here replacing earlier short-duration varieties. Even where water supply was assured under wells, undependable power supply and erratic fluctuations burnt the motor pumps leading to failure of the crop.

The pesticide market is marked by large scale fraud. According to an estimate, more than 100 brands of spurious pesticides are sold in the market. Since the pesticides are given by the dealer-moneylender on credit, farmers are forced to use them even if it is not needed. While the recommended dosage is 6 to 8 times, there are cases where the pesticides are sprayed for more than 15 to 20 times. Pests have become immune to the pesticides due to this excessive usage.

On the other hand, the use of synthetic perethroids against the warnings of environmentalists led to killing of natural enemies of pests like rats, birds, frogs and snakes. "Use of pesticides is more in Andhra Pradesh accounting to 35 per cent of country's total consumption and Guntur is first in India or may be in the world when a district is taken as a unit. Recent estimates revealed that around 13.3 kgs/hectare of pesticides are dumped in Guntur-Krishna-Prakasam region (where cotton crop is concentrated much) while the nation's average was 390 gms/ha," says an entomologist. (Non-pesticidal Approach to Plant Protection - Research Needs, a paper presented at the national workshop on Organic Farming for Sustainable Agriculture by Prof N Venugopal Rao, APAU, Tirupati).

Of late, there has been a glut in the synthetic perethroids market and manufacturers have reduced prices by half. The price of cypermethrin was cut down to Rs 700 from Rs 1,300 per kg.

This year, two pests, Pod borer (Helicoverpa armigera) and leaf-eating caterpillar (Spodoptera litura) attacked the cotton crop. Erratic rains and general drought conditions encouraged wild growth of these pests. The yields have dramatically fell down to 2-3 quintals per acre from the normal 10-12 quintals. The farmers were not able to realise even a fifth of their normal yields.

In trying times like these, the farmers are not provided with crop insurance facilities either. The crop insurance scheme as implemented in Andhra Pradesh has a number of loopholes. The scheme is applicable to restricted areas and specified crops. Basically the scheme is not applicable to commercial crops. Even when it is applied, it is stipulated that the crop should have availed institutional credit.

Less said the better about the cotton market in these districts as anywhere in the country. The cotton market is operated by remote control by the textile mills lobby in the country and international players. The prices are fluctuated according to the whims and fancies of the traders in Coimbatore and Mumbai and their global masters. Cotton Advisory

Board, the apex recommendatory body, is dominated by the textile mills lobby and at the beginning of each season, the board puts out a grossly over estimated projection of demand. At the end of the season, markets invariably experience a glut and prices will go down. Except in 1994-95, in no other season, the cotton farmers got a remunerative price for their yields.

During 1994-95 season, the price had gone up to Rs 3,000 per quintal luring more cultivators. Then the price fell down to less than Rs 2,000 in subsequent years. The farmers in Warangal had protested against the low prices in 1997 also and the Chief Minister himself assured the farmers that he would secure a price not less than Rs 2,000 from the Cotton Corporation of India (CCI) and the Andhra Pradesh State Marketing Federation (Markfed).

However, this season, the minimum support price announced by the central government was Rs 1,530 per quintal, notwithstanding the hue and cry about "high price" by the textile mills lobby and their friends in the media. Both CCI and Markfed started buying small quantities only at a little over the MSP.

Thus this year's losses added to the piled up debts over the last four years. Even a small farmer of 2-3 acres fell in a debt of more than Rs 1 lakh. While those who managed to secure a bank loan faced stringent recovery measures like confiscation of property and ended up in humiliation, those who borrowed from private moneylenders did not find a way out than choosing death. Starting from the second week of December 1998, each day saw at least one suicide death. The death toll rose to three per day in January and February 1999.

Each case of these unnatural deaths of helpless farmers is a pathetic tale in itself. The government's immediate reaction was to brush away the tragedy. Various reasons, other than the real ones, were cited by government functionaries right from the Chief Minister to the district collectors. Natural reasons like drought, excessive liquor consumption, anticipation of ex-gratia and exposure to pesticide while spraying were some of the reasons given for the suicides.

As the suicides persisted, the government had to announce some relief measures like free spraying of pesticides in affected areas, Rs 1 lakh ex gratia each to the victim's families, Rs 1,250 compensation for each acre of pest-affected cotton if the damage is more than 50 per cent, education campaign, and setting up a cotton research institute and testing laboratories.

The state government also approached the Reserve Bank of India and sought some reliefs. The RBI had announced a two-year moratorium on loans to farmers given by commercial and cooperative banks. The RBI had also agreed to extend the repayment schedule to seven years from the present three years and to reduce the interest for small and marginal farmers to 4 per cent. But, by the government's own admission, the loans from these banks account for only 13 per cent of required credit in the state. Thus the RBI relief will be applicable only to the tip of the iceberg.

The Central government opened a second front to dodge the issue by constituting an expert committee to go into the matter and submit a report later. The high-level panel, consisting of bankers, ICAR scientists and senior officials is expected to submit its report by March 15.

However, the promises of the state government and the constitution of a high-level expert committee remind one of a similar exercise ten years ago. When more than 30 cotton farmers committed suicide in Guntur and Prakasam districts in 1988 under similar conditions, a high-powered committee headed by Dr P D Ojha, Deputy Governor, Reserve Bank of India was constituted by the Government of India. Though the report of the committee is not yet made public, the minister of state in the finance ministry, Eduardo Faliero quoted the panel's recommendations in the Rajya Sabha on August 9, 1988. The recommendations sound similar to the present state government's announcements in letter and spirit. Which means that the "short-term measures" and "long-term measures" suggested by the panel were not translated into reality for ten long years!

As things stand at such a pass, one would expect a widespread democratic movement extending solidarity to the victims and protesting against the government's inaction. The general repressive machine, ever operative in Telangana, was in full action against any such democratic initiative. When a committee formed by concerned intellectuals and teachers at the local Kakatiya University tried to give a representation to the district collector in Warangal, the chairman of the committee – a professor of economics, a former Vice-Chancellor and the president of the local bar association and others were lathicharged and several of them were arrested.

While such peaceful protests at the grassroots level are being crushed thus, the high pedestals like the state High Court and the National Human Rights Commission are entertaining complaints filed by concerned citizens over the issue. It is a moot point what will happen to these proceedings. Given the experience of similar suicides a decade ago followed by inaction and another round of suicides, the scenario leaves one in cynicism. The spectacle of indifference and callousness on the part of the vocal sections enhances the hopelessness.

❖ ❖ ❖

II

People's Movements

This section, consisting of eight essays published or written between 1984 and 2012, deals with the origin and growth of various people's movements in Andhra Pradesh with particular focus on the Naxalite/Maoist movement. Whatever may be the professed ideologies and raised slogans of the different social movements, all of them were directly or indirectly influenced by the Naxalite movement's ideas and practice. Even when the ideologues of the sectional movements attempted to show themselves against the Naxalites and heaped bitter criticism, the influence of Naxalites is unmistakable. Thus though one can observe a wide variety of ostensibly rival streams of social movements in today's Andhra Pradesh, a single thread of rebelliousness against status-quo is palpable. The origin and growth of each of these movements require a detailed study.

This section begins with a survey of the Naxalite movement from its beginnings to 1996, sticking to the scope of the multi-volume Comprehensive History of Andhra Pradesh. The essay is included here as it is though much blood and tears have flown under the bridge in the subsequent 16 years. There is a lot to be written about on those 16 tumultuous years.

This section also contains a paper on the Maoist analysis of agrarian relations presented at a seminar in Oxford. This is in response to the arguments that there are a lot of changes in agrarian relations and the original thesis of Naxalbari – semifeudal and semicolonial – does not hold water now. The paper tried to present the history of the characterisation as well as test it in the background of changes and continuity observed in two villages.

When Deccan Chronicle, the largest circulated English daily of Andhra Pradesh launched its edition in Karimnagar, the inaugural issue carried the article included here that dealt with the origin of the movement in Karimnagar, in particular and north Telangana, in general.

Among other essays in this section, two were presentations at academic seminars on concerned issues while two were reports on specific movements of tendu leaf labourers and nuclear power plant protesters.

The idea of negotiations between the Naxalites and the government has been there for a long time and it came to a preliminary level in 2002 before it was aborted by the government. Telugu society enthusiastically welcomed the proposal and K Balagopal dismissed the enthusiasm in his EPW analysis. A rejoinder to his analysis that remained unpublished is also included here to throw light on the dynamics of talks. The idea of talks grew in strength to make its way into the election promises in 2004 and the first round of actual talks were held, before they were scuttled by the government. A detailed exposition and analysis of this round of talks is yet to be written.

In a society where each section is waging its own battle, developing innovative forms of struggle and contributing richly to the broader social movements, this section cannot claim to hold all the relevant material and present a complete scenario. However, here are a few pointers and snapshots to capture the larger picture.

6

Growth of Naxalite Movement in Andhra Pradesh (1967-96)

Introduction

It is impossible to imagine the history of modern Andhra Pradesh without referring to the emergence and growth of Naxalite[1] movement since the latter has directly or indirectly influenced all walks of life in Andhra Pradesh. Evolved from the ongoing tribal peasant movement in the remote corners of Srikakulam and influenced with the ideological path of Naxalbari struggle of West Bengal in 1967-68, the movement aimed at thorough social transformation, spread to several districts in the state before its suppression within four years. The movement simultaneously attracted the attention of masses of all sections in general and middle class intelligentsia in particular, across the state on the one hand and the wrath of the status-quoists and powers that be on the other. The first phase of the movement was suppressed with an unprecedented onslaught by the government resulting in extra-judicial killing of about 400 cadres and leaders and legal proceedings against thousands of tribals, activists and other sympathisers. The repression was followed by a couple of "development" measures intended to wean away tribals from the struggle path, but few of the announced measures translated into practice, without really addressing the basic issues. Thus the movement resurfaced in another part of the state within no time followed by a wider spread and revived in Srikakulam also by the early 1990s, towards the end of this study period.

Commissioned chapter for the forthcoming Vol. VIII of Comprehensive History and Culture of Andhra Pradesh to be published by Andhra Pradesh History Congress in 2012

The first phase of the Naxalite movement in Andhra Pradesh effectively subsided within four years with its high point in 1969. However, because the movement raised fundamental questions about not only the polity and economy but also about culture and society, it attracted quite a few creative and analytical brains and that again led to keeping the flame of the struggle alive even though it appeared extinguished at its starting point. The movement surfaced again within a short time and this time round beginning from Telangana it spread to almost all districts and by its second decade it became a formidable force in the state, despite the proliferation of several splinter groups[2] claiming the legacy of Naxalite path as well as loss of considerable number of cadres in the repression let loose by state and vested interests[3]. At the middle of the third decade, in 1992, the movement again suffered a major setback with the imposition of ban on the CPI (Marxist-Leninist) (People's War), one of the major Naxalite parties and six of its mass organisations. However, the same year witnessed a significant, though short-lived unity of seven splinter groups of Naxalites coming together to form a single party. Out of these seven outfits (CPI (ML) Resistance led by K Ramachandran; UCCRI (ML) Muktigami led by Madhu; CPI (ML) led by Pyla Vasudeva Rao; CPI (ML) Agamiyug led by Koushik Banerjee; CPI (ML) Khokan Mazumdar led by Alok Mukherjee; Coordination Committee of Communist Revolutionaries led by Parimal Das Gupta; and Communist Revolutionary Group for Unity led by Jiten Das Gupta), only the first three were operating in Andhra Pradesh. This unified party again suffered several splits beginning 1995 with the three streams from Andhra Pradesh going three different ways.

Scope and Coverage

The period covered in this survey spans from the beginnings of the movement around 1967 to 1996[4], four years after the ban on the CPI (ML) (People's War) and its mass organisations. Source material used for this survey include varied sources like Naxalites' own published literature, newspaper reports and analyses, government publications, and independent publications. Here it should be noted that there does not exist a single authentic text that provides a comprehensive account of the Naxalite movement in Andhra Pradesh. There have been texts pertaining to a single stream of the movement or a specific period or a specific viewpoint only. Thus this survey had to take from eclectic sources and collate information and analyses to get as cogent a picture as possible.

During this survey period there have been three major streams of Naxalite movement in the state. The first one continues to adhere to the Naxalbari line, with a self critical appraisal and mid-course corrections as well as a strict observance of the demarcation Naxalbari brought into Indian left politics – boycotting parliamentary path. The second and third streams originate from a different line taken in 1967-68 in contrast to Naxalbari and Srikakulam line and opposed the formation of the CPI (ML). However the second stream began claiming Naxalbari legacy after joining a splinter group of original Naxalbari line in 1975. Though this stream followed non-parliamentary path proposed by Naxalbari till 1977, it changed its stand later, with an argument that the parliamentary institutions can be used for people's cause and people themselves have illusions on the parliamentary path. The third stream, originating from the same non-Naxalbari source, adopted ML nomenclature in 1975. All the three streams, irrespective of their support or rejection of Naxalbari contemporarily, came to be known as Naxalite streams by the late 1970s (though it is debatable whether all of them could be called so). The first stream is generally associated with Kondapalli Seetaramaiah (1917-2002), while the second with Chandra Pulla Reddy (1917-1984) and the third with Tarimela Nagi Reddy (1917-1976). Again there have been a number of splits and mergers at individual and group level throughout this period.

At the end of this survey period (1996) the existing Naxalite parties in the state were:

- CPI (ML) (People's War)
- CPI (ML) Party Unity, and
- CPI (ML) Central Reorganisation Committee in the first stream,
- CPI (ML) Janasakthi,
- CPI (ML) New Democracy,
- CPI (ML) Pratighatana, and
- CPI (ML) Praja Pratighatana in the second stream,
- UCCRI (ML), Devulapalli Venkateswara Rao in the third stream, and

- CPI (ML) Unity Initiative, emerged out of a split from the merged second and third streams.

This survey majorly covers the stream of the Naxalite movement represented by the CPI (ML) (People's War), since that gradually evolved into the single largest Naxalite party in the state. Out of the other two parties in that stream, the CPI (ML) Party Unity merged with the CPI (ML) (People's War) subsequently (in 1998) and the other party gradually vanished from the scene.

Pre-Naxalbari context

The three regions comprising of the present day Andhra Pradesh – Telangana, coastal Andhra and Rayalaseema – have a long history of massive people's struggles that can be traced back to the mid 19th century and continuing intermittently. These include Rampa rebellions (1862, 1879, and 1880), Manyam struggle led by Alluri Seetaramaraju (1922-24), various anti-*zamindari* peasant struggles like in Mandasa, Challapalli, Venkatagiri, Bobbili, Nuzvid, Muktyala, etc, tribal struggles led by Ramji Gond (1860) and Komuram Bheem (1941), and Telangana Armed Peasant Struggle (1944/46-51). Participated by thousands of people contemporarily, these struggles formed part of inspiring collective memory in the form of ballads and other folk cultural forms attracting the imagination of later generations. Thus by the time of integration of two regions under different regimes forming Andhra Pradesh, the people of the state had a powerful collective memory of glorious legacy of struggles against exploitation and oppression in their respective regions. Between the state formation in 1956 and the eruption of Srikakulam struggle in 1967 also there have been a number of mass agitations led by opposition political parties, including the then Communist Party of India, on various issues like wages of agricultural labour, land question, demand for industrialisation, trade union issues, as well as against price rise and unemployment, etc. Thus the Srikakulam tribal revolt, its consequent fusion with Naxalbari's political line and its spread to other areas, including Telangana, and coming back to Srikakulam have to be placed in this context of continuity and change of people's struggles as well as massive social churning and collective memory of defiance in the state.

Beginnings

Coming particularly to Srikakulam and Telangana, the first two areas of operation of Naxalite politics in the state, both the areas have decades of distinct history of mass struggles behind them. The popular appeal of the Naxalite ideology and mass participation in the revolutionary practice can be attributed to this history of earlier struggles.

Present day Srikakulam district was divided between Ganjam and Vizagapatam districts till 1936 and became part of Visakhapatnam district and remained so till 1947 under the British. In 1950 it became a separate district. Till 1947 the area also had a number of *zamindaris* like Vizianagaram, Bobbili, Mandasa, Jalantra, Budarsingi, Kurupam, Merangi, Parlakhemundi, Salur, Andra, etc. besides British-ruled *ryotwari* areas. The district consists of two separate regions - forest and hilly part of Eastern Ghats called Agency on the western side and plains and coastline on the eastern side. The tribals and peasants under both the British and the *zamindars* suffered heavy exploitation and oppression and as a consequence, there have been several anti-feudal tribal revolts and struggles in the district during the 19th and early 20th centuries like Achipavalasa (1834), Korravanivalasa (1900), Pentanna (1914), Bobbili (1922), Parlakhemundi (1929-30), and Mandasa (1930-40) before 1947.

Telangana was part of princely state of Hyderabad till 1948 and the feudal empire of the Nizam rulers was mainly divided between *jagir*s (including *surf-e-khas* - king's private property, *paigahs*, *ilaqas*, *samsthan*s, other *jagir*s and sub-*jagir*s) and *diwani* areas. The exploitation and oppression in *jagir* and sub-*jagir* areas under *deshmukh*s, *maktedar*s and other landlords as well as in *diwani* areas were back-breaking and there have been a number of popular uprisings against the exploitation. The spread of political consciousness in Hyderabad in the later part of the 19th century gradually developed into militancy under the influence of the Communist Party of India in the late 1930s and early 1940s leading to the famous Telangana Peasant Armed Struggle 1946-51. It was essentially an anti-feudal struggle and waged against unequal land ownership as well as extra-economic coercions including forced unpaid labour, among other issues. Its major slogan of 'Land to the Tiller' attracted thousands of landless agricultural labour and small peasants and at the height of the struggle, it had its influence in more than 3,000 villages spread across all districts.

In independent India and united Andhra Pradesh, Srikakulam suffered heavily as a neglected district, both administratively and in development, in the remote corner of the state and the condition of two tribal groups – Savara and Jatapu – in Agency was much more pathetic in the late 1950s and early 1960s. The tribals, under the leadership of teachers with communist leanings, began to be organised to raise a protest against the pathetic life meted out to them. The initial stirrings ultimately led to the formation of Girijana Rythu Cooli Sangham in 1958. The leaders of the organisation Palle Ramulu[5], Vempatapu Satyanarayana and Adibhatla Kailasam inculcated a sense of pride and self confidence in the otherwise docile and terrorised tribals. The tribals were suffering from heavy exploitation and oppression at the hands of migrant landlords cum moneylenders cum traders as well as police and forest officials. The Sangham demonstrated the strength of the tribals and was successful in achieving some of their economic demands between the late 1950s and mid 1960s. The demands in this period included returning the lands occupied by non-tribals in the Agency to tribals, distribution of cultivable waste to tribals, moratorium on the debts of tribals as well as provision of credit facilities, provision of agricultural implements and cattle to tribals to enable them in settled agriculture, payment of reasonable remuneration to tribals for the forest produce and providing them essential commodities at fair prices, fair wages, stopping free labour, allowing tribals to use timber for their house constructions and daily use without forest officials harassments, etc.

Though some of these demands were secured in part, the partial fulfillment of the economic demands was going waste with the administration coming to the rescue of the landlords and moneylenders and subjecting the tribals to further repression and harassment. Thus by the mid 1960s the tribals and the local leadership arrived at an understanding of taking up militant forms of struggle including occupying the lands by themselves and fighting the State. However, there was cold response, and admonitions at times, from the party they believed in – the CPI till 1964 and the CPI (M) after that.

At the same time, the national and state level scenario of communist revolutionaries disillusioned with the CPI and the CPI (M) was leading towards a new polarisation and consolidation. Though some of them joined the newly formed CPI (M) in 1964, they had their own doubts about the "revolutionary" and "militant" character of the party and they began raising questions. Charu Mazumdar, the secretary of Darjeeling (West Bengal) district committee of the CPI (M) wrote eight documents between 1965 and April 1967 giving expressions to the new line of thought. The last of these documents coincided with the first spark in Naxalbari on March 3, 1967. On that day, a group of small peasants and agricultural labourers occupied a plot of land under the illegal occupation of a landlord and harvested the crop marking the plot's boundaries with red flags. The same village, within the next fortnight, on March 18, had a peasant convention which upheld the new form of struggle in contrast to the reformist approach taken by the CPI (M). The local *jotedars*, aided by police, wanted to teach the revolting peasants a lesson and on May 25, police opened fire at villagers killing seven women and two children, all tribals. The people of not only Naxalbari, but also neighbouring villages of Kharibari and Phansidewa reacted furiously and attacked landlords and police. Thus Charu Mazumdar's fight against what he termed "reformist and revisionist politics of parliamentary left" in theoretical terms was being translated into practice correspondingly in a rural setting. Charu Mazumdar described the Naxalbari upsurge as "peasants' war of liberation." To strengthen these ideas and consolidate it into an organisational structure Naxalbari O Krishak Sangram Sahayak Samiti was formed in West Bengal and by November 1967 an All India Co-ordination Committee of Revolutionaries (AICCR) was formed. In the meanwhile, the CPI (M) had expelled Charu Mazumdar, Saroj Dutta and others in June 1967. By May 1968, the AICCR expanded itself to new areas in the country and renamed itself as All India Coordination Committee of Communist Revolutionaries (AICCCR) and within the next one year of nation-wide churning a majority of the AICCCR members thought that it was time to consolidate themselves into a revolutionary party and on April 22, 1969 the Communist Party of India (Marxist-Leninist) was formed.

Coming specifically to Andhra Pradesh, while Srikakulam leadership immediately supported and followed Naxalbari line, they had their immediate solidarity base in Naxalbari Sangheebhaava Committee formed by medical students and militant sections in the CPI (M) in Guntur. Srikakulam leadership aligned itself with the newly formed CPI (ML) and announced a four-point programme: seizure of landlords' property; organising Raithanga Sangrama Samitis and other governing bodies in villages; organising guerrilla squads; and annihilation of landlords, police personnel and informers.

On the other hand, Andhra Pradesh Co-ordination Committee of Communist Revolutionaries (APCCCR), led by T Nagi Reddy, Chandra Pulla Reddy, Kolla Venkayya and D V Rao, who were expelled from the CPI (M) in June 1968, was hesitant to sail with AICCCR in toto. Though joined AICCCR initially in November 1968 they opposed the Naxalbari line in general and its application in Srikakulam in particular. They left AICCCR within four months by February 1969 and formed Andhra Pradesh Revolutionary Communist Committee (APRCC) in April 1969 and announced their 'Immediate Programme'. Thus by May 1969 in Andhra Pradesh, there were basically two revolutionary communist organisations, one was the Andhra Pradesh state committee of the CPI (M-L) and the other APRCC. The Srikakulam struggle was led by the CPI (M-L) while the APRCC continued its activity in Godavari valley, particularly in Khammam and Warangal districts.

Srikakulam - Struggle, repression and setback

As already mentioned, the struggle in Srikakulam was initially a tribal struggle, though it also had a strong presence in plain areas of the district. At one point of time there was a brief rupture between the respective leaderships of the different areas also. The objective conditions of the already developing tribal struggle, with an experience over a decade, and the new ideas getting generated through theoretical and political debate happening both at state and national level gave strength to Srikakulam struggle.

Parallel to the influence of Naxalbari line, Srikakulam struggle experienced a major onslaught from landlords on October 31, 1967 and it became a milestone in the history of the struggle. Beginning with 1961, the tribal association used to hold a tribal conference every year and it was scheduled to hold the fifth conference on that date in Mondemkhal. The landlords attacked some of the delegates coming to the conference at Levidi village on the way. When this news reached the conference venue, all the assembled delegates angrily rushed to Levidi and this time round, the waiting landlords fired on the approaching procession killing two tribals – Arika Koranna and Biddika Manganna – on the spot. The State response to this brutal act was indifferent and the culprits were not even arrested till February 1968, adding fuel to the militant resistance of the tribals. The landlords' attack and government's inaction have only strengthened the belief of local leaders and tribals that Naxalbari is the only way available. The incident was coincided with harvest season. Tribals occupied the lands under illegal possession of landlords and harvested standing crops. They also announced that they were not going to pay debts to moneylenders and traders. Grain stocks hoarded at traders and landlords were seized and distributed among poor tribals.

Responding to this tribal resistance, the State forces entered Agency area and attacked several villages and terrorised tribal communities. Arresting and keeping people in illegal custody for days together, subjecting them to severe torture, rape and molestation of women became order of the day. Household properties and grains were either destroyed or taken away.

Analysing the experience of State-landlord onslaught on the movement and tribal resistance that happened for one year, the district plenum in October 1968 resolved that it was high time to launch armed struggle and it was decided to begin the armed struggle on November 25 by seizing the properties of landlords in three villages. Thus the famous Srikakulam tribal armed struggle was officially launched on November 25, 1968.

In the immediate aftermath, the armed struggle spread like a veritable wildfire engulfing hundreds of villages in Srikakulam district. Seizure of properties of landlords, traders and moneylenders, taking away grain from their granaries, burning the promissory notes and other debt instruments, killing landlords and moneylenders as per the "annihilation of class enemy" policy, attack on State forces and taking away arms, etc were the major activities during this period. While these activities were going on till February 1969, Charu Mazumdar visited Srikakulam in February - March 1969 and also attended the state level meeting of communist revolutionaries held at Guttikonda Bilam in Guntur district. This meeting approved Naxalbari – Srikakulam struggles and pledged to take the spirit of the struggle forward. To encourage and enrich that spirit Charu Mazumdar wrote his famous article "*Srikakulam – Will it be the Yenan*[6] *of India?*" published in the March 1969 issue of Liberation.

With the formation of the CPI (M-L) in April 1969, the tribal revolutionaries felt invigorated and the struggle continued and scaled new heights with all militant forms. The contemporary reports indicate that each of the actions was participated by hundreds of armed and unarmed tribals under the leadership of armed guerrilla squads of revolutionaries. By that time hundreds of middle class youth from all the districts of Andhra Pradesh, in the spirit of Che Guevara, volunteered to join the armed squads. As the movement spread spatially and in terms of "violent actions" against landlords and police, the government wanted to crush it with might and went on raising its police force from a mere 500 at the beginning of the struggle to 5,000 Andhra Pradesh Special Police forces. Hundreds of tribals were brought to the camps organised in the big villages and the tribals were subjected to severe torture. When this attempt failed to wean away tribals from the struggle path, the government deployed 10,000 CRPF forces in Srikakulam forest and declared most of the district as "disturbed areas"[7] beginning with Agency area of Patapatnam taluq on June 7 to Parvatipuram, Palakonda, Patapatnam, Sompeta, Tekkali and Icchapuram taluqs on August 20. Prices were announced on the heads of the leaders even as the leaders who were caught were summarily killed without any judicial process. Besides hundreds of criminal cases involving thousands of tribals, Parvatipuram Conspiracy case, a major amalgamated case was registered in 1970. The case combined all the criminal cases against Naxalites booked during 1969 and 1970 and made a large case involving 250 accused and over 500 witnesses. It was charged that the accused entered into a conspiracy at Guttikonda Bilam to commit all these crimes. However, after eight long years of prosecution, out of the 250 accused (100 were already killed in "encounters" by then) the trial court convicted only 15 and even that conviction was struck down by High Court.

Suppressing the movement with such high-handed, extra-judicial and judicial attacks on the one hand, the government also initiated some welfare measures to appease and to make tribals believe its own welfare bonafides on the other. Thus the government has brought in an amendment (popularly known as 1 of 1970) to the existing Land Transfer Regulation Act, 1959, to prohibit transfer of tribal lands. Various land reforms measures including the Andhra Pradesh Land Reforms (Ceiling on Agricultural Holdings) Act, 1973, were promulgated. Several welfare schemes like constructing minor and major irrigation projects, laying roads and establishing schools and hospitals were taken up.

During the same time, there were a number of incidents and processes inspired by Naxalite ideology and Srikakulam struggle in almost all districts in the state. While a number of democrats as well as sympathisers of the mass movement within the political parties raised their voice against the repression, defence committees with advocates and intellectuals were organised at many places to provide legal assistance to the Naxalites. The defence committees gradually developed into an independent civil liberties organisation – Andhra Pradesh Civil Liberties Committee (APCLC) by 1973. In 1970 itself, Viplava Rachayitala Sangham (Virasam, as it is popularly known) (Revolutionary Writers' Association) was formed by young writers as well as some important writers who severed their relationship with Abhyudaya Rachayitala Sangham (Progressive Writers' Association), associated with the CPI. The Revolutionary Writers' Association went on openly propagating the path taken by Naxalbari - Srikakulam and exhorted people to revive that path. Jana Natya Mandali, formed in 1972 added and expanded the cultural and intellectual work to spread the message of Naxalite politics.

Summing up the Srikakulam experience, Sumanta Banerjee, the historian of Naxalite movement in India, said: "By the end of 1969, altogether 15 districts of Andhra Pradesh were affected by Communist revolutionary activities. The situation in Srikakulam and Warangal districts was so grave that the areas affected were declared as 'disturbed areas'. According to Government statistics, the Communist revolutionaries killed 48 people, including landlords, moneylenders, merchants, forest officers and policemen, made 99 attacks on the police and abducted 15 people. In all the abduction cases, according to the Government, the victims were tried in the 'Praja Courts' (people's courts), and punishments ranging from death to penalty of fine were imposed on them. Besides, a large quantity of guns, ammunitions and explosives were also seized by the rebels, during the raids. Both from its power of sustenance and its improvement of organisations, it was evident that the movement in Andhra Pradesh in 1968-69, was a more resounding and clear-throated echo of the short-lived thunder of Naxalbari. While Naxalbari branded the words 'Armed agrarian revolution' on the signpost of the Indian revolution, Srikakulam engraved on it the sign 'guerrilla warfare' to indicate the turn of the road." (Banerjee, 2009, p. 135).

Anyway by 1972, Srikakulam struggle suffered setback due to several reasons including the State repression, loss of key leadership, terror created amongst tribals at large, excesses of and dissensions within the party leadership and welfare measures of the government.

On the other front, the APRCC which broke away from Naxalite line, advocating a gradual, phased and protracted struggle, believed in preparations for a future armed struggle according to its 'Immediate Programme'. It began to organise people in Karimnagar, Warangal and Khammam districts – generally known as Godavari valley. But soon, there was a division within the APRCC and two different lines under Tarimela Nagi Reddy (TN) and Chandra Pulla Reddy (CP) emerged. While the followers of TN attempted to implement the programme in Kondamodalu forest of East Godavari, the followers of CP tried to organise struggles in Warangal-Khammam border. The two lines formally divided in 1973 and the CP group called itself Andhra Pradesh Revolutionary Communist Party and the TN group called itself Communist Party of India (Revolutionaries). In April 1975, the APRCP joined the CPI (ML) led by Satya Narayan Singh, acquired the name of CPI (ML), popularly with a suffix Vimochana, after its fortnightly organ, and continued its activity with claims of Naxalbari legacy. In the meanwhile, the CPI (R) became Unity Centre of Communist Revolutionaries of India (Marxist – Leninist) (UCCRI-ML) in 1975. Though these formations did not support Naxalbari and Srikakulam struggles completely and opposed the formation of ML party in the initial stages, they also formed part of and claimed legacy of the larger Naxalite politics with ML nomenclature. However, both these streams remained a minor force in tribal and rural belts, even as CPI (ML) Vimochana had a considerable influence in students and intellectuals.

Reorganisation

The original CPI (ML) that led Srikakulam struggle almost disintegrated, both at national and state levels with heavy repression on one hand and internal divisions on the other, by 1972 and there were attempts to rebuild the party or at least to coordinate the struggles in various areas. It was Andhra Pradesh State Committee that took lead in this direction and by January 1974, the CPI (M-L) Central Organising Committee was formed with remaining forces of the CPI (ML) from

West Bengal, Bihar, Uttar Pradesh, Kashmir, Punjab and Tamil Nadu to coordinate and unite the revolutionaries in different states. As part of the unity and consolidation efforts, it was also decided to critically review the past experience and pave the way for future. Thus by November 1974 the COC had developed a Self Critical Report and Road to Revolution, a new strategy and tactics document. These two documents humbly accepted the left sectarian mistakes of the past and suggested several corrections. The corrections included setting up mass organisations and adhering to mass line without leaving armed struggle and continuing boycotting parliamentary path, the two distinct features of Naxalbari – Srikakulam line.

Emergency

However, when the attempts of the COC to set up mass organisations and spread its influence both in Andhra Pradesh and elsewhere were beginning to take shape, there was a severe jolt on the movement in the form of proclamation of Emergency in the country on June 25, 1975. The party hardly began implementing its policy of establishing mass organisations with an experiment in forming Radical Students Union (RSU) and preparing to form Radical Youth League (RYL) and Raithu Cooli Sangham (RCS). With the proclamation of Emergency and suspension of fundamental rights, it was not possible for any democratic activity and the RSU could not take up its work openly in educational institutions. Even as half of Virasam members (35 out of around 60) were arrested and any person with remote Naxalite leanings was under surveillance and threat of immanent arrest, the members of RSU chose to go to villages to evade arrest. Particularly, their work in Karimnagar and Adilabad districts in analysing rural agrarian social structures, forms of exploitation and the need to wage struggles paved way for mobilising and organising agricultural labourers and small peasants in a big way. The 20-point programme announced by the government at that time came in handy for these students in their campaign of exposing the shallowness of ruling class policies. By making people demand the implementation of some "welfare" measures of the programme, these students could easily demonstrate that the government was not sincere enough to translate its promises into practice. Based on this realisation the students could exhort people to take up militant struggle path and inculcated the idea of agrarian revolution as the only alternative. These campaigns reaped fruitful results in hundreds of villages with thousands of poor agricultural labour and small peasant masses rallying behind radicals.

Upsurge in Karimnagar - Adilabad

As part of the revised programme of setting up mass organisations and carrying forward the agrarian revolution, CPI (ML) COC formed Radical Students Union in 1974 and within three months of its first state conference in February 1975, it could not function openly due to Emergency provisions. In fact, Radical Youth League was also to be formed and hold its first state conference in July 1975. The energies of these two organisations as well as the party were then utilised to go to rural areas to study the existing socio-economic-political structure and build strong peasant movement during Emergency. Thus RSU cadres went to Karimnagar - Adilabad rural areas and began their study, propaganda and organisational work. The popularity and mass participation of the struggle can be gauged with the successful meeting termed as Jagityal Jaitrayatra held at Jagityal in Karimnagar on September 7, 1978. The meeting was attended by at least 30,000 people and the meeting gave a call to fight prevalent feudal oppression and exploitation.

To understand the forms of feudal oppression and exploitation existing then it would be proper to quote from a contemporary source:

"Here we list out some of the unendurable methods of oppression and exploitation perpetrated by the landlords. These landlords actually deserve to be called as despots of middle ages. Their oppressive activities can be listed endlessly. Here we deal with some prominent practices only:

- Money extortions variously called as gifts, *nazaranas*, fines and compensations.
- Tributes: Annual *mamools* for each caste are fixed. Besides that, a certain amount should be paid as tribute on the occasion of joy, sorrow or dispute.
- *Vetti*: Labour, ploughs, sheep herds and goat herds, milk, provisions, vegetables, and all kinds of services should be rendered to the landlord free of cost.

- Bonded labour.
- Expulsion from village.
- Usury.
- Appropriation of commons and government lands.
- Encroaching patta lands of poor and middle peasants.
- Commission on sale and purchase of land and other assets.
- Brokerage.
- Exploitation of forest produce.
- Processing and appropriation of loans from Land Mortgage Banks and Cooperative Central Banks.
- Charging both the parties huge sums of money in the name of settling disputes.
- Threats and intimidation.
- Atrocities on women.
- Social oppression.
- *Mamools* from traders and contractors of various works.
- Maintaining private armies.
- Keeping licensed and unlicensed lethal weapons.

All these landlords own jeeps, cars, motorcycles and tractors. Many of them have hordes of deadly weapons. They use these weapons freely to ensure their rule over their kingdom. Political power, either at village level or at district level, lies in these landlords' hands. Patel, patwari, sarpanch and other village officers toe the line of the landlord. Officials of banks and government exhibit their efficiency in serving these landlords. They support whatever party that holds the reins. Every parliamentary party aspires for their patronage.

This picture is drawn from the actual experiences gained in Karimnagar and Adilabad districts. Warangal and Nizamabad confirm the picture broadly, except some local variants. Khammam presents much more variance adding landlordism of CPI and CPI (M)." (Kranti Prachuranalu 1981, quoted in 1985)

This situation quite naturally led to widespread movement against the evil practices and the Naxalites gained strength by leading these struggles, which gradually spread not only to neighbouring Telangana districts but also to other districts in the state.

Wildfire 1978 – 1985

While the objective conditions in different districts might have varied in detail and degree, the operation of subjective forces in the form of a well-organised Naxalite party (by this time the CPI (ML) COC became dysfunctional and in the state it was known as the CPI (ML) AP State Committee) and its swelling cadres of various mass organisations provided a fillip to the movement. They also availed the widespread democratic upsurge and euphoric atmosphere that prevailed after lifting of Emergency and while the RSU was revived immediately, the RYL was formed in 1978, the RCS in 1981 and Singareni Karmika Samakhya (Sikasa) in 1982 entering into new walks of life on the one hand and offering thousands of cadres to spread the message of revolution on the other.

A very important process during this time was a unique 'Go to Village' campaign taken up by the RSU at its second conference in Warangal in February 1978. The RYL held its first conference in May 1978 in Guntur and both the organisations together formed small teams of students and youth to go to specific villages with a mandate to study villages, attract masses with songs and other cultural performances, mingle with downtrodden, understand the people's problems, share their knowledge of Marxism and agrarian revolution with masses, and if possible set up local units of mass organisations. The campaign, though attempted to be scuttled by police and village gentry from the beginning, marched in leaps and bounds from 1978 to 1985, when the repression became really grave. Though it was continued later till the imposition of ban in 1992, it was a much scaled-down affair. According to a contemporary account, the 'Go to Village' campaign in 1984 covered as many as 50 lakh people in 2,419 villages with 150 teams comprising 1,100 students and youth. That year alone the student-youth teams helped people set up the RYL and RCS units in 200 villages. In its entirety, the campaign might have covered no less than 12,000 villages and touched at least 3 crore people in seven years.

Even as this mass work – mobilising people and organising them to wage militant struggles – was going on, the Naxalite party working at state level attracted the attention of revolutionaries in other states. The negotiations and debates ultimately led to the formation of the CPI (ML) (People's War) on April 22, 1980. As the inheritor of Naxalbari – Srikakulam line, the party spread its wings to other states as well as consolidated its position in the state. Within two years, the party also formulated an important document called Guerrilla Zone Perspective and made its first attempts to enter Dandakaranya to take its armed agrarian revolution a step ahead.

The period between 1978 and 1985 were crucial for the Naxalite politics in Andhra Pradesh in terms of its horizontal and vertical spread. During this time, the Naxalite influence expanded to almost all sections of people across the breadth and length of the state. It would not be an exaggeration to say that there was not a single group of people or area that did not expose to Naxalite politics during these years. All sections of people – students, youth, adivasis, dalits, middle castes, women, minorities, workers, agricultural labour, and peasants were influenced by respective mass organisations or the Naxalite party in particular and Naxalite ideology in general. There was not a single district that did not witness Naxalite activity.

Two important processes occurred during this time deserve special mention: Indravelli massacre and work among Singareni coal mines.

Indravelli, a big village in Adilabad district, witnessed a brutal police firing on Gond and other tribal communities on April 20, 1981, in which tribals numbering anywhere between 13 and 60 were killed. Tribals of Adilabad under the influence of Naxalites formed Girijan Raithu Cooli Sangham and wanted to hold their conference at Indravelli on that day. Police did not give necessary permission and fired on the processions reaching the place from far off without knowing the refusal of permission. The government sources put the death toll at 13 and independent sources claimed 60. The incident showed the callousness of the government to the problems of helpless tribals and added fuel to the growing Naxalite movement in the state. In fact, Indravelli massacre was part of the long-range repression against this phase of Naxalite movement beginning with killing of cadres by landlords in Karimnagar in 1977, imposition of the Disturbed Areas Act in Jagityal and Siricilla in 1978, widespread arrests and encounter killings all over the state in the later years.

Another major breakthrough during this period was organising coal mine workers spread over three districts – Adilabad, Karimnagar and Khammam. Singareni Karmika Samakhya was formed in 1982 and led a number of struggles. Since the coal belt was adjoining to the areas of ongoing peasant struggles and most of the mine workers came from those peasant families, the working class in coal belt was both influenced by the Naxalite politics and offered a much-needed working class composition to the movement.

Parallel to these mass struggles on various issues, the Naxalite party, true to its ideology of overthrowing the semi-feudal semi-colonial Indian state, believed in armed struggle and continued with its clandestine, armed activities and grew in strength.

Repression 1985-89

At the mainstream political level there were a lot of changes during this time. There was a change of leadership for the first time with Congress losing power in the state after 27 years of unquestioned rule. Telugu Desam Party under the leadership of charismatic movie idol N T Rama Rao occupied the seat of power within nine months of party formation. N T Rama Rao recognised the role of Naxalites in public life and to fully cash their popularity, hailed them as the real patriots and expressed his intention to join hands with them. However there was not much change in the official policy towards Naxalites. Within a short time the government fell due to an internal coup. Reinstated after a massive democratic protest, N T Rama Rao chose to go to polls again and returned to power with thumping majority. With this double victory in two years, the Telugu Desam government post-1985 became arrogant and did not allow any dissent. Since the Naxalites were seen as the real opposition and their growing mass base was proven beyond doubt, the new government wanted to crush them with all its might. The chief minister openly declared that hereafter "no dance, no song and no speech". All the democratic and open expression of Naxalites and mass organisations were curtailed and the number of encounter killings drastically rose. The newly available Terrorist and Disruptive Activities (Prevention) Act was widely and indiscriminately used and hundreds of Naxalite sympathisers were arrested without trial. A tribal hamlet was burnt down by police to threaten tribals for their support to

Naxalites. Encounter killings moved to villages and towns from remote forest areas. The Latin American phenomenon of forced disappearance also began. Though the Naxalites attempted to counter this onslaught with direct attacks on police and State machinery with introducing mine blasts and kidnaps, the Naxalite activity among the masses at large suffered a heavy loss. Even as the mass organisations were functioning, their meetings, mobilisations and struggles were not permitted.

Resurgence 1990-92

During the 1985-89 repression, since there were no visible signs, the Naxalite movement was almost written off by many politicians, bureaucrats and news observers. However, when the then opposition Congress promised to relax the repression and allow democratic rights of the people in general and the Naxalites in particular, people overwhelmingly approved the promise and the Telugu Desam Party which witnessed two thumping victories in two years earlier had to accept its defeat. The new regime initially allowed democratic activity and it was the Naxalite mass organisations that used the relaxed atmosphere to the fullest. While the new government took power in December 1989, the first occasion for show of strength of Naxalites came in January 1990 in the form of twenty years celebrations of Virasam in Hyderabad. The meeting showed that people's trust in and sympathy for Naxalites was not only not declining but spreading. Gaddar, the popular face of Naxalite politics and a powerful balladeer, who had to be underground during 1985-89 repression, came out in February 1990 and again this meeting demonstrated the strength of Naxalite politics. In May 1990, Rythu Cooli Sangham organised its state conference (which was prohibited in Rajahmundry in 1985) in Warangal and it was attended by a record 12 lakh people. Even the ruling class press contemporarily admitted that the Naxalites have a massive support and people are undoubtedly behind it.

The Warangal conference gave a call to develop the scope and forms of struggle in rural areas against feudal exploitation and oppression. The major call was for land occupation and within a short time almost all Telangana districts and some other districts saw hundreds of agricultural labour and small peasants going with red flags and occupying the lands under illegal occupation of landlords. The people began to implement the promise of the governments for decades to occupy and redistribute surplus lands with landlords. While these land struggles were led by the RCS and RYL, there were a number of struggles in villages and towns led by the RYL and RSU.

Simultaneously the party which had already moved into Dandakaranya and going ahead with setting up guerrilla zone there increased its attacks on State.

Ban 1992

The relaxed period between January 1990 and May 1992 clearly showed the government that the Naxalites were indeed a force to reckon with and if their alternative was allowed to grow the movement with its expanding mass base would sweep the ruling politics completely. Even the government's attempts to check their influence in the form of reviving encounter killings, arrests, not allowing public gatherings and protests, failed during this relaxed period. At the political level also there was a change of guard with a new chief minister who reverted back to a stringent policy towards Naxalites. Thus on May 21, 1992, on the first anniversary of Rajiv Gandhi's assassination, the chief minister announced the ban on the CPI (ML) (People's War) along with Radical Students Union, Radical Youth League, Raithu Cooli Sangham, Singareni Karmika Samakhya, All India Revolutionary Students Federation, and Viplava Karmika Samakhya. This was the first ban on a political organisation as well as mass organisations of students, youth and mine workers in the state after independence.

Due to ban the organisations were unable to function in open democratic space and thus thereafter the history of Naxalite movement cannot be written as a process. Only sporadic incidents began appearing in the press. The process became more and more invisible with only events, that too violent and sensational, becoming more visible. Newspapers began reporting more on landmines, blasts, kidnaps, killings and encounters rather than the expression of people's aspirations, people's despairs and resultant struggles. The state to some extent was successful in portraying the image of Naxalites as terrorists who knew killing and dying only. However, though the stream of Naxalite politics became invisible, the Naxalite way of looking at peoples' problems and their distinct solutions remained on the minds of people at large.

Their ideological influence and popularity continued to be the same through literature and culture.

Issues raised by Naxalite movement

Whatever may be one's assessment of success or failure of Naxalite movement in Andhra Pradesh society, one has to recognise their contribution in providing a new perspective to thinking about society. This new perspective spreads to ideological, organisational, social and political levels.

Ideological issues

Semi-feudal, semi-colonial character of Indian state and society: The Naxalites' major contribution to understanding society is their characterisation of the nature of society. While every other political formation almost accepted that August 15, 1947 gave India independence, they argued that India still remained semi-colonial under the same kind of colonial plunder and domination. If India came out of the clutches of one British colonialism, now there are several imperialist countries that exploit and dominate Indian economic and political policies. Even as some Gandhians and old-time patriots argue that India did not get economic independence and needs a second independence struggle, the Naxalites argue that the anti-imperialist struggle that was deceived in 1947 has to be revived to throw out the imperialists and their compradors. Similarly, the Naxalites argue that the stranglehold of feudalism, in the form of semi-feudal production relations, still oppress and exploit Indian masses and to throw it away a genuine anti-feudal struggle has to be waged. Thus the Naxalites' appeal lies in their formulation and leadership of the real anti-feudal and anti-imperialist struggle that can liberate this country.

Inadequacy of parliamentary path to bring about New Democratic Revolution: Another ideological issue brought forward by the Naxalites pertains to the form or forms this liberation struggle has to take. While the traditional left parties argued that one could achieve the goals of democratic revolution in India through parliamentary path, the Naxalites refused this and said it was only a protracted people's war that can bring about a new democratic revolution in the country. The new democratic revolution in Indian specific conditions can only have an agrarian revolution with a slogan of land to the tiller as its axis. The Naxalites argue that since the powers that be would not give up their power to rule, exploit and oppress so easily the struggle against them has to take the form of armed struggle and counter violence, as they believe in the Marxist dictum of "force is the midwife of every old society pregnant with a new one"[8].

Organisational issues

Armed protracted people's war: The Naxalites' contribution to the popular politics in India is that they not only introduced militancy into the mass movements, but also spread the idea of change in system through an armed revolution is the only way, instead of tinkering with social problems in a reformist piecemeal approach. Though it is debatable whether a political party has a right to overthrow a government established by popular mandate expressed in universal franchise through extra-parliamentary methods, the Naxalites have been arguing that their struggle was not against a particular government but against the entire system. They also argue that people are the sovereign power and will have the ultimate right to replace a better system and the revolutionary practice was only an expression of people.

Consistency and continuation of people's struggles: Yet another major contribution of the Naxalite movement to people's politics is that, with its entry it heralded an era where it is impossible to scuttle a movement completely. In Indian history, even if one looks at the struggles from colonial times till Telangana Peasant Armed Struggle, every struggle was stopped in the mid-way, most of the times failed to achieve anything. In fact Telangana Peasant Armed Struggle was officially withdrawn by the leadership. In contrast, even though one or other group claiming Naxalbari legacy stopped its struggle, there are many others who hold fast to it and continue. Thus even after the death of thousands of its activists, surrender or change of mind of dozens of outfits, Naxalite politics continue to operate and gain strength. Usually referred as the spirit of phoenix in Naxalite literature, this power of sustenance and survival against odds gave the movement a glowing attraction.

New type of mass organisations: The Naxalites' contribution to the left politics in the country in organisational sphere is their novel approach to mass organisations. While the traditional left thought that the mass organisations could be organised only on their own economic demands without leading to politicisation, the Naxalites added vigor to the organisations saying that there need not be any watertight compartmentalisation between economic and political demands. Even though economic demands work as the first step of mobilisation, the subjective forces have to be enriched and educated with newer perspectives, including politicisation. Though the Naxalites in the initial stages dismissed mass organisations thanks to the experience of traditional left, in the later years they blended both economic and political demands organically and Sikasa experience is a great example from Andhra Pradesh in this regard.

Social impact

Cultural upsurge: The social significance of Naxalite movement in Andhra Pradesh can be best gauged by the proliferation of people's culture and the respect it commanded thanks to the Naxalite politics. It would be impossible to think of revival and resurgence of people's cultural forms, in the face of onslaught from commercial and cinema influences, without Naxalites taking up the cultural forms themselves. The Naxalites in Telugu cultural field had followed two Marxist thinkers, Stalin who said 'proletarian in content and national in form', as well as Mao who said 'from the masses to the masses'. Thus the credit of conservation, development and innovation of Telugu people's native culture goes to the Naxalites.

Inculcating self confidence and rebellious spirit among masses: A major contribution of the Naxalite movement to Telugu society is that it raised the consciousness of all sections of people so much so that the hitherto downtrodden, oppressed and submissive sections like dalits, tribals, backward castes and women began to rise and question the status quo. Some of these sections might give credit to Naxalites and yet others might not do so, but it is an undeniable fact that it was the Naxalites who taught that it was right to rebel in post-Independence India. While there were no significant people's movements between 1947 and 1967, the post-Naxalbari era has witnessed hundreds of small, sporadic, organised, unorganised, spontaneous people's struggles all over the country, taking Naxalbari consciously or unconsciously as a model.

Sacrifice in an age of selfishness: Another major contribution of Naxalites to social dynamics is their demonstration of supreme sacrifice, that too when the whole society was moving towards more and more selfishness. Hundreds and thousands of youth joined the movement unmindful of the ruthless repression by state forces and even sacrificed their lives just for the cause of a better life for future generations. Even those who do not accept their way of struggle as correct, observed that the sacrificing and selfless traditions they followed, particularly risking their life without asking anything in return, was a noble and exemplary human characteristic.

Impact on governance

In political sphere the Naxalites in Andhra Pradesh had a number of contributions but it would be suffice to mention the impact on governance. Whether it is parroting welfare measures like 1 of 1970 or renewed talk of land reforms or the abrogation of rule of law or violation of democratic rights, the governance in Andhra Pradesh finds itself in such a state because of the Naxalite movement. Subsequent to the Naxalites' struggle the State began to announce a number of welfare measures to address the same land and livelihood issues raised by the Naxalites. The State had openly accepted that it was, through these measures, trying to pull out those sections influenced by the Naxalites. Similarly, in an attempt to crush the movement, the State indulged in a number of violations of fundamental and democratic rights enshrined in the Constitution.

Conclusion

Since the story of Naxalite movement in Andhra Pradesh did not end with 1996 and in fact continued unabated with leaps and bounds, one cannot really sum up this ongoing social phenomenon, that too after another decade and a half. However, to put the nature and impact of the Naxalite movement in a nutshell, the Naxalite movement in Andhra Pradesh began from the wretched of the earth, raised questions on behalf of them, challenged the powers that be from the perspective of the powerless, showed an alternative development and sociopolitical model and in the process, the poor and powerless joined the movement in large numbers and identified themselves with the movement in all spheres.

The movement stood as a shining example of supreme sacrifice in the face of ruthless repression. Thus mass-based alternative politics is the movement's foremost characteristic and its impact is both horizontal and vertical in spatial and social terms. It spread across all regions encompassing all spheres of life and percolated down to the lowest ranks of people at the same time attracting people from upper castes and middle classes also.

Bibliography

AIRSF (1993) – Naxalbari is not Just the Name of a Village, AIRSF, Calcutta.

Aravinda Rao, K (1996) – Naxalite Terrorism – Social and Legal Issues, East West Books, Madras.

Balagopal, K (1988) – Probings in the Political Economy of Agrarian Classes and Conflicts, Perspectives, Hyderabad.

Banerjee, Sumanta (2009) – In the Wake of Naxalbari, Sahitya Samsad, Kolkata.

CPI (ML) Janashakti (1992) – *Eadu Viplava Samsthala Aikyathaa Prakatana*, CPI (ML) Janashakti, Hyderabad.

Desai, A R (1981) (ed.) – Peasant Struggles in India, Oxford University Press, Delhi.

Desai, A R (1986) (ed.) – Agrarian Struggles in India after Independence, Oxford University Press, Delhi.

Ghosh , Suniti Kumar (ed)(1992) – The Historic Turning Point – A Liberation Anthology, Vol. 1, Calcutta.

Ghosh , Suniti Kumar (ed)(1993) – The Historic Turning Point – A Liberation Anthology, Vol. 2, Calcutta.

Kannabiran, K.G. (2004) – The Wages of Impunity – Power, Justice and Human Rights, Orient Longman, Hyderabad.

Kannabiran, K.G. (2010) – *24 Gantalu*, Devulapalli Publications, Hyderabad.

Khusro, A M (1958) – Economic and Social Effects of Jagirdari Abolition and Land Reforms, Osmania University, Hyderabad.

Kranti Prachuranalu (1981) – *Nageti Chaallallo Ragilina Raithanga Poratam – Adilabad Karimnagar Raithanga Porata Samkshipta Charitra*, Kranti Prachuranalu, Secunderabad.

Kranti Prachuranalu (1985) – Crimson Flag Flies Aloft – Brief Accounts of Lives and Struggles of Martyrs, Kranti Prachuranalu, Secunderabad.

Krishna Rao, V. (1989) – Communism in Andhra Pradesh, Cauvery Publications, Hyderabad.

Krishna Rao, Y.V. (ed.)(1986) – *Andhra Pradeshlo Raithu Udyamaalu – Poraataalu*, Vol. 1, Visalandhra Publishing House, Hyderabad.

Krishna Rao, Y.V. (ed.)(1990) – *Andhra Pradeshlo Raithu Udyamaalu – Poraataalu*, Vol. 2, Visalandhra Publishing House, Hyderabad.

Mazumdar, Charu (1982) – Eight Documents (1965-67), Mass Line Publications, New Delhi.

Myrdal, Jan (1985) – India Waits, Sangam Books, Hyderabad.

Nagi Reddy, T (1978) – India Mortgaged – A Marxist-Leninist Appraisal, Tarimela Nagi Reddy Memorial Trust, Anantapuram.

R. S. Rao (1995) – Towards Understanding Semi Feudal Semi Colonial Society, Perspectives, Hyderabad.

Ramalingachari, Vasantada (2005) – *Srikakula Girijanodyamam: Anubhavaalu – Avagaahana*, Comrade Vasantada Ramalingachari Smaaraka Committee, Seshadripuram.

Sabari (ed)(2010) – *Dandakaranya Mahila Udyama Charitra (1980-2009)*, Virasam Prachuranalu, Hyderabad.

Sankar, P. (2002) – *Ee Adavi Maade – Dandakaranya Viplavodyama Charitra*, Pranahita Prachuranalu, Jinkibhadra.

Seetaramaiah, Kondapalli (2005) – *Kondapalli Seetaramaiah Erina Rachanalu* Vol. 1 & 2, KS Memorial Committee, Hyderabad.

Shyam (Nalla Adi Reddy) (2009) – *Shyam Sankalita Rachanalu*, Diksuchi Prachuranalu, Jinkibhadra.

SinghaRoy, Debal K. (2004) – Peasant Movements in Post-Colonial India – Dynamics of Moblisation and Identity, Sage Publications, New Delhi.

Sinha, Shantha (1989) – Maoists in Andhra Pradesh, Gian Publishing House, New Delhi.

Sivarami Reddy, B (2006) – *Mahattara Srikakula Poratam – Charitraka Pariseelana*, Chaganti Bhasakara Rao Prachuranalu, Singarayakonda.

Sudhakar, S and Kodandarami Reddy, M (eds)(1998) – *Moodu Dasaabdaala Naxalbari: Gamyam Gamanam*, Perspectives, Hyderabad.

Vanguard Publication (n.d.) – 30 Years of Naxalbari – An Epic of Heroic Struggle and Sacrifice, Vanguard Publication,

Varavara Rao (1990) – *Srjana Sampaadakeeyaalu*, Perspectives, Hyderabad.

Venkat (2007) – *Srikakula Girijana Raithanga Udyamam*, Tarimela Nagi Reddy Memorial Trust, Vijayawada.

Venkateswara Rao, Devulapalli (1993 - FE 1973) – *Andhra Communist Viplavakaarulalo Mithavaada Avakaasavaadam*, Proletarian Line Prachuranalu, Hyderabad.

Venkateswara Rao, Devulapalli (1993 – FE1982) – *Andhra Communist Viplavakaarulalo 'Athivaada' Avakaasavaada Dhorani*, Proletarina Line Prachuranalu, Hyderabad.

Venugopal, N (2007) – Fake Encounters – Story from Andhra Pradesh, Economic and Political Weekly, Vol. No. October 13.

Venugopal, N (2008) – *Kallamundari Charitra*, Swecchasahiti, Hyderabad.

Virasam Prachuranalu (2010) – *Muppai Ella Dandakaranya Saahiti Samskrutikodyama Charitra* (1980-2010), Virasam Prachuranalu, Hyderabad.

Footnotes

1 The movement began as an attempt to seize land from the illegal occupation of landlords by poor peasants and agricultural labourers in March 1967 in Naxalbari village of Siliguri subdivision, Darjeeling district, West Bengal. In the ongoing debates within the recently formed Communist Party of India (Marxist), these developments in Naxalbari were hailed as a path-breaking effort, and those who subscribed to and followed this path have come to be known as Naxalites.

2 It had become quite common for Naxalite parties to split and further split a number of times, based on some ideological and some personal issues. The splinter groups came to be known not on their ideological difference but after their leader's name, showing an element of unfortunate personality cult. Some groups and parties came to be known after their respective journal's name, if the group survives for some time and launches a journal of its own. Most of the times, police or newspapers gave a name to a party/group and it stuck.

3 During this survey period, the number of Naxalite cadres killed in "encounters" was about 1600 and those killed by landlords could be another 400. Especially during the first phase of Srikakulam almost all the leadership was wiped out. (For details, see N Venugopal, 2007).

4 Though this survey is written much later and after the movement gained considerable strength in consequent decades, it had to stick to this outer limit thanks to the overall conception of the Comprehensive History and Culture of Andhra Pradesh project.

5 Though he can be credited as the pioneer of tribal movement in the area, beginning in 1958 when he was posted as a teacher in Manda village in Palakonda Agency, he left the activity by 1962 due to his differences as well as state repression.

6 Yenan was the base of the Communist Party of China before its victory, between 1936 and 1948. Srikakulam, because of its terrain was expected to become a similar base area for revolutionaries.

7 If the government notifies an area as "disturbed area" under the Andhra Pradesh Suppression of Disturbances Act, 1967, any assembly of more than five persons becomes unlawful. To disperse such an assembly a sub-inspector can open fire to kill. Otherwise police have to take permission of the district magistrate (Collector) for opening fire.

8 Karl Marx, Capital Vo. 1, p. 751.

(Appendix follows)

Apendix : Geneology of Naxalite Parties in Andhra Pradesh (1967 - 96)

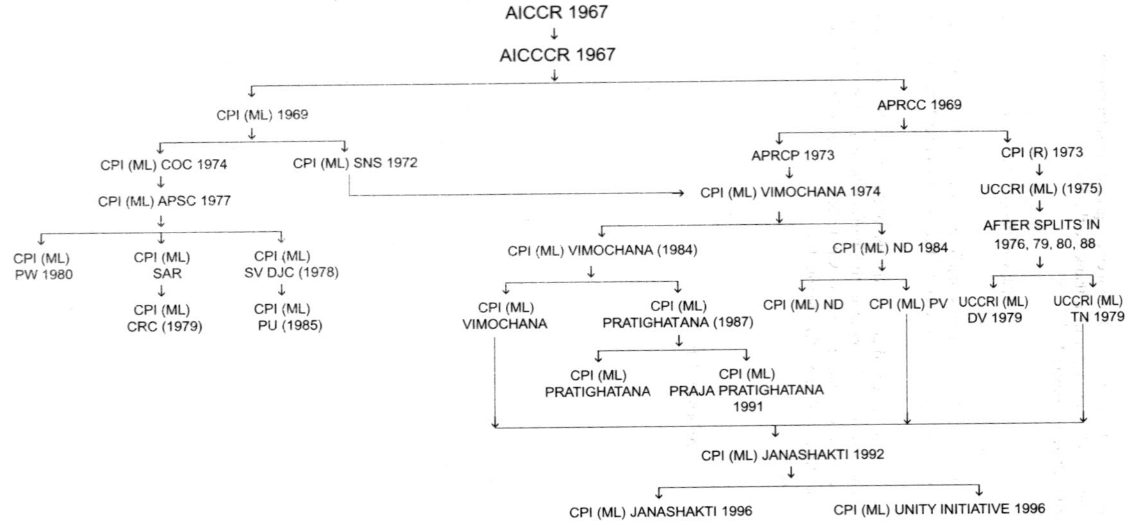

AICCR : ALL INDIA CO-ORDINATION COMMITTEE OF REVOLUTIONARIES
AICCCR : ALL INDIA CO-ORDINATION COMMITTEE OF COMMUNIST REVOLUTIONARIES
CPI (ML) : COMMUNIST PARTY OF INDIA (MARXIST - LENINIST)
APRCC : ANDHRA PRADESH REVOLUTIONARY COMMUNISTS COMMITTEE
APSC : ANDHRA PRADESH STATE COMMITTEE
CPI (R) : COMMUNIST PARTY OF INDIA (REVOLUTIONARY)
UCCRI : UNITY CENTRE OF COMMUNIST REVOLUTIONARIES IN INDIA
COC : CENTRAL ORGANISING COMMITTEE
PW : PEOPLE'S WAR

SVDJC : SRIKAKULAM - VIZIANAGARAM DISTRICTS JOINT COMMITTEE
ND : NEW DEMOCRACY
CRC : CENTRAL RE ORGANISING COMMITTEE
PU : PARTY UNITY
SAR : SA RAOUF
SNS : SATYA NARAYAN SINGH
TN : TARIMELA NAGI REDDY
DV : DEVULAPALLI VENKATESWARA RAO
PV : PYLA VASUDEVA RAO

❖ ❖ ❖

7

Studying the Subject in Motion: Maoist Analysis of Agrarian Transformation 1970s to 2010s

Introduction

Comprehensive understanding of a phenomenon is the precondition to deal with or to bring about any change in that phenomenon. Characterisation of a society, and the agrarian relations if agriculture is predominant in that society, is fundamental to any idea of transforming that society and agrarian relations. Thus it would be obvious that the Maoists, or the Naxalites, one of the major forces attempting social transformation in India, take up the study and arrive at a particular formulation about Indian society and put into practice their transformatory politics based on that characterisation. The Indian Maoists describe the society which they are trying to transform as "semi-feudal semi-colonial". This initial thesis, however, pertains to the obtaining situation in the late 1960s and the early 1970s and there has been a debate that the situation is changed significantly and hence there was a need to alter, if not completely give up, the formulation. There is sufficient evidence that the Maoists have been consistently studying and analysing their subject and concluded that the changes are not so significant or fundamental to alter their thesis.

This paper is an attempt to explore the history of the

*Paper presented at the Conference on **Agrarian Transforamtion in India** held jointly by Goldsmiths, University of London and University of Oxford on July 13-14, 2011.*

characterisation and changes that occurred both in the objective agrarian (or rural) situation and the subjective understanding of the Maoists over a period of four decades. Both the object and subject in philosophical terms are in motion and are undergoing changes over time and a word of explanation on the title of this paper is required before going further. The word Subject has varying connotations and this paper would like to use the word in two different, if not contradictory meanings. Subject, the word in ordinary English, means an object or a field of study, but when it comes to philosophical terminology, subject is an active student or observer or transformer of the object or society or the subject of study. Thus, in a way, the subject and the object change their respective places and become one. Here this paper uses subject to denote both the society, agrarian relations, class struggle (generally regarded as objective conditions) on one hand and the subjective forces, or the Maoists, who are engaged in studying, intervening in, and attempting to change the agrarian relations by leading class struggle.

The paper is divided into four sections and the first section deals with the theoretical, political and economic connotations of the characterisation while the second section elaborates on the concrete and continuous studies undertaken by the Maoists in Andhra Pradesh to understand the changing reality. The third section shares the results of the recent revisiting of two villages which the Maoists have studied three decades ago. The last section ventures to sum up an inconclusive conclusion to locate the characterisation in a larger framework of change and continuity in agrarian situation, entry of new elements and their nature and role, dialectics of appearance and essence and the persisting necessity of agrarian revolution in India.

1. Key concepts – How they evolved

Till now the basic characterisation – semi-feudal semi-colonial – is recognised and understood at at least three levels: 1. Turning it into an empty phrase and repeating it without any proper study of the concrete objective reality and using the same characterisation to understand the complex reality of vast sub-continental proportions, ignoring obvious contra indications in some pockets. 2. Dismissing it as a simplistic, meaningless jargon and completely negating its relevance. 3. Recognising it as a useful, powerful and meaningful tool of social analysis and change and continuously honing that tool through consistent study and practice.

This leaves out the parliamentary left who do not even accept the thesis of semi-feudal semi-colonial nature of Indian society and treat India as an independent, sovereign country and Indian society as one gradually transforming into a capitalist society or "capitalist relations dominant in present day Indian agriculture" or "predominantly capitalist with some feudal remnants", etc. While the semi-colonial semi-feudal thesis[1] marked the dividing line between the parliamentary left and the Marxist-Leninists, or Naxalbari line of 1967, some earlier M-L thinkers and practitioners also began to revise the thesis and started characterising India as a capitalist society or gradually becoming a capitalist society or terming the changes as "significant...that can influence at least the strategy and tactics of Indian revolution", more so in the post-globalisation period[2].

The first trend of dogmatic understanding had harmed the Indian revolutionary movement to some extent and a lot of party literature uses the concept without any study and substantiation and uses the expression as a substitute to concrete study. The fact that only a couple of post-Naxalbari parties and organisations out of about 40 countrywide, undertook concrete studies and published their reasoning in favour of semi-feudal thesis shows the dogmatic phrase-mongering attitude. More than 40 organisations that claim the legacy of Naxalbari continue to use semi-feudal thesis without ever studying and publishing it openly before testing it in their fields of practice.

The second condescending and dismissive approach has been taken by several social scientists, both sympathetic and critical towards the movement. While sociologist Rabindra Ray termed the semi-feudal characterisation a "metaphysic", economist Ashok Rudra called it a "myth". Ray exemplifies this dismissive attitude in making most uncharitable comment – "the characterisation is not so much the description of a state of affairs – an undertaking for which the Naxalites in any case lacked the diligent study and patience – as an injunction to action of a particular kind, i.e. the meaning of the characterisation only emerges with respect to the strategy it entails"[3].

In the same vein, Rudra says, "Marxists are no less capable of manufacturing myths, no less prone to make theories without any empirical substance, no more lacking in the capacity of describing as black what is white and thinking it is day when it is night. Some over-enthusiastic political economists have, by sheer repetition, succeeded in making widely accepted a certain theory of 'semi-feudalism' to explain an alleged stagnation of Indian agriculture, paying scant regard to facts or figures."[4]

The Maoist practitioners, as observed by the critics, might be lacking in sophisticated methodologies and technical explanations with tables, equations, functions, so-called facts and figures, etc. that the social scientists have, but certainly they had their ear to the ground and have undertaken "diligent study with patience." In fact, study and struggle were not separate for them and they did not confine themselves to one at the cost of the other. A survey of their history in Andhra Pradesh shows that they certainly made empirical studies in order to understand the reality and change it.

The third, revolutionary and realistic understanding of the characterisation did not feel content with repeating the expression but tried to test it in concrete reality and emphasised the necessity of concrete study to lead class struggle. The history of their continuous study-struggle-theorisation-further struggle-refining the theory shows that they have taken the thesis with reasonable seriousness it deserved. Though there is sufficient evidence to show that this kind of studies, with varying rigour, were undertaken across the country, this paper would like to present the history of studies in Andhra Pradesh, based on the author's familiarity. At least there have been a dozen proper studies conducted in thirty villages spread over thirty five years in Andhra Pradesh alone. This is not to speak of thousands of villages that the Maoists studied, understood the existing class relations and waged struggles there.

But before going into the details of the studies in Andhra Pradesh, it would be interesting to trace the history of semi-feudal semi-colonial characterisation in Indian communist/ Maoist movement at the country level.

In fact, the characterisation of Indian agrarian scene as feudal and semi-feudal dates back to 1950 when the secretariat of the Andhra Provincial Committee produced a document[5] for the perusal of the Central Committee in the thick of the Telangana Peasant Armed Struggle (1946-51) and the subsequent Letter of the New Central Committee to all party members and sympathisers dated 1 June 1950[6].

In this letter, it was stated that "in the rural areas of India, feudal and semifeudal relations are still dominant. The imperialist rulers have deliberately kept this feudal and semifeudal agrarian framework so as to serve their robber economy... However, this should not blind us to the growth of considerable capitalist relations in the womb of feudalism in India."[7] Based on this understanding the same letter prescribed armed struggle as the strategy to achieve its goal: "The way of going forward successfully is, by the party, boldly initiating mass struggles basing on the level of the consciousness of the masses in different localities, combined with armed guerilla resistance, so as to develop them quickly to a higher phase of land distribution and village people's committees (*jana panchayats*). It is only by this that the revolutionary movement can be defended and extended to wider and wider areas, ultimately embracing the whole country. It is only by adopting armed guerilla warfare that the party would be strengthened and extended. Thus a strong party heading the armed guerilla warfare will be able to unite the toiling masses and mobilise all the anti-imperialist classes, establish liberated bases and organise liberation armies in areas topographically and otherwise suited for them, leading to the final capture of power and complete liberation of the entire country."[8]

This basic understanding of Indian society and the strategy for its revolutionary transformation of 1950, however, did not last long with the party. Within 16 months of this letter, the party officially withdrew its armed struggle, disbanded guerilla squads and surrendered its weapons to the State in Telangana and started participating in parliamentary elections. Later the Communist Party of India (CPI) and the Communist Party of India -Marxist (CPI-M) continued to mention agrarian revolution as a necessary precursor to socialist transformation. The agrarian revolution was seen as a way of hastening capitalist development on the way to socialism and thus India was characterised as capitalist or capitalist with feudal relics.

The programme of the CPI says, "the main aim of government policies has been to replace semifeudal relations in agriculture by capitalist relations. In pursuance of this aim, the Congress governments have substantially curbed feudal interests through legislative measures. Abolition of *Zamindari, jagirdari* and other forms of statutory landlordism, various tenancy laws, laws on land ceiling are all directed towards this aim. But this attack on feudal interests has not been a total one of sweeping them away altogether. It has been a process of compromise and concessions. Hence considerable scope of semifeudal exploitation was left."[9]

The programme of the Communist Party of India - Marxist says: "After independence, instead of abolishing landlordism, the Congress rulers adopted agrarian policies to transform the semi-feudal landlords into capitalist landlords and develop a stratum of rich peasants." "In agrarian relations, the major trend has been the development of capitalist relations in the countryside which is characterised by the proletarianisation of large sections of the rural working masses and a huge increase in the number of agricultural workers as a proportion of the rural population; the accelerated differentiation of the peasantry; production for the market; the large-scale eviction of tenants holding traditional leases; and increased levels of reinvestment of capital in agriculture and agriculture-related activity by the rural rich, particularly landlords, laying the basis for the reproduction of capital on a scale that did not hitherto exist."[10]

This understanding was begun to be challenged from the mid-1960s onwards as part of the churning within the communist movement in general and the newly formed CPI-M in particular. In that process Charu Mazumdar, a leader of CPI-M in Darjeeling district and would be leader of the Naxalbari line, wrote eight documents between 1965 and 1967. In his fourth document (undated, yet certainly of 1965) he said, "the mistake that is often made while analysing the class of peasants is to determine it on the basis of the title deeds of land. This is a dangerous mistake. It has to be analysed on the basis of their earning and level of living"[11]. In the seventh document (again undated, but probably of 1966) he said, "...the peasants are the main force of the revolution in a semi-colonial and semi-feudal country like India." While these two statements were prior to the Naxalbari uprising in May 1967, again in November 1967, after Naxalbari broke out, he wrote "India is a semi-colonial, semi-feudal country. So the main force which can change the colonial condition in this country is the peasantry and their anti-feudal struggle. No change is conceivable in this country without agrarian revolution."[12]

Besides several such references by Mazumdar on the agrarian class structure and semi-feudal formulation, it was the Communist Party of China, in the form of an editorial in People's Daily on July 5, 1967 which said: "India under Congress rule is only nominally independent; in fact, it is nothing more than a semi-colonial, semi-feudal country. The Congress administration represents the interests of the Indian feudal princes, big landlords, and bureaucrat-comprador capitalists."[13]

However, all this was before the formation of the Communist Party of India (Marxist-Leninist) and during the internal struggle within the CPI –M on the nature of Indian State and strategy of Indian revolution. Finally, it was the Political Resolution of the CPI (M-L), which gave a comprehensive definition of the characterisation in one of the two resolutions adopted by the All India Coordination Committee of Communist Revolutionaries (AICCCR) on April 22, 1969, on the basis of which the CPI (M-L) was formed.

The resolution said: "…we stated that India is a semi-colonial and semi-feudal country, that the Indian State is the State of the big landlords and comprador-bureaucrat capitalists… the increasing concentration of land in the hands of a few landlords, the expropriation of almost the total surplus produced by the toiling peasantry in the form of rent, the complete landlessness of about 40 per cent of the rural population, the back-breaking usurious exploitation, the ever-growing evictions of the poor peasantry coupled with the brutal social oppression – including lynching of *harijans*, reminiscent of the mediaeval ages – and the complete backwardness of the technique of production clearly demonstrate the semi-feudal character of our society."[14] "The Indian revolution at this stage is the democratic revolution of the new type – the Peoples' Democratic Revolution – the main content of which is the agrarian revolution, the abolition of feudalism in the countryside…"[15]

That the newly formed party earnestly began its attempts to study and analyse the rural class structure can be seen from a report published in the party organ by June 1969 itself. The study, 'An Investigation into the Nature and Forms of Exploitation: A Report on Class Analysis of a Village'[16] gives a detailed picture of exploitation and the justification of revolutionary politics vis-a-vis parliamentary left.

Again this characterisation was ratified by the Programme of the CPI (M-L), adopted at the party congress held in May 1970, wherein it was stated, "the sham independence declared in 1947 was nothing but a replacement of the colonial and semi-feudal set-up by a semi-colonial and semi-feudal one." The programme refers to the concept of semi-feudal many times and finally says, "the semi-feudal land relations have transformed our country into a land of perpetual famine as a result of which millions of people die of starvation every year."[17]

Within a short time, with the setback of Naxalbari and Srikakulam, the CPI (M-L) got split several times and now there are at least forty parties and groups in the country that claim M-L legacy. As already mentioned not more than half-a-dozen parties have attempted to substantiate the semi-feudal semi-colonial concept as part of their practice. Other questions on strategy and tactics, particularly the participation in parliamentary elections and adoption of mass line, occupied the centre stage and most of the parties did not pay attention to study and analyse agrarian relations to lead effective class struggle.

In this background, the CPI (M-L) in Andhra Pradesh, after the setback of Naxalbari and Srikakulam struggles, tried to revive the party and formed the CPI (M-L) Central Organising Committee (COC) in 1973 along with the remaining CPI (M-L) units in West Bengal, Bihar, and Punjab. During this time the COC developed some novel ideas regarding mass line and agrarian work, consolidated in a document called Self Critical Report in 1974. Under the guidance of this document, mass organisations like the Radical Students Union (RSU) were formed and when Emergency was proclaimed the radical students went to villages, both to study and wage struggles. These experiences and studies formed part of another crucial document *Vyavasaaya Viplavam* (Agrarian Revolution). However, by the time of publication of this document in 1977, the COC became defunct and it had to come as the document of the CPI (M-L) Andhra Pradesh State Committee.

The AP State Committee, after three years of struggles among the peasantry in Karimnagar and Adilabad districts in particular and all over the state in general, attracted the attention of revolutionaries all over the country and the unity thus achieved led to the formation of the Communist Party of India (Marxist-Leninist) (People's War) on April 22, 1980. Voice of the Vanguard, the organ of the Central Committee of the CPI (M-L) (People's War), carried a detailed analysis, beginning with its first issue, on 'Indian Agriculture – Capitalist or Pre-Capitalist?' where it argued the case for semi-feudal thesis based on i. Land utilisation, ii. Holdings, iii. Inputs, iv. Productivity trends, v. Credit, vi. Disintegration of the peasantry, vii. Market, and viii. Utilisation of surplus. The journal also carried a number of studies on agrarian relations and struggles later.

The CPI (M-L) (People's War) and the Maoist Communist Centre of India (MCCI) merged in September 2004 to form the CPI (Maoist) and the party's programme said: "…the direct colonial and semi-feudal system of the British imperialists was replaced with semi-colonial and semi-feudal system under the neo-colonial form of indirect imperialist rule, exploitation and control." "Even today, our country is fundamentally a country of the peasant masses as two thirds of the population live in the rural areas. The overwhelming majority of the peasantry is the most exploited and oppressed class. They are forced to live in most wretched and extremely poor conditions. Despite the hoax of all land reforms, 30 per cent of total land is concentrated in the hands of landlords, who constitute only 5 per cent of the population, while middle peasantry constitute about 20 per cent of the rural population, whereas rich peasantry constitutes 10 per cent. 65 per cent of the total peasantry are landless and poor peasants, who own either no land at all or meagre land. Extreme forms of semi-feudal exploitation are still prevalent in the countryside. The major prevailing forms of such exploitation are extortion of their produce through share cropping, which is robbing them of their produce up to 50 per cent, bonded labour, usurious and merchant capital and other forms of extra-economic coercion. The backward agriculture on fragmented land mainly dependent on primitive methods in some places on vagaries of nature is subjecting a large population of peasantry including an overwhelming number of middle peasants to live a miserable life. The countryside is dominated by landlords, usurers, merchants, and religious institutions. These exploiting sections are the mainstay of the semi-feudal relations of production in the country. All these facts show that our country is a semi-feudal country."

Similarly, the Strategy and Tactics of Indian Revolution by the CPI (Maoist) categorically answered the question 'why do we call India semi-feudal': "Unlike in the West, where capitalism developed by overthrowing feudalism, in India, the British colonialism protected feudalism and used it as its social prop. Introduction of capitalist relations by the British imperialist rulers without basically altering the feudal stranglehold over the vast masses of the peasantry had resulted in semi-feudal production relations. The semi-feudal production relations continued even after the end of direct colonial rule. The imperialists used both the comprador bureaucrat capitalism and feudalism as their social props for their neo-colonial control and exploitation. Due to this alliance between these three main enemies of the Indian people land reforms have not altered the basic structure of agrarian class relations; and usurious and mercantile exploitation of the vast masses in the countryside continues unhindered even after more than half-a-century of so-called independence.

Land concentration in the hands of a few landlords and kulaks on the one hand, poor and landless peasantry of the rural population on the other, continues to characterise the rural scene. As a result, the number of landless agricultural labourers is swelling by leaps and bounds. Due to dearth of jobs, they are obliged to do inhuman labour like bonded servants of the landlords and plantation owners. Due to want of jobs most of them are compelled to live most wretched life, millions of people die or illness caused by starvation and half-starvation.

Another dreadful aspect of the feudal exploitation in India is the usury exploitation that extracts enormous sums of interest from the peasantry. Besides private usurers, various banks and financial companies too exploit the peasantry. Thus rural indebtedness has been increasing by leaps and bounds. Ruthless exploitation by unscrupulous traders is squeezing the vast peasant masses while selling the agricultural produce and buying the agricultural inputs from the market. Servitude and personal subordination of the poor and landless peasant masses, who constitute the overwhelming majority of the peasantry, to the feudal forces in innumerable forms, is perpetuated through ideological institutions and through the coercive arm of the State and even private armies. The life of the peasant masses is shattered continuously by the exploitation and oppression by the gangs of local tyrants, the evil gentry, intermediaries, the police, the courts and by a long hierarchy of government officials – all of whom act as loyal agents of imperialism, feudalism, and comprador bureaucrat capitalism, and by the feudal dictum of various kinds. All these have made the life of the peasant intolerable. The feudal oppression is not in the countryside alone nor is it confined to the peasant masses. In addition, the semi-feudal mode of production itself oppresses the vast masses of the country through the State machinery and through the ideological, cultural and other superstructural aspects. So it can doubtlessly be said that not only the peasantry but the vast masses of the population of the country have contradiction with feudalism.

The feudal exploitation and oppression is hindering not only the development of agrarian economy but also the path of the industrial development of India. Feudalism is one of the main obstacles on the way to the economic and social development of India. Feudalism versus the broad masses of the people is one of the fundamental contradictions in India."[18]

While this programme and strategy and tactics were originally developed by the Central Committee (Provisional) of the CPI (Maoist) in 2004, they were ratified and taken as the foundation documents at the unity congress of the party held in 2007.

Even as late as 2008, when Karnataka Maoist Independent Centre, a split away group from the CPI (Maoist) raised doubts[19] on the semi-feudal characterisation, the Central Committee of the CPI (Maoist) entered into a polemical debate and offered a detailed answer[20]. It said, "when we look at the question of the mode of production we must do it in the context of Lenin's theoretical basis on this issue. The points to be considered as per the Leninist understanding are mainly, nature and extent of the wage labour, nature and extent of capital accumulation and extended reproduction, extent of class differentiation of the peasantry in the countryside, types and extent of tenancy, types and extent of credit/money lending, extent and nature of capitalist commodity production vis-a-vis simple commodity production, extent and nature of land concentration, the extent of artisan population, productivity trends, question of superstructure and nature of political authority asserted in the village, existence and extent of non-economic forms of coercion, extent and growth of industry and manufacturing in the region, etc. Lenin has said that the development of manufacturing acts as an important factor in bringing about agrarian changes. So, while studying the mode of production in rural India we should not just look at it in isolation, but see its interlinking with the rest of the Indian economy, particularly the growth of manufacture and thereby the generation of capitalist relations."

Thus there has been a consistent and unswerving approach on the part of the CPI (Maoist) with regard to the dominant mode of production and consequent strategy of social transformation from mid-

1960s to 2010s. Not only the party, but also a number of political economists independently arrived at and substantiated this semi-feudal thesis with rigorous village studies that observed concrete reality of agrarian relations.[21] The analyses of the political economists are deliberately kept out of the purview of this paper, but exploration of those analyses is much more interesting and rewarding.

2. Studies in Andhra Pradesh

As already mentioned the original thesis of the CPI (M-L) – semi-colonial semi-feudal – continued to be accepted by all the parties and groups that evolved over time, despite their bitter differences over other issues. Besides a number of social scientists, several parties and groups also have contributed to the debate on semi-feudal character of society. This paper confines to the analysis of the present CPI (Maoist) and its earlier forms such as the CPI (M-L) COC between 1973 and 1977, CPI (M-L) Andhra Pradesh State Committee between 1977 and 1980, and the CPI (M-L) (People's War) between 1980 and 2004 with regard to the nature of society, particularly in Andhra Pradesh.

The first known published analysis of agrarian conditions in Andhra Pradesh by the revolutionaries was in 1977, based on their study and participation in agrarian struggles. This document was based on the theoretical understanding presented in Self Critical Report (1974) and Road to Revolution (1976) as well as the concrete study of a couple of villages. The study was first published as a paper in April-August 1976 issue of *Errajenda* (Red Flag), the clandestine organ of the CPI (M-L) COC, AP State Committee and a revised and enlarged document *Vyavasaaya Viplavam* was released in May 1978[22].

Vyavasaaya Viplavam not only scanned the history of agrarian relations in the state for centuries, but also undertook specific study of the existing state of agrarian relations in one village each in Nalgonda and Krishna districts, and two villages in Adilabad district, and concluded that it was semi-feudal society in general. The document provided a graphic presentation of several characteristics of existing agrarian relations and drew its conclusion based on those empirical facts. The observed facts include backward nature of agricultural production without assured irrigation; use of archaic implements and methods; inequality in landholdings; rising input costs in agriculture since major share of inputs like fertilisers and chemicals being imported; erosion of soil nutrients because of chemical use; agriculture becoming unremunerative and uneconomic; shortage of livestock to the needs of agriculture; inadequacy of capital infusion in agriculture; shortage of credit facilities; continuation of feudal practices like unpaid and bonded labour, faulty weights and measures and usurious money lending; unsustainable pressure on land and agriculture that resulted in not providing work to agricultural labour for at least half of a year; increasing debt burden and a number of feudal superstructural practices.

Based on this picture, the book argued the case for land to the tiller in particular and a thorough going agrarian revolution in general as part of new democratic revolution. It listed six essential tasks of agrarian revolution: 1. Redistribution of all land in the country on the basis of land to the tiller. 2. Providing protected irrigation facilities to all the arable land in the country. 3. Raising the agricultural production to the optimum level through introducing modern technology and methods. 4. Annulling entire debt burden on the peasantry. 5. Stabilising prices. 6. Industrialising the country.

The Self-Critical Review and *Vyavasaaya Viplavam* prepared a strong basis for developing a broad-based militant class struggle with a genuine mass line in rural Andhra Pradesh, particularly in Telangana during 1977 to 1980. During the same time the party had not only strengthened the existing Radical Students' Union, but also formed Radical Youth League (RYL) and Rythu Cooli Sangham (RCS - Union of small peasants and agricultural labour). In 1978, for the first time in the history of Indian revolutionary movement, the RSU and RYL have taken a historic decision to organise 'Go to Village campaign' to send student and youth teams to villages to spread the message of revolution, and to organise the rural masses into mass organisations as a first step towards developing class struggle. Beginning the summer of 1978 for about a decade this was a regular practice. Thousands of students and youth used to form into small teams of about 8 to 10 members attend a two-three day preparatory workshop to get educated on the rural society, agrarian relations, Marxist philosophical perspective, political economy and the concepts of agrarian and new democratic revolution. Each team, in a week to ten days time, would visit as many villages, mingle with people, learn from them, organise them and teach them. The teams invariably consisted of political commentators, singers and organisers, most of whom got their initiation into village level mass mobilisation for the first time. In thousands of villages these campaign teams set up local, village units of RYL and RCS and the state level RCS was formed in 1981. The complete account of this gigantic programme is yet to be written, but it would suffice to say that 'Go to Village Campaign' sowed the seeds of revolution in the villages of Andhra Pradesh. This programme inevitably and naturally led to studying the existing agrarian relations in the villages and identifying the motive force, probable friends in the united front as well as enemies of the class struggle in the village. Study, mobilisation, organisation and struggle formed part of a single integrated praxis.

As part of these experiences, the party again conducted a detailed study of four villages (Gouravelli, Manikyapur, Ramavaram, and Kotthapalli) in Karimnagar district and published the findings in *Dunnevaanike Bhoomi Dakkanide Raithaangaanki Vimukti Ledu* (Liberation of peasantry is not possible until tiller gets the land) in April 1982. An abridged English translation of this booklet was published in Voice of the Vanguard in 1983. Continuing the analysis of rural problems, this booklet said, "these four villages symbolise the average rural economic relations in the district." The concerned issues identified by the study in these four villages include i. Inequality in landholding, ii. Inequality in the ownership of livestock, agricultural implements, etc., iii. Unbearable debt burden on each of the families, iv. Lack of credit facilities, v. Gulf between income and needs of most of the villagers, vi. Insufficient work opportunities to the agricultural labourers throughout the year, vii. Lack of healthcare facilities, viii. Low level of educational facilities, ix. Failure of land reforms, x. Existence of farmhands in a sort of bondage, xi. Concentration of land in a few hands through feudal practices like low wage, fraudulent weights and measures, and usury, xii. Untouchability, xiii. Occupational castes, and xiv. Traders and employees.

The party also published *Naagetichaallalo* (In the Furrows) (1981), *Karimnagar – Adilabad Raithaanga Poraataalu Vardhillaali* (Long Live the Peasant Struggles of Karimnagar–Adilabad) (1982), *Munumunduku Saagutunna Raitaanga Poraataalu (Peasant Struggles Marching Ahead)* (1983), and *People's War Tho Cheyi Kalipi Nadustunna Lakshalaadi Janasamoohaalu* (Millions of People Join Hands with People's War) (1990), among others, that offered detailed accounts of agrarian struggles in Telangana in particular and Andhra Pradesh in general. Naturally these accounts elaborated, though not in quantitative terms, the existing class relations and various forms of class struggles in rural areas. Besides these expositions from the party, there have been a number of poems, short stories and novels written by sympathisers and observers. All this literature vividly portrayed the struggles against the existing semi-feudal relations in the countryside. These anti-feudal struggles were suppressed by extra judicial killings of hundreds of activists and people in the name of "encounters", arrests and torture of thousands of people, rape and molestation of women, harassment of thousands of sympathisers, burning of villages, destruction of property, etc. This repression culminated in the legal promulgation of ban on the party and six mass organisations in May 1992. Thereafter the party and its mass organisations could not function openly and publish their viewpoints in legal channels, except during short respites in 1995 and 2004.

However, even under such repression the party cadres continued their activity of mobilising and leading people on various issues and taking the class struggle to higher levels. As part of this mobilisation, organisation and leadership, they also have undertaken studies of concrete reality. According to a recent draft document[23], during the last twenty years, the party has done village studies in Kondapur, Laddunur, Khila Shahpur, Adavi Kesavapur villages and Eturunagaram area in Warangal district, Gorrepalli in Karimnagar district, Molachintapalli in Mahabubnagar district, Mangi area in Adilabad district, and an overall study of Nizamabad district. The document also shows that the party has also taken into consideration several studies conducted by independent social scientists across the state. There are many more studies published in the columns of *Kranti* (Revolution), monthly organ and *Errajenda* (Red Flag), theoretical journal of the CPI (Maoist).

After analysing all these studies, the document concluded that "as a result of serious class struggle in the state in the past, old feudal system has undergone some considerable changes. Forms of extra-economic coercion like *vetti* (unpaid labour) have disappeared. Several old landlords shifting their properties to towns, considerable changes in village class structure, and the entry of distorted capitalist relations into production to some extent have led to changes in semi-feudal relations. Class contradictions of 1960s, '70s and '80s as identified in

Vyavasaaya Viplavam are no longer in the same style and at the same level. Due to these changes in the villages, the old picture that existed for centuries of one big landlord on one side and vast masses of people on the other and the ensuing revolutionary struggles of the people is changed and a new phase of struggle has begun. Some of the rich and middle peasantry have become new landlords and bossing over the village. Today's class struggle needs to target them. A new broad united front according to the changed class structure in the village is developing. Today peasantry has to wage a struggle mainly on land to the tiller slogan, but at the same time, their struggle has to target imperialist, comprador bureaucratic capital and fight on various issues that distress peasantry…"

3. Revisiting two villages

In the context of this consistent history of study – practice - further study and further practice adopted by a revolutionary party, this paper wanted to revisit two villages for which there exists a benchmark study conducted in 1980-82. Out of the four villages (Gouravelli, Manikyapur, Ramavaram, and Kotthapalli) studied earlier we revisited and studied Gouravelli and Manikyapur.

Before going into the findings, it would be necessary to state some qualifications regarding the earlier study and the present revisit. Except the published booklet, we don't have any other supporting material to understand the methodology it employed, basis of classification of peasantry and if there was any mismatch between the reality and perception. The study was a political document which combined economic and political data with a defined political perspective. It clearly and categorically identified the basic classes that have to be mobilised in the struggle and those that have to be fought. It clearly showed the necessity of transformation of the existing agrarian relations and stated a definite political programme that can bring in the transformation. The current study does not have similar agenda and it is so limited that it just wanted to check what changed and what didn't in the objective reality identified thirty years ago. Thus this paper listed out fourteen parameters from the benchmark study and observed what happened to each of those parameters, in terms of change and continuity. This study also tried to identify other changes that occurred in the village, even if a corresponding benchmark parameter does not exist.

Labour

When compared to 1981 situation, the number of wage labourers increased and in a sense they are free to be employed by any employer. In both the villages more than half households are wage labourers, but the agricultural operations in the villages are not able to provide them work for not more than 90 days in a year. Several of the male occupations like ploughing, watering, and harvesting are taken over by mechanisation and it is female labourers who get work in operations like sowing, weeding. Construction, service occupations, migration and MGNREG scheme have been providing work to the wage labourers, but on the whole it is reported that one does not get work for less than 6-7 months in a year. There is a push from agriculture and a pull from urban and service sectors but there is an apparent mismatch. It is also reported that interest in as well as the skills needed for farming activities are on decline. Labour necessity and absorption in agriculture decreased considerably. Money wages have increased but in terms of real wages it is either stable or declining. In 1981, there used to be farmhands on annual contract and living almost in a bondage to the landlords and rich peasants. There were 106 farmhands in Gouravelli and 66 in Manikyapur but now the number of farmhands has come down drastically to 10 and 26 respectively.

Land

In 1981 stark inequality in landholding existed with landlords constituting 5 per cent of the village population having 44 per cent of land in Gouravelli and 5 per cent landlords having 39 per cent of land in Manikyapur. At the other end of the spectrum, in Gouravelli 50 per cent of the population was landless and small peasantry and in Manikyapur 48 per cent was in that category. Now, the landlord category, which holds more than 30 acres of land, does not exist in both the villages, as a result of fragmentation within families or sale of land by landlords over the last 30 years. However, the magnitude of landlessness and small landholdings has not come down drastically. The small landholdings are so uneconomical that they can also be classified as almost landless. The continuity in landlessness and small landholding can be seen in Gouravelli where 100 households out of the total 490 are landless and 85 dalit households own 56 acres only. In Manikyapur out of 600 households, 150 are landless and 50 among them are dalits. There is a remarkable change in landholding with regard to the growth of middle peasantry, but their agricultural operations are in crisis due to lack of irrigation and high cost of inputs. The landholding is retained even when the families migrate to towns and settle in other occupations so as to show other income as non-taxable agricultural income. The importance of landholding as a security and a source of prestige is also not diminished. On the whole, there is a change in the composition of inequality in landholding on one hand, while inequality continues on the other.

Table 1

Gouravelli – Landholding 1982 and 2012[24]

Holding	Households 1982	Total area 1982 (acres)	HHs 2012	Total area 2012 (acres)
Landless and Small peasants	298	239	361	355 acres
Middle peasants	184	796	212	1226
Rich peasants	44	610	20	300
Landlords	39	1158	3	60

Table 2

Manikyapur – Landholding 1982 and 2012[25]

Holding	Households 1982	Total area 1982 (acres)	HHs 2012	Total area 2012 (acres)
Landless and Small peasants	280	435	307	307
Middle peasants	43	223	319	1393
Rich peasants	25	182	16	240
Landlords	24	577	10	320

Livestock and agricultural implements

In 1981, livestock and traditional agricultural implements like wooden ploughs and bullock carts played a prominent role and the study listed the individual ownership of these assets. Now, livestock for agricultural use and traditional implements lost their relevance and that is visible in drastic decline in numbers. There were 1,076 bullocks in 1981 in Gouravelli but it is reduced to less than 182 now. The number of bullock carts has come down from 112 to 2. Similarly in Manikyapur 479 bullocks have come down to 397 and carts from 71 to 4. However, over the years dairying has grown in both the villages and milch animals are considered to be income generating assets and they are spread across all families, of course with some inequality. With regard to agricultural implements, most of them are mechanised and either owned by rich peasants or leased out by seasonally migrating traders.

Table 3

Gouravelli – Some indicators of change

Indicator	1982	2012
Farmhands	106	10
Agricultural livestock	1076	182
Bullock carts	112	2
Oil pumpsets	146	0
Debt	Rs. 8,95,000	Rs. 4.4 crore

Table 4

Manikyapur – Some indicators of change

Indicator	1982	2012
Farmhands	66	25
Agricultural livestock	479	397
Bullock carts	71	4
Oil pumpsets	73	0
Debt	Rs. 8,69,700	Rs. 2.26 crore

Technology

There is a phenomenal increase in the usage of modern technological implements, both in agricultural production process and daily life, over the last thirty years. While there were oil pumpsets only in agriculture in 1981, now there are electric pumpsets, borewells, tractors, HYV seeds, chemical fertilisers, synthetic pesticides, drip irrigation systems, and harvesters in agriculture and two-wheelers, three-wheeler autos, trolleys, mobile phones, television sets, video equipment in daily life are ubiquitous. The change in cropping pattern is also quite visible. The coarse cereals like bajra and jowar have completely disappeared and commercial crops like cotton and horticulture have emerged in a big way.

Process of Accumulation

Except for the landlord and big/rich farmers agriculture is not sustainable and there is no surplus to accumulate. Since both the villages have less than 5 per cent farmers who can be described as landlords and big farmers, process of accumulation is not high. However, there is income and surplus generation in dairying and savings from government schemes and employment. In Manikyapur small and middle peasants shifted to cattle trading, horticulture contracts, dairying and real estate businesses and able to earn considerably. In a rough estimate, a village on an average is able to generate a gross income Rs 7 crore per annum from agriculture, toddy, dairying, wage labour and services and thus there is at least Rs 2-3 crore available surplus for extraction.

Surplus Extraction and Investment

Surplus extraction is taking place in a number of ways like liquor trade, mobile phone service, two-wheelers, fuel, private education and healthcare, modern commodities, television cable, festivals, marriages, celebrations and religious functions besides low wages, under valuation of resources, and siphoning of common resources. Most of the spending is on consumption and luxury. The surplus extraction is taking place through ownership of means of production, caste, political and bureaucratic connections. In Manikyapur alone Rs 50,000 per day (Rs 1.8 crore per annum) is being siphoned off from the people by liquor shops. Thus the surplus generated and savings in the villages are not being reinvested in productive activity in general. Manikyapur shows a rare example of middle peasants purchasing 500 acres of land from the neighbouring villages to augment their agricultural operations.

Debt burden

Over the last thirty years the increase in debt burden has been manifold. In 1981 all the households had debt burden and on the whole Gouravelli had a debt of Rs 8.95 lakh and Manikyapur Rs. 8.7 lakh. In disaggregated terms, 298 landless and small peasant families had Rs 1.64 lakh debt in Gouravelli. Now in Gouravelli, self help groups alone have disbursed a credit of Rs 86 lakhs. Added to this are bank loans, microfinance loans, private and personal loans. The total debt burden on 120 dalit families in the village is Rs 50 lakh. No need to mention that this debt did not meet productive and agricultural purposes. Most of it was used as consumption expenditure, and on rituals, healthcare and education. This huge debt is clearly unsustainable and without any deposit. The interest repayments are being handled through earnings from the government programmes like the MGNREG scheme, old age pension scheme, etc.

Credit

In 1981, one of the main reasons for agricultural distress was lack of institutional, low-cost credit facilities and people were suffering under usurious money lending from landlords. Now, usurious moneylender-landlord nexus is conspicuously not visible, but the new channels of money lending and circulation have entered the rural scene. This study found at least 13 types of credit facilities with interest ranging from 0 per cent to 36 per cent. Some of the old practices of credit like future trading in paddy, sale of fertilisers and pesticides on credit and concealed interest, purchase of grain by grain merchants are still continuing. The new channels of credit include self help groups, women's thrift groups, and micro finance organisations. There is a certain improvement in institutional credit facilities like lead bank mechanism attached to each village, but this credit is being cornered by dominant sections of the village and even today the institutional credit is able to cater to 40 per cent of the needs only.

Social indicators

The earlier study observed a huge gulf between income and needs of most of the villagers. The income generation in villages was not even providing bare minimum necessities of people like food, clothing and shelter. Now, the number of income-generating activities has gone up, but poverty is much more conspicuous. Earlier there were no healthcare facilities in the villages and now there is some change in this scenario with good roads and a couple of non-medical professionals working in the villages. However, modern, trained medical care is not available now and the villagers have to travel distances to get expensive private medical help, where public healthcare facilities are either not available or insufficient. In 1981, education was at very low level and the number of educated youth, school going children in that age cohort was pathetic. In contrast, there is a remarkable change in the number of educated in the villages now and the interest shown by the villagers to send their children to schools.

In 1982 feudal practices were predominant and landlords used to grab lands through these practices. "All their wealth has accrued over the years through feudal practices like payment of wages in kind, deception through fraudulent weights and measures, partly unpaid labour, bonded labour, etc," said the 1982 study. Usury and exorbitant rates of interest were also included in this list. This scenario seems to have changed as the practice of wages in kind is discontinued (except the services of barbers and carpenters being partly paid in kind), the scope for using fraudulent weights and measures largely diminished, scope for partly unpaid and bonded labour vanished and high rates of interest appear to be concealed.

However, land concentration in the hands of non-cultivating "farmers" is more and these non-cultivating rural gentry are able to extract surplus through new methods like mediation in political and administrative affairs, contracts of public works, management of rural financial operations, trading, leasing out tractors and other implements, real estate, etc.

Untouchability and caste discrimination were most visible in 1982, but now there seems to be a change in caste discrimination with most of the castes losing out their traditional occupations and becoming labourers. The problem of untouchability does not appear as stark as it

Table 5

Changes in studied villages

Indicator	Disappeared	Increased	Decreased	Newly emerged
Wage labourers		✓		
Farmhands			✓	
Middle peasants		✓		
Landlords			✓	
Landholding inequality			✓	
Farm livestock			✓	
Wooden plough / Manual water harvesting implements	✓			
Tractor and farm implements		✓		
Artisans			✓	
Debt burden		✓		
Institutional credit		✓		
Self Help Groups				✓
Microfinance				✓
Moneylenders			✓	
Dairying		✓		
Employment		✓		
Welfare finance		✓		
Healthcare		✓		
Education		✓		
Open feudal practices			✓	
Untouchability			✓	

existed earlier and in both the villages the practice of untouchability was not seen. The earlier study found the importance of occupational caste groups in agrarian economy and particularly carpenters, blacksmiths, potters, and weavers played a major supporting role in farm activities. However, over the last thirty years the need for several occupations diminished, if not vanished, and the caste groups are either engaged in non-agricultural activities or migrated to towns. In most cases caste identity and discrimination persists more in ideological sphere than in occupational sphere.

New elements

There are certainly some hitherto non-existing elements like migration, service sector growth, entry of new commodities, and welfare schemes of government evolved over the last thirty years. Their role in changing or continuing agrarian relations has to be analysed. Of late the rural areas are throwing out more and more people outside and they are going in search of a gainful employment elsewhere. However, this push-pull factor is not employing this surplus population in any meaningful livelihood and there is no corresponding growth of secondary or industrial sector to provide them employment. In both villages studied, hundreds of people migrated but not even a single person got an employment in industrial sector. The growth of service sector in nearby towns as well as in villages is able to engage the time and energies of people and extracting surplus, not leading to any significant improvement in their level of living. The numerous welfare schemes are turning them into beneficiaries, alms seekers, dependents and unproductive instead of helping them develop into complete, creative and productive force.

4. Conclusion

The current study, against a thirty-year old benchmark, observed that there are several significant changes in both the villages despite considerable continuity. Quite interestingly the indicators that completely disappeared from the rural scene are very few compared to those that emerged over time, meaning that the new has not completely replaced the old. Most other indicators have shown either positive or negative growth in quantitative terms. One wonders whether this indicates the absence or inadequacy of a qualitative change in relations of production. The prescription given in both *Vyavasaya viplavam* and 1981 study to bring about such a qualitative transformation in agrarian structure namely, redistribution of land on the basis of land to the tiller; providing protected irrigation facilities; raising the agricultural production to the optimum level; annulling entire debt burden on the peasantry; stabilising prices; and industrialisation appears to be still mostly relevant in both the villages.

There are quite a few significant and obvious changes in the countryside in general and agrarian production systems in particular. However, the changes in nature of relations of productions and social relations do not seem to be in correspondence with these visible changes, giving yet another proof of the dichotomy between the essence and the appearance. But the difficulty is that the changes in appearance are quantifiable whereas changes in essence are mostly in quality.

As already pointed out by many scholars, one or two village studies cannot provide a complete picture of the country as a whole. At macro level the question of dominant mode of production in India in general and semi-feudal or capitalist character in particular has to be located in a larger framework of change and continuity in agrarian situation, obstacles to industrial and independent capitalist growth in the imperialist stage, the nature of Indian ruling classes and the growth and nature of Indian working class. Similarly entry of new elements and their nature and role have to be carefully understood and analysed with more concrete observation into essence.

Bibliography

(This includes several Telugu sources, indicated in italics)

Andhra Pradesh Raithu Cooli Sangham, 1983 – *Munumunduku Saagutunna Raithaanga Poraataalu*, Kranti Prachuranalu, Secunderabad.

Arvind (ed.), n.d. – Agrarian Question in India, Communist League of India (M-L), Delhi.

Balagopal, K, 1988 – Probings in the Political Economy of Agrarian Classes and Conflicts, Perspectives, Hyderabad.

Basu, Pradip, 2000 – Towards Naxalbari (1953-1967) – An Account of Inner-Party Ideological Struggle, Progressive Publishers, Calcutta.

Bhaduri, Amit, 2010 – Essays in the Reconstruction of Political Economy, Aakar Books, Delhi.

CPI (M-L) Central Committee, n.d. – Semi Feudal Character of Indian Agriculture, Resistance Publications, place not given.

CPI (M-L) Janasakthi, 1994 – *Siricilla Raithaanga Poratam – Poorvaaparaalu,* CPI (M-L) Janasakthi AP State Committee, Hyderabad.

CPI (M-L) (People's War), 1982 – *Dunnevaaniki Bhoomi Labhinchanide Raithaangaaniki Vimukti Ledu,* Kranti Prachuranalu, Secunderabad.

CPI (M-L) (People's War), 1982 – *Karimnagar – Adilabad Raithaanga Poraataalu Vardhillaali,* Kranti Prachuranalu, Secunderabad.

CPI (M-L) (People's War), 1983 - Indian Agriculture: Capitalist or Pre-Capitalist?, Voice of the Vanguard, Vol 1, Issues 1, 2 and 3, March, April and May.

CPI (M-L) (People's War), 1983 – Struggle for Land is the Centre of All Peasant Struggles, Voice of the Vanguard, Vol. 1, Issues 5-6, July/August.

CPI (M-L) (People's War), 1985 – *Bharata Arthika Vyavastha – Ardha Valasa Ardha Bhoosvaamya Vidhaanam,* Kranti Prachuranalu, Secunderabad.

CPI (M-L) (People's War), 1990 – *People's War tho Cheyi Kalipi Nadustunna Lakshalaadi Jana Samoohaalu,* Kranti Prachuranalu, Hyderabad.

CPI (M-L) Vimochana, 1992 – *Bharata Vyavasaayarangapu Ardha Bhoosvaamika Svabhaavam,* Vimochana, Hyderabad.

CPI (Maoist), 2004 – Party Prorgramme. Available on www.bannedthought.net/India/CPI-Maoist-Docs/Founding/Programme-pamphlet.pdf

CPI (Maoist), 2004 – Strategy & Tactics of the Indian Revolution. Available on www.bannedthought.net/India/CPI-Maoist-Docs/Founding/StrategyTactics-pamphlet.pdf

Damas, Marius, 1991 – Approaching Naxalbari, Radical Impression, Calcutta.

Diwakar, D M, 1994 – India – A Semi-Feudal Semi-Colonial State, Manak Publications, Delhi.

Ghosh, Suniti Kumar (ed.), 1992 – The Historic Turning Point – A Liberation Anthology, Vol. I, Author, Calcutta.

Ghosh, Suniti Kumar (ed.), 1993 – The Historic Turning Point – A Liberation Anthology, Vol. II, Author, Calcutta.

Gupta, D N (ed.), 1995 – Changing Modes of Production in India – An Historical Analysis, Hindu College, Delhi.

Karnataka Maoist Independent Center, 2006 – Dialectics of Revolution, Bulletin 1, December.

Lenin, V. I., 1977 – The Development of Capitalism in Russia in Collected Works, Vol. 3, Progress Publishers, Moscow.

Mao Tsetung, 1971 – Selected Reading from the Works of Mao Tsetung, Foreign Languages Press, Peking.

Mazumdar, Charu, 1982 – Eight Documents, Mass Line Publications, New Delhi.

Overstreet, Gene D. and Windmiller, Marshall, 1960 – Communism in India, The Perennial Press, Bombay.

Parameshwar, 2002 – *Bhooporaatamlo Vaastavaalu – Vakreekaranalu,* Viplava Rachayitala Sangham, Hyderabad.

Patnaik, Utsa (ed.), 1990 – Agrarian Relations and Accumulation – The 'Mode of Production' Debate in India, Sameeksha Trust and Oxford University Press, Bombay.

Prasad, Pradhan H, 1989 – Lopsided Growth – Political Economy of Indian Development, Sameeksha Trust and Oxford University Press, Bombay.

Rao, M B (ed.), 1976 – Documents of the History of the Communist Party of India, Vo. VII, 1948-50, People's Publishing House, New Delhi.

Rao, R S, 1995 – Towards Understanding Semi Feudal Semi Colonial Society, Perspectives, Hyderabad

Rao, R S, 2010 – *Kotthachoopu,* Veekshanam Publications, Hyderabad.

Ray, Rabindra,1992 – The Naxalites and Their Ideology, Oxford University Press, Delhi.

Reddy, N Rajasekhara, 1977 – What is CPI's Programme?, Communist Party Publication, New Delhi.

Revolutionary Communist Party, 2008 – Opportunists Never Understand Dialectics of Revolution – Central Committee, CPI (Maoist), June.

Rudra, Ashok, 1992 – Political Economy of Indian Agriculture, K P Bagchi & Company, Calcutta.

Sanyal, Kalyan, 2007 – Rethinking Capitalist Development – Primitive Accumulation, Governmentality & Post-Colonial Capitalism, Routledge, London.

Sau, Ranjit, 1986 – Economy Class Society, Universities Press, Madras.

Seetaramaiah, Kondapalli, 2005 – *Vyavasaaya Viplavam* – Kondapalli Seetaramaiah Memorial Committee, Hyderabad.

Seetaramaiah, Kondapalli, 2005 – *Aatma Vimarshana Report Taditara Teermaanaalu,* Kondapalli Seetamaiah Memorial Committee, Hyderabad.

Sen, Samar and others (eds.), 1978 – Naxalbari and After – A Frontier Anthology, Kathashilpa, Calcutta.

Shah, S. A. (ed.), 1983 – India – Degradation and Development, M Venkatarangaiya Foundation, Hyderabad.

Singha Roy, Debal K., 2004 – Peasant Movements in Post-Colonial India – Dynamics of Mobilisation and Identity, Sage Publications, New Delhi.

Thorner, Alice, (1982) – Semi-Feudalism or Capitalism? Contemporary Debate on Classes and Modes of Production in India, in Economic and Political Weekly, Vol. XVII, No. 49, 50 and 51, Decmber 4, 11 and 18.

Venugopal N, 2008 – *Kallamundari Charitra – Naalugu Dasaabdaala Viplavodyamam – Samakaalika Vyaakhyalu*, Swechchaa Sahiti, Hyderabad.

Notes :

1 It is interesting to note that the initial M-L party documents put it semi-colonial semi-feudal, several other variants with different sequence and unhifenated phrases appear in both academic and party writings.

2 These include a wide range from the Communist League of India (M-L), an offshoot of the CPI (M-L) Central Organising Committee to Karnataka Maoist Independent Centre, a split away group from the CPI (Maoist).

3 Ray, Rabindra, 1992, p. 176.

4 Rudra, Ashok, 1992, p. 82.

5 Rao, M B, 1976, pp. 775-944.

6 Rao, M B, 1976, pp. 628-68.

7 Rao, M B, 1976, p. 644.

8 Rao M B, 1976, p. 649.

9 Programme of the CPI.

10 Programme of the CPI-M.

11 Mazumdar, 1982, p.18

12 Ghosh, 1992, p. 78.

13 Ghosh, 1992, p. 229.

14 Ghosh, 1992, p. 46.

15 Ghosh, 1992, p. 47

16 Ghosh 1992, p. 196-208.

17 Ghosh, 1992, p. 10-17

18 CPI (Maoist), 2004.

19 Karnataka Maoist Independent Centre, 2006, p. 42-45

20 Revolutionary Communist Party, 2008, p. 9-14.

21 They include R S Rao, Amit Bhaduri, Pradhan H Prasad, Nirmal K Chandra and Ranjit Sau.

22 The book was reprinted more than half-a-dozen times until the party was banned in May 1992. While it was published for the first time under the name of CPI (M-L) Andhra Pradesh State Committee, and post-1980 reprints under the CPI (M-L) (People's War) without naming the author, after the death of Kondapalli Seetaramaiah in 2002, KS Memorial Committee published this book as his work.

23 A draft of this yet to be published internal party document, *Andhra Pradesh lo Vyavasaya Utpatti Sambandhaalu* (Production Relations in Agriculture in Andhra Pradesh) was circulated in July 2009.

24. Gudatipalli, a hamlet of Gouravelli in 1982 was subsequently seperated into an independent village and hence descrepancy in figures of 2012.

25. Villagers of Manikyapur purchased lands of neighbouring villages and hence descrepancy in figures.

(The author gratefully acknowledges the intellectual and moral support given by the late Prof. R S Rao, who mooted this idea and encouraged and helped in developing some of the formulations. His untimely demise on June 17, 2011 leaves a void in this paper as well as in the life of this author. Dr M Bharathi's contribution in the preparation of the paper is gratefully acknowledged. The paper also owes its existence to the author's associates Y Ramachandram and D V Ramakrishna Rao, who have taken the complete burden of meticulous study of villages in several rounds. The author is grateful to the villagers of Gouravelli and Manikyapur who extended cordial help in sharing the information about their life and miseries. Help and cooperation of hundreds of activists of the Maoist movement who helped the author in developing this concept over the years is also acknowledged with gratitude and admiration. The author thanks Alpa Shah, Barbara Harriss-White and Jens Lerche whose comments on the first draft helped revise the paper thoroughly. The responsibility for any errors, however, rests with the author.)

❖ ❖ ❖

8

The Dream for 'Land, Livelihood and Liberation'

The Naxalite movement in North Telangana signifies many things to many people. Some would like to see it as nothing but an expression of violence – a land mine here and a blast there or an encounter here and a murder there. Some others would identify the movement with the people's aspirations in the area in the context of the lack of development. Yet others would see social oppression as the root-cause of the movement and treat it as a manifestation of a sense of self-respect. There are of course other viewpoints, which deserve to be ignored, of looking at the movement as a lumpen outburst of rural riff-raff, a manifestation of disgruntlement, an easy way of making money and gaining power by wielding guns, etc. Thus there is a wide spectrum of looking at the movement from a law and order to social, cultural, economic and trivialising perspectives. Starting from the police officials to the media, every concerned party has played its role in propagating these ideas about the movement. The professed objective of the movement of attaining land, livelihood and liberation for the masses, has taken a backseat in the popular perception.

One could argue that there is a grain of truth in all these points of view. Even as all of them contain a part of truth, none of them approximate the whole truth. The truth of the origin and growth of the movement in the region lies elsewhere. Unless one deciphers the historical, ideological, social, economic, political and cultural origins, it is almost impossible to arrive at a reasonably sound understanding of the movement. It would

---

Published in Deccan Chronicle, May 27, 2001.

not be easy to comprehend the reasons for violent outburst of the movement, if it is not located properly in its specific historical context.

The region has been the hotbed of revolutionary ideology for a long time now. The historic Telangana Peasant Armed Struggle (1946 – 51) against the autocratic rule of the Nizam and the feudal landlords spread to major parts of North Telangana, though it began in small pockets of the erstwhile Nalgonda and Warangal districts. Following the Police Action in 1948, the then Communist Party of India, spearheading the struggle expanded the movement into Karimnagar and Adilabad districts. Thus, aspirations of the peasants of almost all the North Telangana districts for a better life and genuine land reforms were aroused by the end of the struggle. Unfortunately, the struggle was withdrawn without meeting those aspirations or consolidating whatever little achievements were made. On the other hand, the people were fed with illusions of *Bhoodan* and tenancy reforms. In fact, Hyderabad state was the first region in the country to bring out legislation for land reforms. However, both the initiatives did not materialise in positive sense.

The people, particularly the landless, were peeved by the withdrawal of the struggle and the failure of the successive governments in implementing land reforms. This obtaining situation by the mid-1960s was a veritable tinderbox that got ignited by the Naxalites. That is why the people of the North Telangana districts were the earliest takers of the clarion call of Naxalbari. Telangana became a major flash point along with Srikakulam, Bhojpur, Musahari, Debra-Gopiballabhpur and Waynad.

However, the first phase of the Naxalite movement witnessed a setback in Telangana too, as elsewhere. But within a couple of years, the revolutionary forces consolidated their forces and started working at grassroots during the dark days of Emergency. In several places in Karimnagar district, the activists of Radical Students Union (RSU) started campaigns amongst people and prepared them to demand the implementation of Indira Gandhi's 20-point programme. The welfare programme was never implemented and the Radicals exposed the failure to spread their ideology of agrarian revolution.

Later the withdrawal of the Emergency and a brief period of free democratic activity led to open mobilisation by several revolutionary organisations. The RSU's' 'Go to Villages' campaign resulted in the formation of Radical Youth League (RYL) and Rythu Cooli Sangham. The CPI (ML) (People's War) was in the making by that time and the underground revolutionary organisation was known as CPI (ML) AP State Committee. At the same time, peasants and landless labourers of some of the pockets in Karimnagar district were being organised by CPI (ML) Vimochana, a predecessor organisation of CPI (ML) Janashakti.

Thousands of meetings and awareness campaigns all over the districts of Karimnagar and Adilabad during those days between 1977 and 1980 could be the real foundation for the current struggles. In fact, almost all the revolutionary organisations claim their origin to this mass upsurge of Karimnagar and Adilabad districts. By the early 1980s the struggle and organisation spread to almost all the districts of North Telangana and adjoining parts of Maharashtra and Madhya Pradesh.

The movement's growth, in the face of severe repression and killing of hundreds of activists in real or fake encounters, should be located in this background of solid mobilisation that took place two decades ago. Liquidating the leaders of the movement, arrests, forced and voluntary surrenders, ban on a Naxalite party and several mass organisations did not deter people from rallying around the banner of revolt. The factors, which strengthened the movement in those early days, are still persisting in the rural areas of North Telangana and thus the struggle could neither be wished away nor suppressed through law and order means.

The major factor behind the spread of the movement is the land question. The various land reform legislations introduced in the last five decades were never implemented in letter and spirit. The landlords discovered all the loopholes in the legislations and manipulated the powers that be. In fact, in most of the cases there was no marked difference between the rulers and the landowners. In almost all the North Telangana districts landlordism was rampant and even now there are several landlords who own hundreds of acres, legally or illegally. Thousands of acres of wastelands, government lands and village commons were appropriated by the landlords. The struggle was basically to reclaim the land in unauthorised possession to the landless peasants. This was successful to a very large extent in the 1980s. During the next decade, the struggle tried to occupy excess lands of the landlords and distribute it among the landless. However, both these attempts hit roadblocks as the State machinery did not want these reforms.

While the land struggles met with more failures than successes, the Naxalite movement had gained significantly in its second area of operation – livelihood. From tendu leaf labourers in the forest areas of the region to coal miners in the Singareni belt to agricultural labourers, almost each walk of life had its own struggle for better wages and working conditions. In the last two decades, there is not even a single struggle on economic demands in the region that did not have direct or indirect support from the Naxalites. Thus the movement had touched the lives of each and every section of the working population in the region. The growth and both horizontal and vertical expansion of the movement could be traced to these struggles. The small and big agitations, essentially on wage demands, had a two-way effect as those sections achieved the demands with the support of the Naxalites and the latter could make their presence felt in ever new sections.

The third aspect of the Naxalite movement is their adherence to the cause of liberation. They want to liberate the society from the clutches of feudalism and imperialism. This cannot be done through parliamentary elections and the overthrow of the system could only be materialised through a protracted armed struggle, the Naxalites believe. Thus, it is logical on their part to form an army and fight the present system. The critics feel that this militarist trend is taking the Naxalites away from their mass politics. Whatever maybe the arguments and counter arguments, it is again the North Telangana region that witnessed remarkable events including armed clashes and the formation of People's Guerilla Army.

The politics of liberation does not necessarily mean armed struggle to overthrow the present system but also include a vision for the future. The movement seems to be focussing on realising its vision through developmental activities like forming village development committees and taking up welfare measures like co-operative agriculture, healthcare, primary education, minor irrigation facilities, etc. Their current slogan of "All power to the village committees" is a hallmark of liberation and genuine decentralisation.

❖ ❖ ❖

9

Social Movements and Radical Questions

Various social movements played a great role in the making of modern Andhra Pradesh and transformation of social values in all spheres. Andhra Pradesh was formed in 1956 by merging two distinct political and regional entities existing then and both the areas separately had glorious histories of social movements during the early part of that century. The social movements of the first part of the 20th century were waged on social and religious reform, language identity, gender equality, caste oppression, peasant rights, workers' rights, and democratic rights as well as political issues and in the process raised several radical questions. The questions are described as radical not only in the sense that they were unconventional, original and much-ahead of their times, but also for the fact that their solutions would have brought about a radical rupture with the existing norms. This contention can be proved by taking each and every social stirring in coastal Andhra starting with Kandukuri Veeresalingam's social reform activities and in Telangana with Library Movement and Andhra Jana Sangham activities. It is also true that most of these activities were sectional and limited to a minority in society in terms of participation and influence. However, a single and continuous thread of dynamic social movements that brought radical questions on to the social agenda time and again, informs the history of Telugus in the modern period.

Coming to the making of Andhra Pradesh, Telangana Peasant Armed Struggle (1946-51) and Mulki Agitation (1952) in Telangana

---

Paper presented at ICSSR-sponsored Seminar on 'Movements, Social Transformation and Making of Modern Andhra Pradesh' at Centre for Economic and Social Studies, Hyderabad, 17-18 March, 2007.

and agitations for separation of Telugu-speaking areas from Madras as well as *Visalandhra* (1948-53) in coastal Andhra were the immediate precursors to the state formation and all these social movements had raised radical questions in their own way. Telangana Peasant Armed Struggle began as a movement against feudal practices including predominant extra-economic coercion like *vetti* and highly inequitable agrarian relations and developed into an armed struggle aiming state power, with significant mass base. It was radical not only in its basic questions on land, livelihood and liberation, but also in terms of its pioneering spirit that stands as a beacon for all peasant movements in the sub-continent.

We would like to describe the Mulki Agitation, on which unfortunately much study has not been undertaken, as a social movement that raised radical questions because, it was almost the first stirring that asserted the rights of the sons of soil in post-1947 India. Separation of Telugu-speaking areas from Madras state and merger of Telangana with coastal Andhra can also be called radical ideas, at least in the 1950s, if not now, for the simple fact that the ideas were informed by nationality question based on language and culture and rejection of the rule by others. That was also unconventional at that time.

To look at these movements from a different angle, the forms of struggle taken up by these movements also help in describing them as radical. All of them opted for mass mobilisation, fasting unto death, taking up awareness campaigns through publications, holding public meetings and seminars, picketing and obstructing government work, using indigenous and modern weapons, and attacking symbols of power and wealth – all signs of exceptional social movements.

Thus Andhra Pradesh inherited a legacy of social movements with radical questions and the following five decades also witnessed a number of social movements, on almost all social issues, with similar disposition. Almost all social sections either participated or supported these movements. While some of these movements were spontaneous, sectional and local, yet others were organised, comprehensive and regional, if not state-wide. One important factor of all these movements is that, either at the time of conception or during the course, they raised radical questions in every walk of life and attempted to offer meaningful solutions. There are at least five basic types of these social movements and one could discover several instances where they raised radical questions and transformed the way one looked at society. Though there are some overlapping issues as well as separate, particular local or regional issues, all the movements can be broadly categorised as: i. Movements on regional identity issues, ii. Movements on tribal issues, iii. Movements on caste issues, iv. Movements on gender issues, and v. Movements on class issues, particularly the Naxalite movement.

In this paper, for want of time and due to limitations of this session, we would like to take up the Naxalite movement and attempt to show how it raised radical questions. First of all, the movement has to be put in its proper perspective, refuting some popular misconceptions. That the Naxalite movement recognises itself as an agrarian revolution goes without saying and we think that is the reason this paper is scheduled in this session on agrarian/farmers' movements. But we would argue that the Naxalite Movement is much more than a set of ideas regarding agrarian relations and if one reduced the movement to land question alone, one would tend to believe naively that a successful land reform programme would see the end of the Naxalite movement. This is far from truth, for neither a successful land reform programme is possible under the given state of relations of production, nor is it the single agenda of the Naxalite movement. The second popular misconception, propagated by the state and media, is that the Naxalite movement is basically a movement that preaches and practises violence. Though it is true that counter-violence has a major role in the ideology and practice of the Naxalite movement, reducing it to that single factor would tantamount to denying the radical questions it raises and the social transformation it envisages.

Here it would not be possible to examine all the radical questions the movement raised since they are too numerous, but we would like to take up five basic aspects of the movement and show in what way they are radical. These five aspects are land, livelihood, liberation, organisation and forms of struggle and in each of these the Naxalite movement brought forth new questions, new modes of thinking and new solutions. The history of four decades of the Naxalite movement in Andhra Pradesh vouches for this novel thinking and it could be substantiated by hundreds of examples. But we would like to give at least two instances of radical thinking in each of these aspects.

Even as the land question occupies a place of prime importance in the left political practice ever since the Telangana Peasant Armed

Struggle, the attention it drew over the following decades is quite uneven, both in ruling parties and the parliamentary left. Interest in land question received a blow among Communists when the Telangana Peasant Armed Struggle was officially withdrawn in 1951. Landlords whose lands were occupied by landless peasants and tenants have taken back their lands. The land question did not fare on the agenda of the then Communist Party of India. Surprisingly, it was the Congress governments all over the country that initiated land reform programmes and it is generally concluded that tenancy reforms were successful. Andhra Pradesh was not formed by then and both the administrative areas had enacted separate land reform measures, particularly tenancy reform regulations. After the formation of Andhra Pradesh, it was only during the early 1960s that the then CPI began an agitation in rural areas but it was not primarily on land question, but against rise in land revenue and water cess – primarily issues of landed peasants.

One has to see the fundamental nature of land question raised by the Naxalite movement in this background. The struggles for land led by the Naxalites began in the late 1960s and witnessed massive participation during 1977 to 1992, with a respite from 1985 to 1989. These land struggles were so widespread that they covered the entire state from Adilabad to Chittoor to Srikakulam, including at the unlikely places of Krishna and West Godavari. The period of 1985 to 89 saw heavy repression on the movement with sweeping use of the Terrorists and Disruptive Activities (Prevention) Act on the landless peasants and their supporters. Again, in 1992 one of the major Naxalite parties in the state – the Communist Party of India (Marxist – Leninist) (Peoples War) and six mass organisations, including Andhra Pradesh Raithu Cooli Sangham, were banned. Though the other Naxalite parties and other peasant-agricultural labourers' associations were allowed to operate openly, they also had to work under constant threat and thus it was the State that put down all the questions on land with iron heel.

Here it would not be out of place to mention the government's attempts to legislate in favour of protection of tribals from land alienation (1970), prescribing land ceiling (1973), distribution of government land to landless, particularly Dalits (1977) and getting the lands occupied by landless poor registered (1990), were in direct response to the questions raised by the Naxalite movement.

But, post-new economic policies, the land reform ideas have received a short shrift in the corridors of power. Post 1992, there was not even a mention of land reform in official documents, even as the Naxalite movement was going ahead with land occupations and land struggles.

Again, during a brief respite when the government and two Naxalite parties wanted to hold talks on various issues of social concern, the land question occupied primary position. The CPI (M-L) (Peoples War) which became the CPI (Maoist) by then and the CPI (M-L) Janashakti participated in the talks and they submitted a detailed paper 'Land Distribution – Development of Agriculture: Our Perspective' along with two annexures: i. Our specific proposals, and ii. Details of alienated land around Hyderabad.

This important document, one of the first presented by the parties engaged in struggle to the government, was a real eye-opener to anybody who thought there was nothing in the Naxalite movement except violence. While the government, with the vast resources it commands, could neither produce any status paper on land question, nor refute the Naxalites' arguments properly, the Naxalites who were on the run continuously and arguably without any resources produced a well-debated and substantiated paper. Again this paper was radical in more than one way, but it would suffice to refer to the specific proposals where for the first time in the country's history of land reforms the Naxalites argued to eliminate all the absentee landlords if they had any other source of income. The paper also suggested identification of surplus lands in villages rather than through an all-pervasive legislation and in revenue offices. The paper also suggested to begin the distribution of land from Dalits and registration of distributed land on the names of women. Though the talks failed and government did not invite the parties for the second round as promised, the subsequent land distribution by the government included these two suggestions.

The issues of livelihood cover a wide range of hundreds of small and big and widespread and sporadic issues from domestic violence to State violence. Livelihood is normally denoted by financial aspects and there is a tendency to consider struggles on wages, allowances, working conditions and terminal benefits as agitations on livelihood. But the Naxalite movement has enlarged the scope of the struggles for livelihood in terms of aspirations of better life, whether it is freedom from oppression, gender equality, fight against all forms of subjugation. They are radical in redefining the scope as well as their spread across all sections of society. Whether it was the struggle against rape of Rameeja Bee by police in Hyderabad or the rape of a servant maid by the son of a mining officer in Bellampalli or a struggle for raising the wages of tendu-leaf pickers in the forests of north Telangana, or a struggle for the self-respect of Dalits, or a struggle for better wages for agricultural labourers or a students' struggle for better hostels and improved living conditions, or a struggle for house sites for poor or a struggle against price rise, or a struggle against liquor, or a struggle for improving the working conditions of coal miners, or a struggle against the ill-effects of globalisation and privatisation, or a struggle for remunerative prices for farmers – name any struggle, the influence of the Naxalite movement is there and similar movements in other states can be compared to identify the radical nature of these struggles in Andhra Pradesh.

While the struggles on land and livelihood are described as "economic struggles" in the Naxalites' parlance, the movement is marked by its "political struggles". These are struggles for liberation. The Naxalites think that the present social and economic order has to be completely overthrown and a new social and economic order has to be created and they think toiling masses are chained in a number of oppressive situations and they have to achieve their own liberation. Somewhere Karl Marx charactersied this as radical rupture with the status quo and in fact this aspect of the Naxalite Movement is their real radical element. The Naxalites treat all their economic struggles as consciousness raising exercises on the way to achieve this liberation. That's why one has to extricate themselves from the popular and naive misconception that the Naxalite movement can be contained by solving the questions of land and livelihood, in whatever broad and inclusive way they are defined. The Naxalite movement's major aim is to achieve liberation, meaning throwing away the yoke of the existing social and economic order and its political manifestation, and establishing a people's State. The Naxalites think that the current political expression is democratic only in form and not in essence and thus they think it is not a people's State. In this sense, this is the most radical question that is posed to the current State and thanks to the influence of the Naxalite movement in Andhra Pradesh for the last forty years, each and every subsequent movement even if it says it opposed the Naxalites, has included the nature of the State in its discourse. Thus the Naxalite movement not only raised a fundamental radical question but also made all the other movements follow the same lines. One could argue that the Naxalite movement's single most contribution to all the social movements in Andhra Pradesh is its idea of questioning the character of the representation of the State in a radical way.

In terms of organisation and forms of struggle also the Naxalite movement has added new elements in the tradition of social movements in the state. Until the Naxalite movement came on to the scene in Andhra Pradesh, the political parties did not know that there was scope for non-parliamentary political processes and in itself the idea was a radical posture. Even those parties which did not participate in electoral politics did have an ambition of fighting elections one day and till that time no single party openly gave a call for boycotting the electoral political process branding it as fake. The Naxalite movement was so radical in giving such a call and it showed an alternative political path where political mobilisation at the grassroots level would pave the way for a mass upsurge, coupled with establishing a people's militia and liberating countryside and then encircling urban power centres to ultimately seize State power. The movement has conceived this strategy as a protracted, long-drawn peoples' war with probable tactical shifts on the way. In fact, after some adventurous mistakes in the early years, this process began earnestly during the late 1970s and early 1980s with a massive support from poor and downtrodden. However, brutal State repression, unmindful of fundamental rights and directive principles of Constitution, was successful in terrorising people from joining or supporting this alternative political process openly. Gradually space for this political process was shrunk and the Naxalite movement and the people who subscribed to the ideology and practice had to search for alternative routes for this process, giving scope to much more illegal and clandestine activity instead of open, legal, democratic and constitutional activity. In the process, this gave rise to violence and counter violence spiral killing thousands of people. The movement continued with this activity for the last two decades, despite losing thousands of its cadres, and this again is a sign of its radical departure. The movement did show that there was a possibility in Indian polity and society to practice an alternative route, even with supreme sacrifices of youth, at a time when the mainstream youth were careerist and self-seeking, the movement presented an example of self-less sacrifice.

Besides its social, political and economic questions, the significance of the Naxalite movement lies in its radical cultural paradigm, where this self-less sacrifice is juxtaposed to the all pervasive selfishness, acquisition, consumerism and careerism. In fact, this idea of sacrifice has become a radical touchstone for all social movements.

❖ ❖ ❖

10

Tendu Leaf Labourers in Telangana Working Conditions and Struggles

"It is the experience of all the states that the nationalisation (of Tendu Leaf Trade) not only brought extra revenue to the states, but also ensured payment of reasonable minimum wages to the collectors ..." as observed by National Commission on Agriculture. But the experience of Andhra Pradesh does not confirm this. Tendu leaf trade was nationalised in AP according to The Andhra Pradesh Minor Forest Produce (Regulation of Trade) Act, 1971(APMFP) "to make provision for regulating in the public interest ... by creation of a state monopoly trade ..." Let alone a pretentious phrase like "public interest", even the two results traced out by the NCA were not the effects of nationalisation. The facts show that "extra revenue" was brought about by the bidding capacity or generosity of the contractors. In fact, they alone have the power to monitor and manipulate that "extra revenue to the State". On the other hand, nationalisation has not ensured payment of reasonable minimum wages to the collectors. In fact, higher – far below the "reasonable" and "minimum" – wages were achieved by the relentless struggle of collectors over the years. Of course, to make the observation of NCA true, the state government is fixing the wages correspondingly lower than those achieved by the collectors. This reality of "State monopoly" and the experiences of the eight year-struggle are worth considering for all those interested in people's movements and the struggles in unorganised sector.

Published in Economic and Political weekly Vol XIX No 46, November 17, 1984.

I

The leaf of *Thuniki* (Tendu, as popularly known, or abnus in legal parlance), a medium-sized tree found in the dry forests is most suitable for wrapping tobacco in indigenous beedi making process. Tendu trees are common in north and north-east forest belt of Andhra Pradesh and adjoining forest areas of Maharashtra, Madhya Pradesh and Orissa. The leaves sprout up during April-May are the appropriate kind for the purpose. The trees should be pollarded just before the season to facilitate leave growth. In about forty-five days the leaves will be ready for plucking. Actual plucking lasts for ten to forty-five days. "Pollarding or pruning is usually undertaken during the month of February/March and plucking usually starts about the middle of April and continues up to the first or second week of June". This is how, the total activity is restricted to three months in maximum. This strictly timed profit making gives rise to the avarice of the contractors. At the same time, it forces the contractor to negotiate with collectors.

According to the NCA report, a decade ago, the annual collection of tendu leaves was estimated to exceed 3 lakh tonnes, of which AP was contributing about 14 per cent. But the collection marked an enormous growth over the years and in 1983, AP alone produced 2.38 lakh tonnes of leaves. In five districts of North Telangana, tendu leaf trade is a flourishing trade. Of these five, Khammam occupies the first place, in proportion of forest area to the total geographical area, with 47 per cent to be followed by Adilabad (42 per cent), Warangal (28 per cent), Karimnagar and Nizamabad (21 per cent each). Forest department of Andhra Pradesh government controls this forest stretch by dividing it into four circles and seventeen divisions. This forest accounts for the major share of total beedi leaves produced in the state. (It was as high as 95 per cent in 1980-81.) Government revenue on beedi-leaves per annum is more than one seventh in relation to total revenue from forests. Between 1978-79 and 1981-82 it was 17 per cent, 13 per cent, 13 per cent and 20 per cent respectively (see Tables). According to Section 4 of the APMFP Act, "the government may, for the purposes of purchase of and trade in, any minor forest produce, on their behalf, appoint an agent for each unit..". In other words, the government auctions off the rights to collect and trade the leaves to aspiring *guthedars* (contractors), who are so-called agents in the "public interest". Though the procedure, for appointing an agent, prescribed by the Act is a lengthy one, it is

Table 1
Value of Beedi Leaves, Circle wise - 1980-81

(in '000 Rs.)

S.No.	Circle	Value of MFP	Value of Beedi Leaves	Value of Total Forest Produce
1.	Adilabad	16,492	12,307	88,412
2.	Warangal	14.171	13,329	52,408
3.	Khammam	11,935	6,756	36,452
4.	Nizamabad	8,650	5,534	15,215
	Total	51,238	37,926	1,92,487
	Andhra Pradesh	85,541	39,675	2,87,096

never followed; except on paper. The whole forest area is subdivided into a number of units and a contractor can bid for any number of units. The bidding price is called 'royalty'. Every year just before the commencement of season, the government appoints an advisory committee to recommend the price. This committee comprises of traders of MFP and growers of tress giving MFP. According to Section 7 of the Act, "the government shall by notification and after consultation with the committee fix the price at which any particular MFP shall be purchased by them or by any authorised officer or agent ...". It is a moot point what a committee comprising of contractors recommend as the wages to be given to collectors. The contractors appoint employees (*kalledars)* in every village, supervisors *(girdavars)* over them and at accessible places they open the depots. "There shall be set up in each unit such number of depots and at such places as the government may be taking into consideration the convenience of the growers of the respective MFP. A price list of such produce fixed by the government ... and the hours of business shall be prominently displayed on notice board kept for the purpose at every such depot ..".

Prior to nationalisation there was no government fixation or check on wages. Now the government fixes the wages and apparently supervises the payment and bears the responsibility for the damage of produce, if any. The contractors have not lost anything with this kind of nationalisation. For, they are the people on the committee to recommend wages and the forest officials who have to supervise the payment can be easily bribed. Not only that, the nationalisation entitles them to claim compensation for "damages" from government. And apart from fixing the wages, the contractors have invented a number of methods of exploitation.

They pay very low wages to the collectors. Prior to 1976, the wage-rate was a paltry 3 paise for collecting a bundle of 100 leaves. Even though, it is 15-22 paise now, it is still a meagre amount, as any contractor earns more than 25 paise on every 100 leaves bundle. All the members in a collector's family are engaged in the labour. The elders go out for collecting and younger ones sort and pack them. The actual collectors have to walk at least 2-3 km to collect the leaves and the plucking is a laborious work of examining each and every twig. If we consider a family's total capacity of collecting per working day (it is anything over 10 hours!) the wages family receives becomes less than the statutory minimum. As can be expected, authorities neither try to see that the prescribed wage-rate is followed nor do they supervise the implementation of respective minimum wage Acts.

The other way of profit making that the contractors indulge in is illegal collection, thereby escaping the royalty and sales tax payment. For every unit, the government fixes a specific target, and this target figure is to be calculated by local forest officials. In almost all the cases, the officials give a lower figure in connivance with the contractors. And besides the target quantity they collect large sums of leaves which they sell in free market. They don't have to pay royalty and sales tax on this income. At times, they do not sell the leaves, because the leaves are used in their own beedi factories. In some units where 10 lakh leaves (100 tonnes) target was prescribed, this kind of illegal collection was estimated to fetch a quantity as high as 5 lakh leaves.

To guage the extent of exploitation and profit one should look into the figures, calculated on the basis of a 10 lakh leaves unit in Karimnagar district during 1984 season.

Royalty and Sales tax to be paid to the government - (Rs 230 per 1000 leaves bundle) - Rs 2,30,000

Packing, storage, transport and other miscellaneous charges (calculating at moderate Rs 75 per 1000 leaves) - Rs 75.000

Wage Bill (at the average rate of 12.5 paise per 100 leaves) - Rs 1,25,000

The total costs incurred by the contractor - Rs 4,30,000

At the market the leaves are sold in units of kilograms and 10 lakh leaves weigh about 100 tonnes.

The market rate per kilogram is Rs 6.04 and the contractor's earnings are Rs 6,04,000.

Thus, even without indulging in illegal collection, a contractor can make a profit of Rs 1,74,000. But no contractor contents himself with just this profit. As a 10 lakh target unit can yield five lakh more leaves, the contractor can pocket Rs 2,02,000 more. The total period needed for realising this profit is three months and that too, in a single unit. There are as many as thirty units in Karimnagar district alone. Apart from these major areas of exploitation there are other usual extra-economic exactions. Over the years, this kind of exploitation had become an unquestionable custom. *Kalledar* collects a large sum of bundles without paying the wages. To maintain this appropriation contractors and *kalledars* have discovered at least a dozen excuses. Collectors have to give two or three bundles free of wages on every amount of a rupee-earning bundles as a token of gratitude for permission to pluck *(Gulla Katta)*. In every season contractors declare two or three days as *vetti* days, on which no wages are paid and all the labourers are made to do compulsory work. *Pechchu Katta* (additional bundle), *gampa katta, pothi katta, gutha katta* (sum bundle), gali katta (bundle to Air goddess) and *mithi katta* (interest bundle) are some of the different names given to this kind of exploitation.

Another way is that the contractors demand free bundles as an offering to village deities such as *Pochamma Katta, Maisamma Katta,* etc. Apart from these ways, *kalledars* raise many objections such as 'the leaf is not tender', 'it is too tender', 'it has holes' and 'the bundle doesn't have 100 leaves' in order to get those bundles free. All the manifestations of the above exploitation were rampant till recently. Some of them continue to exist, though not as they did previously. A relentless fight against this exploitative system during the last eight years is the sole reason for the retreat of contractors.

II

When the state of Emergency was promulgated on June 26, 1975, many activists of Radical Students Union (RSU) had to go underground to evade arrests and "encounters". Some of these activists went into the interior parts of Karimnagar district. They conducted village surveys, analysed the class composition in villages, organised people to rise against exploitation and at places led people to achieve partial and economic demands. The RSU and peasant activists campaigned throughout the area. In 1976 tendu leaf collectors in 40 villages went on strike demanding higher wages. The contractors were made to concede demands. The following two years saw a greater consolidation at village level and the struggles were waged at village level. Only in 1979 the concept of total unit strike came into light. In 1979, collectors in Thungur, Bhukthipur, Nerella and Rachapalli units of Jagityal taluq waged a unit level struggle. A total strike was organised in 35 villages under these units. The strike was on two basic demands—implementation of eight paise per bundle wage-rate and scrapping of the custom of free bundles. Strike continued for three weeks and the contractors accepted to pay seven paise per bundle and not to demand any free bundles.

This success turned out to be more than exemplary as Manthani and Metpalli taluqs in the same district and one unit in Chennur taluq of Adiiabad district followed suit in 1980 season. As the contractors and wage rates in different units varied collectors in a particular unit had to fight for the same wage rate which their counterparts in another unit had achieved. Similarly the unit which succeeded in getting a higher wage-rate the previous year had to fight for a still higher wage-rate.

In 1981 the struggle was co-ordinated and an unified strike call was given in Karimnagar and Warangal districts. Jagityal, Metpalli, Sirisilla, Manthani, Husnabad, Huzurabad, Peddapalli and Mahadevpur taluqs of Karimnagar district and Mulugu, Parkal and Etur Nagaram taluqs of Warangal district observed the strike. Although wages demanded were different, dernand for scrapping of free bundle custom remained common. Organisers of the struggle got the support of growers by demanding the payment of income from leaves in *patta* lands to actual *pattadars.* Adilabad district also experienced a widespread struggle in 1981. 150 villages in Utnoor, Boath, Khanapur and Nirmal taluqs, bordering Maharashtra, went on a strike for five days and achieved nine paise wage-rate. *Kalledars* also participated in the strike demanding higher salaries and achieved a 100 rupees rise.

Same year saw the strike spread to Kamareddi and Bheemgal taluqs of Nizamabad district, Asifabad taluq of Adilabad district and

Table 2
Tax Levied under the General Sales Tax Act, 1957 on Beedi Leaves

(in '000 Rs.)

	1967-68	1979-80
Total turnover of beedi leaves	2,846	28,500
Tax levied	91	2,094

spread over to Sironcha taluq of the then Chandrapur district in Maharashtra. One reason for this extension was migration. Usually contractors set up residential depots at interior sites, called labour *kallam.* The collectors who work in this labour *kallams* are generally not natives but migrant labourers. Collectors of Madhya Pradesh and Maharashtra who used to migrate to Karimnagar and Adilabad for better wages, now started fighting for better wages in their own areas. In a few places, it is the other way round also. 1981 is also the first year which showed the contractors the consequences of their not complying with the agreement. In Thadicharla unit the contractors accepted all the demands and the strike was withdrawn. But, once the strike was called off, they refused to comply with it. Furiated people burnt down three lots of leaves belonging to the contractors.

1982 saw expansion of the movement. The struggle started with the initial activity of pollarding. The wages for this are time-rate and far below the minimum wages. The cutters went on a 40-day strike in Metpalli, Jagityal, Chennur and Vellam Kunta units and achieved a raise in wages. Struggle committees were formed at unit level in the entire area of conflict. An effective leadership from among the labourers was developed through struggle committees. Other pending problems were taken up. The contractors who did not keep their promises to pay the income to the *pattedars* were fined, the fines were collected immediately and the amount was deposited with the village struggle committee for common use. As the labourers went on strike at the time of pollarding, contractors of Vellam Kunta unit brought pclice force before plucking started and tried to check the impending struggles.

In 1983 a planned co-ordination committee supervised the struggle. A few struggle committees, entirely of women, were also

Table 3
Circle wise Comparitive value of Beedi Leaves before and after Nationalisation

(in '000 Rs.)

S.No.	Circle	Value of MFP			Value of Beedi Leaves		
		1970-71	71-72	80-81	1970-71	71-72	80-81
1.	Warangal	3,709	12,333	14,171	3,052	12,058	13,329
2.	Kothagudem/ Khammam*	4,001	11,005	11,935	493	7,495	6,756
3.	Adilabad	1,225	8,133	16,492	3,354	10,256	12,307
4.	Nizamabad	**	**	5,400	**	**	5,534

Notes : * Earlier Khammam Circle was known as Kothagudem.
** Nizamabad Circle was not formed then.

formed. *Kalledars* and watchers also expressed their solidarity with the strike and at places joined hands with the strikers. Struggle spread to Visakhapatnam district in Andhra Pradesh and Bijapur taluq of Bastar district in Madhya Pradesh, where a one-week strike under the leadership of struggle committees was organised. The strike was total and successful in Karimnagar, Adilabad, Khammam, Warangal and Nizamabad in AP and Gadchiroli in Maharashtra. At many places labourers demanded petromax lamps and big cooking utensils for common purpose and succeeded in getting these. Three lots of leaves of a contractor were burnt down in Nizamabad district. Had not the contractor come down to negotiate and accepted all the demands, the fourth lot also would have gone to ashes. Despite severe repression from CRPF and APSP, 1984 season observed more of a militant and successful struggle. Wages for pollarding were increased in the whole area. The wages before the strike were so paltry that even a 100 per cent increase was less than the minimum wages. In Adilabad district, wages for women labourers were increased to Rs 4 from Rs 2 and wages for men labourers were increased to Rs 5 from Rs 2.50. In Karimnagar the corresponding increase was Rs 2 to Rs 4, and Rs 3 to Rs 5.

Strike in 50 units comprising of 700 villages in Adilabad district was total. Struggle committees were organised in every village. The strike achieved a wage-rise to 15-17 paise from existing 12-15 paise per bundle of 100 leaves. Time-wage rate for miscellaneous works was also increased. In some villages the struggle succeeded in securing petromax lamps, big bed sheets and utensils and increase in wages of 12 to 20 paise per bundle. In Nizamabad district villages belonging to 25 units in Kamareddi, Domakonda, Bheemgal, Nizamabad, Banswada, and Bodhan went on strike. Wages went up to 18-20 paise per bundle in all the units. In some units the wages in previous year were 8-9 paise. In one village, by name Ramsagar in Koratpalli unit the labourers achieved a wage-rate as high as 24 paise. *Kalledars* could secure a 150 per cent increase and watchers a 100 per cent increase in their monthly salaries.

III

But the story is not devoid of its consequent enmity from the contractor-forest official-police combine. Contractors, by employing hired hoodlums, terrorise the labourers and beat up the leaders. Forest officials threaten the labourers to seize the household wood as forest timber, threaten not to give the leaves and grass to thatch the huts, and not to give any firewood. Contractors' henchmen take up the false propaganda in every village that all the other villages have called off the strike. Above all this kind of terrorising tactics they enjoy help of the police. Over the last eight years police tried various terrorising methods to stem the struggle. They raided villages, arrested hundreds of people, and have put up camps at plucking sites and beat up the leaders of struggle committees publicly to achieve demonstrative effect. But these methods are insignificant compared to the methods adopted this year.

Just before the season this year, N T Rama Rao's Telugu Desam government requested the Centre to sanction three batallions of CRPF. The CRPF batallions were used in the forest areas. The APSP camps, which were put up before CRPF's entry, were continued. These forces indulged in combing operations at places where campaigns were held. In Adilabad district alone 30 APSP camps and five CRPF camps were put up. Policemen of these camps tore up the posters, assaulted the people, combed the surrounding villages trying to force the people give up the struggle. In Karimnagar district the police actively succeeded in appointing former activists as *kalledars*. These activist-turned *kalledars* in turn try to divide people using their past "contacts". The people arrested by the police were kept in illegal custody for twenty days in some instance. Police camps were put up in 40 villages in Nizamabad district. Forest officials and police obstructed people from taking their cattle for grazing in the forest. Besides these 40 camps, 400 CRPF and APSP personnel were commissioned to comb the adjoining forest areas in search of Naxalite squads. Dirtrict Superintendent of Police toured each and evey village in the struggle area. At his behest the landlords in one village caught a Radical Students team who were on their routine Summer Village Campaign' and handed over them to the police. In another village the landlords' goondas attacked the students, and handed them to police. At two places police fired on campaigners at point-blank range.

Yet the struggle has notched success. Over eight years wages have gone up on an average to 22 paise from a paltry 3 paise. Many kinds of unpaid labour have been discontinued.

❖ ❖ ❖

11

Politics of Nuclear Power in Andhra

Symbols serve strange purposes. At times the same symbol may be used for two antagonistic aims. August 6 and 9 are the dates which symbolise death and destruction. People remember Hiroshima and Nagasaki on these dates and recollect the untold suffering caused by nuclear devices. The parliamentary parties in Andhra Pradesh as a routine observed August 6 as Hiroshima Day against nuclear weapons and in the same breath they chose August 9 to demand nuclear power plant - a potential nuclear armoury. On that day almost all the parliamentary parties in the state were to participate in a meeting proposed at Nalgonda to ask the central government to expedite the planned nuclear power plant at Nagarjunasagar. Though the meeting was postponed for some other reason, the intention of the organisers was reflected in a detailed article in favour of nuclear power plant published in Visalandhra on that day.

As N Raji Reddy, minister for power, government of Andhra Pradesh recorded on the floor of the legislative assembly there is an 'opposition' from some sections of the public to the location of the plant at Nagarjunasagar, who apprehended danger to the irrigation project and human, plant, and animal life". Precisely to counter the opposition to the power plant the power monger classes of Andhra Pradesh cheated "... a section of the public which is supporting the establishment of the plant at Nagarjunasagar due to acute power shortage

Published in Economic and Political Weekly, Vol XXIII, No. 36, September 3, 1988.

in the state and also on the account of the proven record of the atomic power plants all over the world". This is just in tune with the style of functioning of N T Rama Rao, who invents 'people's wishes' as a pretext for his actions.

The parties supporting the demand included Telugu Desam, Congress (I), CPI, CPI (M), MCPI, Janata Party, and ISCUS along with the Atomic Energy Commission. And arguments in favour of the plant in particular and nuclear power in general were indeed ridiculous.

In fact, M R Srinivasan, chairman, AEC, N T Rama Rao, and N Raji Reddy could not compete with these active supporters. According to an editorial in *Visalandhra,* daily organ of the CPI, Nalgonda district committee of CPI, in a resolution, condemned the propaganda of some elements against the establishment of the nuclear power plant. It appealed the people "not to get provoked by such unwarranted misgivings and not to give heed to such opportunist leaders. It also asked the centre to go on with its plan speedily".

The support did not end at that level. It was promptly translated into practice. Again to quote, "a decision was taken at . . .the state conference of ISCUS to form a broad-based front to strive for the setting up of nuclear power plant at Nagarjunasagar . . Every unit of ISCUS in the state has not only to take initiative but also should make efforts to bring in all the concerned sections onto a united platform..". Actually the postponed meeting was to be hosted by ISCUS, Nalgonda unit in which state level leaders *of* CPI, CPl(M), MCPI, Congress (I), Telugu Desam, Janata Parry and a scientist from Nuclear Fuel Complex, Hyderabad were announced to speak. General secretaries of the state unit of ISCUS have written articles in support of power plant in Visalandhra and Udayam, another daily.

Besides ISCUS, the district units of AIYF and AISF also urged the government to expedite the plan. They even branded the opponents as 'reactionaries'. And also, the president of Nagarjunasagar Employees and Labour Union (AITUC) wrote a long article in Visalandhra.

Prajasakti, the CPI (M) daily editorially commented that the agitation against the power plant was "groundless either on scientific considerations or in view of past experience. Pursuing such an agitation based on blind beliefs would be an obstacle to our development."

Mystifying Science

Leaving aside the usual rhetoric, the arguments put forth in favour of the power plant should be examined seriously as they consist of falsehoods, distortions and evasion of inconvenient facts. The arguments are intended to mislead people by mystifying science.

The major argument of the supporters is that going in for a nuclear power plant was imperative because of the acute power shortage in the state. The state had to impose severe power cuts during 1987-88. The situation was temporarily better for only the first week of June 1988. Editorials of Visalandhra and Prajasakti, the articles by Vemulapalli Sri Krishna and P Rama Koteshwara Rao, general secretaries, ISCUS and speeches of M Omkar, leader, MCPI and N Raji Reddy repeatedly quoted this fact to promote nuclear power.

It is true that Andhra Pradesh has been experiencing a power crisis for the last three years. But until 1983-84 the state had surplus power. In that year, Andhra Pradesh produced excess power to the extent of 1.6 per cent. According to 1987-88 statistics, the state has an installed capacity of 3614.5 MW of which hydel projects generate 2422 MW and thermal plants, 1192.5 MW. The minister for power in fact, stated on the floor of the assembly that the generated units from an installed capacity of 2421 MW were sufficient for the needs of Andhra Pradesh. He categorically accepted that power generation was more than the consumption in the state.

On the other hand, Andhra Pradesh has been recording a high percentage of losses in transmission and distribution. According to CMIE's *Current Energy Scene in India* (1985) the Andhra Pradesh State Electricity Board lost 23.1 per cent in 1982-83 and 21.3 per cent in 1983-84. Due to its predominant dependence on hydel power good monsoons gave Andhra Pradesh a surplus even after these losses. But 1984 onwards hydel power could not be generated as much as in the past due to the failure of the monsoons.

It is obvious that the power crisis in the state is not real. Yet the remedy for the apparent power crisis lies elsewhere. Proper maintenance to check transmission and distribution losses, reducing the dependence on hydel power and exploring alternative renewable resources of energy on one hand and building up minor hydel projects on the Godavari on the other, would solve the power problem. The investment would also be much less than that on a nuclear power plant.

The nuclear protagonists' argument is creating an impression that the entire benefit from the nuclear power plant would come to Andhra Pradesh. This is a distorted representation of the policy. The power generated by the nuclear power plant will go into the national grid and nobody knows exactly how much of the proposed 1000 MW comes to Andhra Pradesh.

The other argument put forth by the supporters is that the nuclear power plant would not create any problem of human displacement. According to Visalandhra, "there is no habitation within the radius of 1.6 km at the proposed site of the nuclear power plant. Arrangements are being made to see that no population centre comes up within the radius of 5 km. Density of population within the radius of 30 km is meagre." Another edit-page article in the same newspaper says that there is a possibility of townships being formed around any major industrial location and hence the idea of not having a population centre is senseless. Yet another article in the same daily says that ". . . if the nuclear power plant is established, people belonging to seven or eight villages and hamlets around Chalakurthi within the radius of 5 km may have to be evacuated and rehabilitated. But can we afford to turn back in our invaluable forward march because of the fear of rehabilitation?" Although these statements are either 'official' or have appeared prominently, they contradict each other.

To add to the confusion, M R Srinivasan has estimated the number of the people to be displaced and rehabilitated, i. e., the people who live within the radius of 1.6 km at 1050. But this figure is also a gross underestimate. Surprisingly the editorial of Visalandhra basing itself entirely on the speech given by M R Srinivasan reduced the number to zero. In fact one village and eight hamlets are to be totally evacuated. The nuclear power plant is proposed at Pottichelma, a village Chalakurti and seven surrounding hamlets, namely, Naayakuni Thanda, Mailonikunta Kindi Thanda, Mailonikunta Pai Thanda, Kaapagudem, Bethelameedi Thanda, Voorabai Thanda and Kunkuduchettu Thanda are going to be erased from the map. As per 1981 census the population of Chalakurthi was 4605 and with the population of the surrounding hamlets the estimated population is about 5500. In addition to this 25 villages and hamlets around Chalakurthi were warned about probable evacuation. Population in these areas would be around 20,000. Vijayapuri, the town at Nagarjunasagar dam site, a population of around 40,000 lies within the radius of 16 km of the plant. So clearly the problem of displacement cannot be wished away or ignored.

Cost Factor

Another argument put forward by the nuclear supporters is regarding the cost factor of nuclear power. They claim that nuclear power is the cheapest of all available sources of energy. This argument has been repudiated time and again at national and international debates. It has been substantially proved that nuclear power is not as cheap as the protagonists state. Raja Ramanna, the foremost promoter of nuclear power in India has given computed costs with utmost care. According to him a unit (Kwh) of nuclear power from a 2X235 MW nuclear power station commissioned during 1990s would be 65 paise. Out of this amount, 47 paise goes to fixed charges and 18 paise to operating expenses. ('A 15-year Programme for Nuclear Power in India' by Raja Ramanna, *Indian Journal of Power and River Valley Development,* November-December 1984, p 453). This is a gross underestimate as the cost for decommissioning and the cost over-run due to time lag has not been taken into consideration. Experience of decommissioning in UK and other places shows that the cost of decommissioning is almost as much as, if not more than the cost of installation. So an additional 47 paise has to be added to the unit cost of nuclear power. That means the total cost of a unit of nuclear power at moderate rates comes to 112 paise, without considering the cost overrun. The cost over-run is unpredictable as the several factors like the time taken for construction, etc, are beyond the control of the powers that be.

In comparison, a unit of power from a thermal plant costs 34.90 paise and from a hydel project costs 14.61 paise. ('Usefulness of Hydro Power - Its Economics, Peaking Capabilities and Operating Efficiency' by T C Agarwal and Shafiq Ahmad *Indian Journal of Power and River Valley Development,* September-October 1984, p 426). Another case study on mini-hydro power projects which compared the costs estimated the costs to be 29 paise to 40 paise in mini hydro power projects, 26 to 39 paise in large hydro projects, 36.76 paise to 40.37 paise in thermal power projects per unit on average. ('Economics of Mini-Hydro Power', by M P Garg, *Indian Journal of Power and River Valley Development*, September-October 1984, p 436-437). Even if all these figures for thermal and hydel power are doubled, they show that these sources are much cheaper than the nuclear power. The promoters of the nuclear power plant argue that having a power plant is a privilege for the state. Once again to quote Visalandhra, "the nuclear power plant set up at Kalpakkam was actually to be allocated to Andhra Pradesh. But, because of the unfounded prejudices about the site at Nagarjunasagar, we have lost that opportunity.." The same line of argument is repeated in other articles as well. It is being argued that the nuclear power plant would bring about industrial development and thereby usher in a new era in Andhra Pradesh. These statements are intended to arouse the sentiments of Telugu people on the one hand and to disseminate the ruling class definition of development on the other.

Almost all the advanced countries except France and Japan, of course for their own illegitimate needs, have either stopped or toned down their atomic power programmes. People of all countries are gradually realising the potential danger of the nuclear estate. In these circumstances, the supporters are deliberately arousing regional passions knowing well that straight forward arguments cannot gain currency. But as D D Kosambi said: " . .The prestige of having atomic power stations does not compensate the extra expenditure or the extra danger involved". Not content with underrating the extra expenditure the nuclear power mongers are now engaged in belittling the other dangers as well.

M R Srinivasan declared in Hyderabad while speaking on 'Environmental Aspects of Nuclear Power' that there were only two accidents—Three Mile Island and Chernobyl-in all the 400 nuclear power plants all over the world and everyone enthusiastically joined in the chorus. Any one who has gone through a minimum of information on nuclear power will understand that hundreds of accidents of various intensities have taken place in plants all over the world. There are at least 10 recorded major accidents and according to Patterson, "by the end of the 1960s there had been major accidents in Canada, the UK, the US, and Switzerland. The reactor types involved had included. .. combinations of virtually all the major varieties of reactor design". (Walter Patterson as quoted in Pragathipara Vidyarthi Kendra and Progressive Youth Centre, Karnataka, *The Brink of Disaster,* 1987, p16.)

Even the Indian nuclear power stations have witnessed a number of accidents. The normal functioning of the plants has also contributed to nuclear radiation over exposure. As K Balagopal said in a protest meeting, "every industrial establishment will have a major product and generally pollution will be its byproduct. But in a nuclear reactor the major product is pollution and power is its byproduct."

The supporters have ignored the recorded damages of the past nuclear power programmes and accidents as well. They ridicule the fact of radiation effect through water which flows into the reactor to cool the condensers. They said that there would not be any increase in the temperature of the water due to hot effluent water. They claimed that Tarapur plant has been cent per cent safe for the last 19 years. All these statements are falsifications of truth.

In fact, all these defence arguments attempt to mystify science. "These are issues to be settled with technical knowledge through debates and clarifications. But it is not fair to endanger the interests of the people through arousing sentiments with ignorance", says one of the general secretaries of ISCUS. In the same tone Visalandhra says "people like the chairman of AEC who are in responsible positions are experts in science and technology. They are experienced. When they have scientifically assured us that there was no objection to setting up the nuclear power plant...". And Prajasakti says "When we ourselves are not scientists we should move ahead according to the advices from and consultations with the efficient men of learning- ..". What a contrast this to Kosambi who said "this is no longer a technical problem, but a social one" with reference to atomic power as early as 1960.

But this confusion is not a consequence of an error of judgement. The supporters, particularly the communists have not erred in looking at nuclear power as a technical problem only. The problem involved is power and that mystifies anything which comes into contact with it. The people who have power and those who aspire for power try to mystify science also and thereby they attempt to use it as a weapon in their hands. When that weapon has a long record of destruction, supporting it becomes a deliberate act and amounts to a conspiracy against people. On the banks of Nagarjunasagar such a conspiracy is being hatched and all the conspirators are clever enough to pose as progressives and men of science. And also they have the means at their disposal to brand the people who raise their voice against the conspiracy as "reactionaries and obscurantists".

After the usual accusations it is but natural that anti-nuclear power plant agitationists were indicted as agents of CIA. " ..It was proposed to have mutual co-operation in atomic sphere between India and the USSR in 1979. Gradually the proposal gained strength and in 1988 April, final talks were held between the representatives of both the countries. Signing of the mutual agreement is due. The government of India wants to build up 10 more nuclear reactors. The proposed plant at Nagarjunasagar is one of them... The Indo-Soviet mutual cooperative agreement is a thing not relished by American imperialism. Creating an unhealthy atmosphere against this agreement by some or other means and ultimately scuttling the programme is the aim of CIA. That is why the problem of setting up nuclear power plant at Nagarjunasagar is being presented in the light of the Chernobyl disaster...", says an edit page article in Visalandhra.

There is a suspicion that this is the real cause behind the supporting arguments of the CPI, CPI (M), and MCPI. They must have been supporting the plant as they expect that it comes from USSR. But, T Shivaji Rao, one of the spokespersons of the anti-nuclear power plant agitation thinks that it would be a Canadian reactor. But then, it is not important from which country it is imported. What has become real is the clearly laid out battle lines. 'Left and democratic forces' find themselves on one side arguing in favour of nuclear power, displacement of people, pollution and threat to the right to life. On the other side are the 'reactionaries, obscurantists and CIA agents' asking for a scientific debate, social awareness about the merits and demerits of the nuclear power plants, and people's right to information and life. The beginnings of a people's movement against the plant-meetings at Vijayawada, Guntur, Nagarjunasagar, Hyderabad, Kodad, Mothkur, Haalia, etc- have been quite promising. To consolidate the movement a collective leadership under the name, Action Committee Against Nagarjunasagar Power Plant, has emerged. One hopes that the prediction of its convenor, K Purushotham Reddy comes true: "The Atomic Energy Commission will see its Waterloo at Nagarjunasagar".

❖ ❖ ❖

12

Naxalite Movement and Working Class: Observations from Andhra Pradesh

The ML movement, as it was known in the earlier decade, or currently popular Maoist movement has tremendous impact on various walks of social life and it is but natural that its impact on labour in general and agricultural labour in particular is unmistakable. As the impact on society is all pervasive, holistic and complexly interwoven between various spheres, it is almost impossible to separate the labour scenario and search for exclusive impact. However this paper attempts to identify the long lasting exclusive impact of the movement on the agricultural labour as well as labour in unorganised sectors. Given the magnitude and complexity of the subject, this paper restricts itself to sharing some observations from history of Naxalite movement with regard to labour. Posing some questions for debate and future action is also attempted.

At the outset, it has to be borne in mind that the social dynamics and all social phenomena cannot be quantified and given out in discernible numbers. There will be tangible as well as intangible impacts. The tangible effects can be gauged approximately and the quantitative results appear 'objective' and the intangibles will be more in qualitative terms and always tend to be regarded as 'subjective'. To put it in other words there may be measurable economic results and non-measurable social and political results.

Paper presented at the national seminar on Rights of Labour in Globalising India, organised by Center for Human Rights, University of Hyderabad, during February 28-29, 2012.

The ML movement in Andhra Pradesh in the last four decades had both these kinds of effects on labour. The movement describes itself as a struggle for land, livelihood and liberation and labour has relationship with these three elements in distinct ways. Most of the labour, whether in villages or migrant in towns and cities, predominantly has land hunger and given a chance they would like to have their own piece of land. This characteristic is more than proved in the popularity of the slogan 'Land to the tiller' given by the movement. Livelihood is directly related to the pathetic existence of labour and the movement articulated the labourers' demand for higher wages in order to get better livelihood. Even when the movement could not function openly, due to repression and ban, the need for unity and sense of confidence it inculcated in the labour in general continue to inspire them to take up further struggles. Even if one achieved land and better livelihood, the movement taught the masses that it was not possible to sustain the victories without liberation and transformation of system. By liberation it was meant the overthrow of the existing exploitative and oppressive system to bring in an egalitarian social order.

Thus any study of changing labour conditions vis-à-vis the Naxalite movement has to locate itself in the context of these three slogans and the interaction labour will have with them. While the land and livelihood questions are basically economic and the achievements could be tangible, the liberation element is mostly social and political and cannot be measured, except in terms of rise in political consciousness or ultimate systemic transformation.

At the outset it would be useful to identify a couple of difficulties or obstacles in studying the impact of Naxalite movement on labour struggles in Andhra Pradesh:

i. It is difficult to relate the strategy adopted by the Naxalite movement, agrarian revolution involving capturing villages initially to encircle cities later, to the industrial working class, located in urban centres.

ii. The Naxalbari line began from an aversion towards mass organisations which degenerated into pure economism away from politics under the influence of parliamentary left. This aversion distanced the Naxalites from trade unionism in industrial centres.

iii. Since the working class movement needs to have a country wide organisation and the Naxalites' failure to set up an all-India party, with strength in urban industrial centres resulted in non-functioning of Naxalite trade unions.

iv. Even when the importance of trade union and working class activity was recognised, it was treated as part of general urban work and not an independent necessary work.

Though these difficulties existed at the conceptual and organisational levels all over India, the experience in Andhra Pradesh throws light on a couple of perceivable welcome departures. The Naxalites in Andhra Pradesh recognised the need for mass work and continued their pre-Naxalbari working class contacts and formed organisations of labour, though small and local, at various places. Thus even from 1970 there was considerable activity among working class in textile, jute, railway, transport sectors, besides PSUs. The broad based mass activity during the post-Emergency and the powerful examples of agrarian struggles in the neighbourhood gave a fillip to these sporadic initiatives and the Naxalite politics entered various working class sections, particularly in local, ancillary, unorganised and informal sectors. Transport, railways, jute mills, cement factories, rickshaw pullers, porters, Singareni coal miners, and truck drivers came under the influence of the Naxalite politics. Since the society in Andhra Pradesh is mostly agrarian and almost all the industrial centres are encircled by rural areas where a valiant anti-feudal struggle was going on, it was but natural that the workers got easily influenced by the peasant struggles around. Moreover, most of the workers came from peasant and landless families and brought the memories of struggle back home with them to the industries. Indeed, some of them were activists at home and were driven out of homes due to repression and they found a new fertile ground for their radical politics.

One could also divide the working class struggles under the influence of the Naxalites as struggles for wage rise, struggles for betterment of working conditions, struggles for implementation of statutory regulations, struggles for land, and struggles against repression. Wage rise and better working conditions were key demands both in rural areas for farm hands, daily wage labourers and in small industrial units. Fighting for the implementation of statutory regulations and job protection were essentially urban and industrial issues.

However, there was a mixture of issues with regard to tendu leaf labourers and Singareni miners. It is difficult to treat these two sections of workers either completely as rural agricultural or urban industrial. Because of this ambiguous nature, these sections faced extra economic coercions also. They defy to be brought under the definition of free labour in classical sense. They are tied to pre-capitalist semi-feudal relations. They have one leg in agriculture and another in industry. Describing them industrial proletariat is a debatable issue. This is not only the question of Singareni coal mines but several industrial sectors in Andhra Pradesh even today have the same characteristics.

Even if one looks at proper industrial segments in and around Hyderabad and Visakhapatnam the problems persist. Most of the working class is situated in ancillary, small, local, informal units to serve industrial and service sector majors. Either the employers use this tactic to avoid labour welfare conditions or it is more profitable to organise production in this way. This situation prohibits setting up a unit of an organised all- India trade union. Thus the workers are forced to form local committees, joint action committees, issue-based action committees, etc leaving them unorganised forever, or getting them organised for a limited period of time and issue.

One has to locate the work of the Naxalite movement on the working class and its impact in this background. Some of the Naxalite formations in Andhra Pradesh tried to set up larger state-wide trade unions and yet others started units of post-Naxalbari all India based Indian Federation of Trade Unions. However, all these efforts did not turn into a force to be reckoned with.

To give a specific case study, it would be proper to understand the workings of Singareni Karmika Samakhya (Sikasa) that worked as a mass organisation of the CPI (ML) (People's War) during 1979 to 1992 openly, and as a clandestine organisation later. The remarkable element of this organisation was that it was born out of struggles and not set up first to organise struggles later.

Singareni coal mines are spread over four districts of north Telangana - Adilabad, Karimnagar, Warangal and Khammam – on the banks of the Gadavari. The hundred-year old mines have seen militant trade unionism as a continuation of the peasant armed struggle being waged in the rear. During 1940s trade unionism under the influence of the then Communist Party of India began here and after 1950s it was degenerated into pure economism under the parliamentary left. Again with the upsurge of the Naxalite movement in north Telangana and since most of the miners came from landless and small peasant families involved in agrarian struggles, Singareni miners started taking militant path by late-1970s. Small and sporadic struggles against various anti-labour practices like employing temporary, contract and casual labour, officers behaving like lords (indeed, the officers had to be addressed *dora*, lord!) and treating miners as servants in officers' houses, high handedness of the officials, police and private goons, unbearable and unhygienic working conditions in the pits, lack of minimum facilities like drinking water, housing, transport, and healthcare, illegal suspensions, dismissals, picked up in the post-Emergency period. In May-June 1981 the miners went on a historical strike for 56 days under the leadership of Sikasa.

Gradually these economic struggles led to political struggles and under the leadership of Sikasa coalminers waged a number heroic battles on various economic and political issues. Whatever may be the recognised union at that particular time, the calls given by the Sikasa used to have much more impact. But in 1992, when the CPI (ML) (People's War) was banned by the government, Sikasa was also banned along with five other mass organisations. Severe repression on members of Sikasa and the miners suspected to be close to Sikasa continued for many more years and even the clandestine activity of Sikasa was crushed with iron heel. When a leader of clandestine Sikasa was taking shelter in a miner's quarters in Mancherial, Adilabad district, huge force of police and paramilitary personnel cordoned off the house, fired hundreds of rounds at the house, finally climbed up the roof and poured petrol and burnt the house along with the miners' leader.

With this kind of barbaric repression, miners sympathetic to Sikasa were forced to join other unions and any kind of militancy was suppressed brutally. Taking this repression to their advantage, leaders of other unions turned labour aristocrats.

The Sikasa experience has also taught valuable lessons in secret versus open functioning in trade union affairs.

Indeed post globalisation the working class in Andhra Pradesh has been suffering severe onslaught in terms of closure, disinvestment, retrenchment, and restructuring of several industrial units, anti-labour amendments to welfare measures, setting up of Special Economic Zones, etc. There has been great erosion of labour rights and decline in the bargaining capacity of the workers. In one word, during the last two decades there has been a growing need for labour resistance and struggles. The tangible and intangible influence of Naxalite ideas and practice in Telugu society appears to be a hope to rekindle the working class struggles.

❖ ❖ ❖

13

Talks and People's Consciousness

What Balagopal could not see in "immature" talks!

Though it is belated, condescending and dismissive at places, K Balagopal's 'People's War and the Government – Did the Police Have the Last Laugh?' (*EPW*, Feb 8, 2003) makes an interesting reading. The piece begins with and perpetuates some faulty assumptions and ends up in characteristic cynicism, unmindful of the dynamic debates and enthusiasm the talks generated. Balagopal had a word or two, mostly uncharitable at that, for each of the players in the talks and attributed "political immaturity" as "the hallmark of writers and poets close to the *revolutionaries* in Andhra Pradesh." As a writer and poet close to the *revolutionary movement* (I hope readers take note of the difference between being close to the *revolutionaries* and the *movement*), I would like to clarify a couple of points, whether they demonstrate my "political immaturity" or otherwise. (In my critique on Balagopal in 1999[1], I said he was aspiring to become an ombudsman to pass judgements on everybody. I am sorry to find that the comment more appropriate with regard to this essay with his condescending comments on everybody from police officers, Chandrababu Naidu to each of the CCC members to Gaddar and Varavara Rao to the government emissaries to Marxism to Telangana people.)

One of the problems with Balagopal's article is its scant respect for facts and actual developments. It would have been better if he stated the facts correctly and went on to give his own analyses. (In fact, his own perception on talks moved from one extreme to the other, as

---

Written in 2003. Unpublished.

appeared in his Telugu articles over a period of one year. With that somersaulting perspective he might not be able to stick to consistency of facts! Moreover, he ridicules others for "characteristic ability to denounce yesterday's truth in favour of today's realisation" forgetting that it applies to him more than anybody else!).

He used to be well known for his accuracy and highly respected for his meticulous research into whatever he wrote and spoke. But in this article, his information on the process of talks, the roles of different players, perceptions of various sections and the final outcome of the process, seems to be far from perfect, on many counts. His exposition is punctuated with silences, half-truths and distortions. His penchant for theorisation is once again visible with 'violence spiral', 'hidden agenda of revolutionaries', 'cynicism of Telangana people,' 'people getting caught between police and Naxalites', so on and so forth. In the tradition of good speculative theoreticians, he seems to have lost track of facts. At one place, he says "the emissaries met and talked *three or four* times" showing his contempt for facts and accuracy and his dismissive attitude towards what he was writing.

Balagopal's respect for facts also comes out when he talks about "middle class' critique of the movement being unknown in the state" (nothing could be farther from truth as the state has abundant written and oral criticism of the movement by middles class intelligentsia since 1940s), "faith in universal worth of individuals being foreign to Marxism" (a run of the mill falsehood repeated umpteen times by ignorant commentators) and "revolutionaries' methods that pushed the state to repudiate law and legality" (it would be suffice to prescribe his own writings in EPW a decade and a half ago whether this was true).

But all that is besides the point and I would not like to dwell much on that. There are some serious issues in which the record had to be set right and I will touch upon some of them. The debate on some profound issues he raised, as I showed in my earlier critique, has been there since Bernstein and it could be continued on relevant fora. However, issues like the history of the talks, role of the Committee of Concerned Citizens (CCC), talks between the emissaries of the CPI (M-L) (People's War) and the Government of Andhra Pradesh (GoAP), formation of Peace Initiative Committee (PIC) and the final outcome of the whole process should be clarified.

Talks and rise in consciousness

Before going into those issues, one crucial aspect has to be mentioned. Though the police apparently had had the last laugh, the process of talks undoubtedly led to considerable rise in the level of consciousness of people. The letters to the editor in *Vaarta*, mentioned by Balagopal, were only a part of that rising consciousness. Though he mentioned the letters, he does not seem to recognise their underlying significance. The letters demonstrated the blossoming of democratic spirit among people, and one only hopes a democrat like Balagopal took note of, and celebrated, that positive contribution. What he did not mention include a number of books, booklets and pamphlets published during those six months, meetings held by different organisations and formation of a new organisation to intervene in the process. There were at least 10 booklets published during that period and more than thirty meetings took place all over the State, giving a chance to over 200 speakers to express their views. The number of pamphlets and statements by various people's organisations putting forth their own agendas and adding to the People's War agenda were countless. It was a veritable cauldron of ideas ranging the whole spectrum. One should only read Telugu newspapers to find out what kind of dynamism informed those momentous weeks. Even if a battle were lost, it would be worthwhile to identify the rise in consciousness that was brought about by that battle.

Who initiated the talks?

Balagopal is only partly correct in giving complete credit to the Committee of Concerned Citizens (CCC) for the talks. Though CCC has shown commendable perseverance (though Balagopal would qualify that as "unreasonable") in pushing the talks further, it is factually incorrect not to mention other players and the actual unfolding of the idea.

If one traces the history of talks[2], one would go back as early as July 1996 when a High Court bench made a recommendation to the government to arrive at a negotiated settlement with the Naxalites. Delivering a judgment in a case under the TADA involving Naxalites, Justice M N Rao pointed out that "while leftwing extremism is viewed as a problem by the administration, it is increasingly being perceived as a solution to their problems by the alienated masses."

The judge also felt that "a peace commission with representative character inspiring confidence in all sections of the society including the Naxalites and the police and backed by State power and consent, we believe, can bring about immediate cessation of police encounters and violence by Naxalites and then only in the resultant peaceful atmosphere, a meaningful search for permanent solution is possible."

There were at least three important points in this judgement: *Recognising Naxalites as a solution, asking for immediate cessation of police encounters and violence by Naxalites, and a meaningful search for permanent solution.*

The state government not only did not heed to this suggestion, but also reimposed the previously relaxed ban on People's War and six mass organisations within three weeks of this judgement. (Thus Andhra Pradesh has a dubious distinction of having banned the organisations of students, youth, agricultural workers, and miners). The CCC, by its own admission, drew its inspiration from this judgement and started an earnest endeavour to bring both the parties to negotiating table.

Subsequently, there were two other significant developments from the high offices of the State regarding the problem. On the occasion of the Republic Day 1997, both Krishna Kant, the then Governor of the state and Justice Prabha Shankar Mishra, the then Chief Justice of AP High Court, expressed their concern and suggested to the government to negotiate a peaceful settlement.

In April 1997, a division bench of AP High Court consisting of Justice Prabha Shankar Mishra and Justice D H Nasir constituted a 15-member advocates' panel, under the chairmanship of a senior advocate, K Pratapa Reddy to go into the problem. The panel visited affected Telangana districts and came out with a number of suggestions, mostly against the revolutionary movement and a couple against the police repression also. The committee's report was left to gain dust in the corridors of power. Similar was the fate of a Cabinet Sub-Committee's *Report on Leftwing Extremism* two years later in late 1999. It is believed that these two reports written by influential and high-powered bodies were consigned to ignominy just because both of them suggested "to stop fake encounters" and "to take action against all those who are guilty in fake encounters as per the law in force" even though the thrust of the reports was against the people's movement and in favour of police.

All through these developments, not discouraged by the failure met by such powerful committees before them, the CCC persevered in its resolute effort to make their point at both the ends. The committee's efforts in appealing to both the Government and People's War and "to intervene in the climate of social turmoil and violence in rural Andhra Pradesh, specially in Telangana, in the interests of the common people of the state" are commendable.[3]

"The CPI-ML People's War responded positively to the news of the Committee's efforts in the press by releasing a set of seven demands to be met by State Government so that an atmosphere for further talks could be created. This was the first sign that a solution was after all possible," said the First Report of the CCC in May 1997.

In fact, the attitude of People's War towards negotiations seems to have undergone change. In February 1995, Nalla Adi Reddy, the then Secretary of the AP State Committee, said in a media interview that there was no need for the party to go in for negotiations. "We are putting forth our demands publicly. Let the government come out with its stand on these demands. Our party doesn't think there is any need for talks," he said.

The demands he placed before the government at that time were: Lifting of ban on People's War and mass organisations; Stopping fake encounters and ordering judicial enquiry into earlier killings; Enquiry into the attacks on Dalits; Withdrawal of paramilitary forces from Telangana villages and stopping "surrender" dramas; Giving up repression on people's movements; Withdrawal of cases against peasant activists and release of political prisoners, and Implementation of genuine land reforms instead of phony *Bhoosamaradhana* programme announced by the government then.

However, when the CCC started its efforts to create conducive atmosphere for talks, there was a visible change in the attitude of People's War and it started responding positively. The CCC visited Telangana districts to study the obtaining ground reality and started correspondence with People's War on one hand and the GoAP on the other. The correspondence culminated in the CCC having direct discussions with People's War in January 1998 and with the GoAP in April 1998.

While the going till then seemed smooth and everybody expected something would evolve out of this effort, there was no reprieve in the repression and the CCC itself had to say in an *Open Letter to the Chief Minister of Andhra Pradesh* on June 1, 1999 that, "it is more than a year since the Committee met you. Unfortunately, your Government has not only not acted on any of the assurances given to us but did not even respond to most of the specific appeals made by us from time to time."

As the efforts of the CCC regarding the proposed talks between the government and People's War gained momentum, Andhra Pradesh Civil Liberties Committee (APCLC), People's Union for Civil Liberties (PUCL), some senior Editors and prominent intellectuals in the State also made similar appeals. Responding to these appeals People's War had come out with a concrete proposal as part of required modalities for talks during May 1999.

"Our party places some proposals before people as a basis to bring in peaceful atmosphere and improvement in the situation:

a. Lift the ban on our party and mass organisations and allow us to have open activities like other political parties. Before talking about talks, it is a principle of natural justice to seek required free and equal treatment and political status.

b. Stop encounter killings. Register all encounters under Sec. 302 and proceed against the concerned police officers, as per the directions given by AP High Court in Madhusudan Raj's encounter case. Supreme Court also ratified the High Court's direction. National Human Rights Commission also identified six clear cases of fake encounter and directed the government to initiate proceedings.

c. A number of our party cadres are in jails for over five years now. Both Supreme Court and AP High Court ruled that the TADA would not apply in their cases. The prisoners also got bails but not allowed to come out. Thus we reiterate our earlier demand to release them unconditionally.

d. Provide *pattas* to landless peasants for the lands occupied by them. Though peasants have occupied the lands, they are not allowed to till them due to severe repression unleashed by police and consequently thousands of acres of land is lying fallow. Even as the landlords are willing to leave the land, the government and police machinery are stopping them to do so.

e. Lift all the police camps and withdraw Central para military forces. When Chandrababu Naidu asked for an additional 50 companies force to reinforce the existing 23 companies, Union Home Minister Indrajit Gupta accepted.

f. Stop all the raids on villages, destruction of people's property and illegal arrests immediately.

g. Either the Disturbed Areas Act or the proposed Leftwing Extremism (Prevention) Act are aimed at the democratic activity outside and we demand the government to stop all those initiatives."

While these offers and responses appeared to be going in right direction, there was a big jolt to the entire process in the form of the infamous "Koyyur encounter" in which Nalla Adi Reddy (Shyam), Arramreddy Santosh Reddy (Mahesh), Seelam Naresh (Murali), three Central Committee members of People's War along with a militant, Lakshmirajam, were killed in Karimnagar district in December 1999. The three leaders were picked up in Bangalore, brought to Hyderabad and tortured severely before killing them and throwing their dead bodies in Karimnagar forest. To make the encounter appear real, a militant from a nearby village was also killed along with them. Two of these three leaders were in fact involved in discussions with the CCC and their killing, in a way, temporarily scuttled the peace process.

People's War in its turn killed the then Home Minister A Madhava Reddy in a land mine blast in March 2000 and surprisingly, the State Government offered to revive the peace process immediately. Within a couple of weeks of this killing, in a press conference in New Delhi, revolutionary balladeer Gaddar and poet Varavara Rao were asked by the press whether there was any scope for talks.

"The talks would materialise only if the encounter killings are stopped and a proper trial is assured for the arrested activists. The State government has been talking of talks for a long time but it seems to lack required sincerity. If the government were really serious about talks it would not have killed the Central Committee members who were the most authorised and proper persons to be involved in talks," they said. A section of the press also reported that both Gaddar and Varavara Rao offered to mediate, in the event of talks becoming real. (This is how Gaddar and Varavara Rao came into the picture of the talks, at least two years before the actual nomination, but not stealthily and undeservingly as Balagopal tries to suggest).

The State Legislature was in session then and the Opposition parties responded positively to these statements and advised the government to accept the offer. On the floor of the house the Chief Minister N Chandrababu Naidu announced that the government was ready to invite Gaddar and Varavara Rao to an All Party Meet on extremism and seek their views on the issue. Both of them declined to attend the proposed All Party Meet and put forth four demands to make the climate amenable for talks. The demands were stopping fake encounters, booking all encounter killing cases under Sec. 302, instituting judicial enquiry by a sitting Supreme Court judge into all encounter killings including "Koyyur encounter" and lifting of ban on CPI (ML) (People's War) and six mass organisations. However, the government neither sent a formal invitation to them nor stopped the repression on the movement.

Again in the aftermath of Madhava Reddy's killing and following the acceptance by the Chief Minister on the floor of the House to hold talks, the CCC and Senior Editors continued their efforts to bring both the parties to negotiating table. People's War responded to these efforts with a set of eight demands and the CCC said that it "was disappointed to find there was no change at all in the approach of the Government." During 2001, the CCC went on gathering support for its demand for talks and held discussions with various political parties, mass organisations and intellectuals. Following the feedback, the CCC again appealed for talks in October 2001. While the atmosphere this time was maturing towards positive, December 2001 saw violent incidents from both sides, including People's War killing Ragya Nayak, a tribal MLA belonging to Congress, putting a brake on the initiative.

Thus at least four sets of demands have been floated by People's War or its sympathisers between 1995 and 2001. That almost all the demands were within the purview of the rule of law, the Constitutional obligations on the government and principles of natural justice speaks volumes of the state of affairs in Andhra Pradesh. It is strange to see that these demands well in the purview of the Constitution were raised by the so-called anti-Constitutional bodies and the so-called Constitutional government dilly dallied on them. Even as these demands were being put forth, the police machinery and ruling classes in the state were castigating People's War of raising "unreasonable demands and preconditions." Even some well-meaning intellectuals and leader writers in newspapers bought these ideas.

2002 round of talks

In the recent round, the CCC had again, in January 2002, appealed to both the government and the People's War to come down for talks and end armed conflict. "Even though there have been positive responses, there is no basic change in the overall situation. In the last session of the Legislative Assembly, different political parties called for the commencement of the dialogue and the government announced that the decision would be taken after convening an All-Party Meeting. These developments gave rise to expectations and the committee hoped for a positive outcome...The committee hoped that both the sides would do everything possible to create a conducive climate for the dialogue," the CCC said.

The CCC had made six suggestions each to the state and People's War. The suggestions to the state were "to stop encounters, to stop combing operations, to stop all forms of harassment, to take actions dealing with the life and liberty of people strictly in accordance with law, to review cases against villagers and to permit all non-violent, peaceful and democratic activities." The suggestions to People's War were "to stop all killings including police personnel, alleged informers and political activists, to stop attacks on police stations, destruction of government and public property, to stop use of land mines, claymore mines and other explosives, to stop extortions, not to interfere with any democratic activity of any political party, not to do any thing that would give an impression that development, administrative and other welfare activities are being obstructed."

Responding to this appeal People's War, for the first time, expressed its willingness to come for the talks "unconditionally". The *Open Letter to CCC* signed by the spokespersons of both Central Committee and AP State Committee said, "we have been expressing our preparedness for talks in the recent times, particularly since May 2000, and putting our specific proposals before you and people at large. It is long since the government left the initiative in the half-way after starting a dialogue with your committee and editors."

This time round People's War had put forth two proposals for the talks: "1. The government should stop all raids, arrests and encounter killings and create favourable atmosphere for talks. 2. All combing operations in villages and forest areas should be stopped forthwith. Harassing people and activists of mass organisations alleging they have links with the party, torturing in police stations and asking them to come to police stations without any court orders, keeping some of them hostage in the process to kill them in fake encounters should be stopped immediately...There are no other conditions except stopping encounter killings and attacks on people for undertaking talks."

However, the CCC and the leader writers in newspapers found that the Peoples War's statement had asked for stopping of armed activity on the part of the government, but kept quiet on whether they were going to stop armed actions. Within a week after these objections and comments, the party had given another statement saying that they were willing to "cease fire" from the second week of February provided the Government also stopped encounter killings and raids on villages and combing operations. The party accused the government of double-speak, as it was not interested in solving the basic problems of people. "While we are coming forward for talks taking the protection of people's democratic rights and solution of basic problems as priority, the government wants to avoid talks putting blame on us," said the statement.

Even though the underground party without any high-tech communication network responded so fast to the comments on its earlier statement, the government with all the communication infrastructure and modern gadgets at its disposal, could not come to a conclusion even after two weeks. One does not know whether it was a deliberate procrastination or technical difficulty, the government went on deliberating with top brass of police, cabinet ministers and ruling party and finally, it was decided to call an All Party Meeting. However, this meeting had to be postponed for about two weeks as the Chief Minister was scheduled to go to the US. Ultimately the All-Party Meeting took place on February 12 and the GoAP had not come to the meeting with any prepared agenda. The meeting ended in exchange of views between political parties and the government with another meeting scheduled after 10 days.

All the political parties in the state welcomed the proposal for talks and the response was overwhelming. A senior poet and civil libertarian Padma Vibhushan Kaloji came forward and offered his good offices for negotiating between both the parties. Vaarta, the second largest circulated daily newspaper in Telugu, had asked people to respond on the proposal and almost ran a campaign, in which hundreds of people wrote to the newspaper in favour of the talks and probable modalities of the talks.

On the other hand, the then Director General of Police H J Dora expressed doubts on the offer from Peoples War. "The seriousness of the offer for talks is being examined since the deeds and words of the outfit have never matched in the past," he said. At least three lower rank police officers also spoke against the talks, unconcerned of political decisions and service rules.

Even as the debate on talks was going on and everybody was expecting a decline in State violence and repression on people in general and activists of mass organisations and party cadre in particular, the ground reality on the part of the police did not show any such positive tendency. Even as the GoAP was apparently showing its willingness to talks, the police machinery in Warangal, Karimnagar and Nizamabad districts was going ahead with severe repression on teachers, writers, journalists, peasants and ordinary people. Combing operations, midnight searches, illegal arrests, illegal summoning of people to police stations, torturing for days together and killings continued unabated.

The instances of repression show that either the government didn't want to rein in the police or the latter didn't care for any democratic political process. Whatever might be the analysis on the apparent division between the police machinery and the elected government, one expects that the government demonstrated a modicum of sincerity and stopped repression on the mass organisations when it accepted to talk to a party that believes in armed struggle. But the question on everybody's mind was why should a government talk to an armed struggle or vice versa?

Compulsions

Apparently the government had some compulsions to take the offer. Whether one saw it as a fear of death in the face of mine blasts and ambushes in the rural terrain or the questioning consciousness on the part of rural masses, the political leaders were unable to visit rural areas of Telangana, without police protection. In the process it was the tail that wagged the dog but not the other way round. The political leadership appeared, at least for some time, to change this scenario before the next elections, due in 2004.

Another major compulsion on the GoAP was the context of the World Bank - dictated reforms and inviting MNCs to come to the State. The MNCs wanted peace zones and it seemed they were hesitant to come even though the state was highly resource rich and offered a good market and the government was willing to crawl before them. Particularly after symbolic attacks on Coca Cola's plant as well as on the facilities owned by the Chief Minister himself and a Central Cabinet minister in 2001, the MNCs were forcing the government to take all measures to make the state "peaceful".

At least a section of police force (most probably their families) didn't want to live under this perpetual pressure situation and wanted a solution. This section no longer believed that use of force would finish the movement. However, another section of police officers did not want this conflict to end, as they were able to enjoy unlimited power, not only over people but also on the political establishment, as well as unaccountable money, vehicles and paraphernalia, in the name of crushing the movement. The money spent on anti-Naxalite operations is believed to be in the range of a couple of hundreds of crores, without any legislative scrutiny.

On the part of People's War, there have been various assessments on why they were opting for talks. The assessments ranged from "tactical retreat" to "fatigue" to "winding up the struggle." There have been over a half-a-dozen publications from the party and other revolutionary organisations which give a perspective on the talks. The argument basically is that "no arm is untouchable in the armoury of revolutionary struggle and talks are also a part of struggle."

Talks between emissaries

Whatever may be the compulsions on both sides, it was remarkable that they actually accepted to come down to a negotiating table and thrash out issues. In fact, there were some apprehensions at that time that how a legally established government could hold talks with a banned party and it was also suggested that the ban be temporarily lifted to set up natural justice – equality between both the sides – before the talks. Of course, the government did not heed this suggestion. The talks should be placed in this historical perspective.

However, there was no precedent as to how to go about the talks. The learned counsel who ridicules the idea of "debating competition" was in fact ridiculing the idea of talks itself at that time. Quite naturally, the People's War thought the talks would not gain anything except exposing the government. Thus they wanted to put forth the legitimate and minimum democratic demands like rule of law and land reforms. But when posing them initially was looked as putting pre-conditions they said they were coming unconditionally but the modalities have to be decided by people in public life. They may be vociferous supporters of revolutionary politics, but describing them as "persons with a known penchant for their adversorial stances" as Balagopal does is cheap, to say the least. Even the People's War statement naming them as its emissaries to decide modalities says "they stood by toiling masses for over three decades now, as participants in democratic and revolutionary movements and mainly in revolutionary literary and cultural sphere."

The emissaries from both sides met on June 5, June 9 and June 20 and each time the meeting was preceded by an encounter killing resulting in protests from the People's War's emissaries. The actual work of setting modalities was not taken up since each time there was an irritant from the government's side. Even a cursory glance at the notes submitted by the People's War emissaries on all these occasions shows that they were far from adversorial.

Formation of Peace Initiative Committee

In the meanwhile, another group of intellectuals and public personalities formed themselves into Peace Initiative Committee (PIC), to take the talks further. Recognising the pioneering work done by the CCC in bringing both the parties to a negotiating table, the PIC said, "these talks cannot be an affair between the government and the People's War…Problems faced by larger sections of population should form part of the talks. Their aspirations and needs should have a place in the talks. Resolving people's problems should be the single agenda either for the government or for people's movements. Peace Initiative

Committee was formed to mobilise public opinion in that direction and to bring out people's aspirations."

Peace Initiative Committee held a lot of public meetings both in Hyderabad and in at least 12 centres all over the state in which hundreds of people from various walks of life participated and expressed their views. PIC has become instrumental in giving expression to a cross section of population not only on the talks but also on the entire political economy of development and underdevelopment that harms peace and security in a society.

Final outcome of the talks

Though Balagopal tried to trivialise the importance of the talks, at least in four areas the talks have made significant impact: Importance of negotiations for a party in armed struggle, people's movement's adherence to its words, rise in people's consciousness, and achieving a democratic space for political discourse.

For the first time in the history of Andhra Pradesh or for that matter in the history of revolutionary movements in the country, a movement was recognised as a force to reckon with and invited for talks. Whatever may be the questions on the moral authority of the powers that be, the invitation certainly is a recognition of the adversary's credentials. It was not just the arms in the adversaries' hands that forced the government to invite them to the discussion table. History has seen many armed groups dying down under brutal onslaught and at very few points of time the rulers felt a need to talk. The mass base of revolutionary movement should be given this credit and the talks have established this credential, if not anything else.

The talks proved that the People's War would stick to its promises. Whatever may be the mistakes and inadequacies of the party, it announced cease-fire twice during the talks and strictly adhered to its words. The party not only announced but also implemented cease-fire from the second week of February to March 14 (withdrawn after Tupakulagudem 'encounter' in which six activists were killed) and from May 10 to July 20, whereas the government did not make announcement and continued the killing spree during this time.

From the people's point of view and the overall consciousness among Telugu society, the talks have been a significant development. Telugu people have been waging valiant fights against enemies of all kinds for a long time. However, they have not sufficiently learnt how to talk, while engaged in war. May be because of this unprecedented nature, the 2002 round of talks appeared off the mark a couple of times, but the whole process was a great educator and unquestionably the society has gone up this learning curve.

Another important achievement of the talks was that people's politics were voiced from the seat of power for the first time. While the whole discourse against the people's movement was focussing on violence spiral, the talks could bring it back to the real issues and put it in a proper perspective. The People's War's emissaries could hold press conferences right in the state secretariat and elaborate the revolutionary politics. It would have been unimaginable to explain certain political beliefs in crowded media gatherings using all the state paraphernalia, in a state where you can be arrested, harassed or killed on the suspicion of having those beliefs. For the first time in the 22-year history of the People's War, the talks tried to erase the blot on its name. (It is always referred wrongly as "PWG" in the press, while its name is Communist Party of India (Marxist-Leninist) (People's War). The police call it, pejoratively, "People's War Group" or "PWG" and media have been gulping it unquestioningly, as if other political formations are parties and this alone is a "group"!)

Most importantly the talks proved or reiterated two points – People's War's larger political, social and economic interests than violence as being propagated and the keenness to appear reasonable on the part of the People's War while the government did not show any such inclination.

Notes :

1 N Venugopal (1999) - *Kallola Kaalamlo Medhavulu – Balagopal Udaaharana* (Intellectuals in Troubled Times – Balagopal's Example), Viplava Rachayitala Sangham, Hyderabad.

2 For this, see my earlier 'Is it a Problem or a Solution?', available on the net www.cisdl.org/conference/proceedings_english/session17/venugopal-p-e.pdf

3 For details of their efforts see *Committee of Concerned Citizens - Third Report 1997-2002,* December 2002, Hyderabad.

❖ ❖ ❖

III

Repression

The six essays in this section deal with the most brutal repression let loose by the state against the Naxalite movement in Andhra Pradesh.

The first essay gives an account of the widespread practice of Andhra Pradesh police in extra judicial killings, calling them encounters euphemistically. The ruling classes of the state adopted this form of killings with impunity as the only response to the questions posed by people's movement under the leadership of Naxalites. The encounter killing policy was launched by Congress Home Minister J Vengal Rao in 1969. Since then all the powers that be have been thinking that they can silence the questions by liquidating the voices that raise the questions. However, even after killing over 5,000 cadres and leaders in these fake encounters the movement did not lose its mass base in the state.

Another essay talks about the all out repression under the chief ministership of N T Rama Rao when he openly said 'No song, no dance and no speech'. Beginning with killing a civil libertarian – pediatrician in his clinic in broad day light, the repression regime continued for the next four years and this essay portrays a sample of that.

In the next decade under Chandrababu Naidu's rule an attempt was made on the life of popular legend, poet-singer-performer Gaddar and an essay here deals on how and why the rulers wanted to kill Gaddar.

Two other essays present the scenario of repression in the next decade under Y S Rajasekhara Reddy's rule. Grey Hounds in search of Naxalites in Visakhapatnam forest raped tribal women and no political, administrative and judicial machinery came to accord justice to the victims. Under the same regime, Revolutionary Writers' Association along with other mass organisations was banned.

The last article in this section is a review of a book written by a former police officer on the Naxalite movement. The review shows that even the intellectual and research pretences also justify the repression and misrepresent the movement.

14

Fake Encounters - Story from Andhra Pradesh

The shocking revelations about the brutal killing of Sohrabuddin Shaik, his wife Kauser Bi and friend Tulsiram Prajapati by Gujarat police with probable help from police officers of Rajasthan and Andhra Pradesh caught the attention of everybody, thanks to the arrest and booking of the erring police officers with criminal charges including murder. Even as the case is being debated on all the fora including parliament and media, it appears strange that most of the commentators seem to regard the case as almost the first of its kind and Indian police were almost law-abiding saints with no knowledge of extra-judicial killings before Sohrabuddin's case. An occasional reference to similar fake encounters in Jammu & Kashmir, Punjab, Uttar Pradesh, West Bengal and Maharashtra is also made but there is some sort of a silence on the fake encounters in Andhra Pradesh, probably the worst affected state with hundreds of fake encounters that snatched away lives of about four thousand people during the last four decades.

Thus the newly discovered fake encounter case of Sohrabuddin Shaik forces one to recollect the gory history of killings of political opponents as well as "unmanageable" people by policemen, in the name of 'encounters' in Andhra Pradesh. Several mass organisations in the state have been describing all these encounters as "political murders" since the police officers responsible for this kind of cold-blooded murders have received cash prizes, unnumbered vehicles and unaccounted fuel, accelerated promotions, gallantry awards, plush

Published in Economic and Political Weekly, Vol XLII, No. 41, October 13, 2007.

postings and other rewards from the powers that be. In the last forty years, chief ministers, home ministers and policy makers in the state changed so much so that apparently opposing political parties also came to power, but the encounter killings as a policy of governance has not changed a bit. There are home ministers, belonging to both Telugu Desam and Congress, who on record defended encounters as a means to maintain law and order!

History of encounter killings in Andhra Pradesh

Killing people in cold-blood and describing the incident as "an encounter where an exchange of fire took place at the end of which the police discovered some dead bodies" dates back to the early part of the last century. Perhaps it was the British who invented this devious method of killing people and a popular instance of so-called encounter took place in May 1924 when Alluri Sitarama Raju, who led a tribal rebellion against the British, was killed. However, later-day research explored the reality and showed that he was caught and killed in cold-blood without any exchange of fire. Later, during the 1940s, more than 3,000 cadres and people who participated in the Telangana Peasant Armed Struggle (1946-51) were also killed in 'encounters', most of them being fake. While it was the Nizam's police that used the liquidating method during 1946-48, two thirds of these encounter killings took place under the military rule and subsequent civil rule of Government of India between 1948 and 1951 and thus the then Hyderabad state has the dubious distinction of the first state to kill its own people in the name of encounters in post-1947 India.

Inheriting this horrifying tradition, Andhra Pradesh police revived similar killing policy again in 1968 and by May 1969 the policy became predominant. In one of the first major incidents of encounter killings, Panchadi Krishna Murthy, a leader of the CPI (M-L) which led Srikakulam struggle and six of his associates were killed on the early hours of May 27, 1969 after being arrested a few hours earlier in Sompeta railway station as they got down from a train from Calcutta. It is said that the higher ups including the then home minister (later chief minister) Jalagam Vengala Rao received a message on the arrest and responded with a cryptic answer: "bump them off". The district police bumped the arrested persons off and announced that they died in exchange of fire in an encounter. The First Information Report (FIR)[1] on this incident, filed by the Inspector of Police, Sompeta, which formed part of the documents of the infamous Naxalite Conspiracy Case (also known as Parvatipuram Conspiracy Case), makes an interesting reading:

"On information that Panchadi Krishnamurthy and several other communist revolutionaries, who committed dacoity with murder at Borivanka on the night of 19th May, 1969 and several other offences in the Sompeta Circle were moving in Pathakota hills. I proceeded with SIs Sompeta and Ichapur and APSP to Pathakota hills on 26th May 1969 at about 10 pm to apprehend wanted accused. I searched in Pathakota hills but could not find them there. As I was returning with my staff at about 3 am on 27th May 1969 a mob of about 30 armed with guns, country bombs and spears advanced towards us between Jalantrakota and Pathakota hills. They fired with guns and country bombs from a distance of 50 yards. I declared the mob an unlawful assembly and gave a warning that fire would be opened if they do not surrender or disperse. The warning did not have any effect and one person who was identified as Panchadi Krishnamurthy by Sri Jagannadharao, SI, Sompeta hurled another country bomb, shouting "Comrades, Kill Police, Kill Police." As the entire police party was about to be killed and as the Communist Revolutionaries were surrounding the police from all sides I fired from my revolver four times, giving order to 15 APSP PCs also to open fire. Each of them fired one round with 303 rifles but as the mob was still trying to advance the SI Sompeta fired 3 rounds and SI Ichapuram fired two rounds. The mob immediately ran away as some people were found falling down shouting, "Long Live Mao" "Long Live Revolution" "Kill people, kill landlords". Immediately the SIs and I flashed 3 torch lights and found seven persons lying dead. One of them is identified as Panchadi Krishnamurthy. I sent SI Sompeta with 10 APSP PCs to search for the other Communist Revolutionaries. I have found one loaded ML gun, two country bombs and one spear and five gelatine cartridges and some explosive materials at the scene, where the deceased were lying. I am sending them herewith. Some communist literature bags were also found there..."

This version has almost become an unavoidable *verbatim* pro-forma for later FIRs and the story was repeated *ad nauseam* for hundreds of times over the last 38 years with mere change in names of places and persons.

Euphemism of encounter

Encounter, if it is real, involves an accidental chance happening and by definition it is unplanned, unexpected and fortuitous and one cannot have an encounter at will. But police in Andhra Pradesh have turned the noun into a verb of intention and plan and known for threatening people with getting them encountered! Most of the encounters took place when the deceased were arrested a few hours, if not days, before the so-called encounter. In several cases family members and friends of the would-be 'encounter' victims issued statements alerting the press about the arrest, apprehending probable elimination, and demanding the police to produce the arrested persons in a court of law. A day or two later police would announce that the same persons got killed in encounter. If it were a real encounter, the family members and friends should be highly clairvoyant to imagine before hand that their near and dear were going to face police by chance and open fire to get killed. In some cases activists whose arrest information appeared in news papers suddenly faced police and got killed in encounters. It is another strange aspect that out of the thousands of encounters, not even in a couple, the police officers were injured demonstrating the extreme and incredible efficiency of police in always killing their opponents and without even getting bruised once. If one analyses the FIR quoted above the opponents were more in number, almost double, than the police, and apparently with equal fire power. Even then there were seven casualties on one side and not even a scratch on the other!

Surprisingly, there have been times when such a chance happening did not take place at all! There were no encounter killings between December 1989 and June 1990, a couple of months in early 1995, and between May 2004 and January 2005. This absence of encounters for months together clearly shows that it was a government policy that allows or prevents encounter killings. If the government were willing to kill revolutionary activists, it would allow and for whatever political compulsions if it wanted to stop, it could do that.

Legal position

Legally police in India are authorised with crime investigation and law enforcement only but not punishment, which is the jurisdiction of law courts. In fact, police are not even allowed to keep suspects in their custody for more than 24 hours even for investigation purposes.

While that is the case with regard to apprehension, police do not have a right to snatch the life of a person who is under their custody or who happened to bump into them with arms. Restriction on right to life in India, a legal sanction of killing a beyond-doubt confirmed criminal, is allowed only in accordance with the "procedure established by law" as per the Article 21 of Constitution of India and that too in "the rarest of rare cases" as per a Supreme Court verdict in 1983. Thus if an ordinary citizen kills another citizen the culprit would be tried according to the procedure established by law and in this regard law of the land does not provide any exception to any public servant, even if he is a part of law enforcing authority.

However, the law enforcing agencies can take shelter in using reasonable and minimum force to disperse a mob or unlawful assembly. But even then they have to take the permission of a magistrate to open fire and even in that case they should not aim at people to kill. Section 100 and 300 of Indian Penal Code allow self-defence to ordinary citizens as well as police personnel but the need to self-defence has to be substantiated and proved in a court of law, with the burden of proof lying on the defender.

In any case, first of all, all killers, including police personnel, have to undergo legal proceedings, and they have to prove that the killing happened in self-defence only. No ordinary killer would be pardoned if he said he did that in self-defence. Even then he has to undergo judicial proceedings and face the charge of murder and prove his innocence by showing reasonable evidence to the act of self-defence.

Even as the theoretical legal position states so, in practice, police officers in India have been sanctioned impunity. They can kill and condone themselves by claiming self-defence and not registering any complaint. This impunity is dangerous not only to the deceased persons but also to the society at large. Police officers in Andhra Pradesh have been enjoying this socially-destructive impunity for a long time now.

Some illustrative cases

While over 3,000 alleged Naxalites and their sympathisers and another 1,000 ordinary people (so-called dacoits, ISI agents, factionists, rowdy-sheeters and eve-teasers as well as ordinary people) were killed in encounters over the last 38 years in over 2,000 incidents, one can easily say that over 90 per cent of these incidents are evidently fake. Even when the deceased had weapons on them, there is ample evidence that they did not use the fire arms against the police and the latter could have overpowered and arrested them without any harm. There are hundreds of incidents where eye witness accounts and circumstantial evidence published along with the police hand-out showed that the victims were picked up from their homes, offices, streets, when they were not alone and within a couple of hours they were shown as killed in encounters.[2] Some times it is also alleged that the victims were given poisoned food so that they can be arrested without resistance. A few incidents of fake encounters are listed below to show the magnitude of falsehood spread by police hand-outs.

K Parsaiah and M Ravindra Reddy, activists of the CPI (ML) Re-Organising Committee were arrested on July 19 and July 21, 1981, respectively. Both of them were produced before the magistrate at Suryapet in Nalgonda district on July 23. This mandatory production before a magistrate, even though it happened in violation of 24-hour maximum duration of police custody, was done at midnight and the production before the magistrate itself was a euphemism as the arrested persons were kept in a police jeep that stood outside the magistrate's residence and only the papers were taken before the magistrate. The magistrate signed the papers and remanded them. Within a few minutes both of them were shot dead and police released the usual encounter statement.[3]

Pingili Bhoopathi Reddy and Kavatam Saraiah of the CPI (M-L) Re-Organising Committee, both public activists attending various court cases, were arrested on May 27, 1985 when they were sleeping in their lawyer's residence in Warangal and within hours they were shown as killed in encounter in Narsapur, about 60 kms from Warangal.[4]

Gulam Rasool was a reporter in a Telugu daily *Udayam* and his exposes on the nexus of land mafia and police made him an enemy of the police, particularly a DSP working in the suburbs of Hyderabad. Rasool took an aggrieved party to the district police headquarters two days before his encounter and he had a heated exchange with the same DSP. Two days later, on December 28, 1991, his dead body was found on the outskirts of Hyderabad as "unidentified" killed in encounter. His friend Vijay Prasad Rao, who was pillion riding when Rasool was arrested was also killed since he was the key eye witness to the arrest.

Since Gulam Rasool was a working journalist and was on duty at the time of arrest, his participation in an encounter was an obvious lie, journalist community protested and the government appointed a judicial commission. The terms of reference were *ab initio mala fide* and the commission came out with an irrelevant conclusion that the deceased were Naxalites, ignoring to find out whether an encounter took place actually or it was a cold-blooded murder.[5]

T Madhusudan Raj Yadav, the then state secretary of the CPI (M-L) Pratighatana, was killed on July 27, 1995 in Gandhinagar, a busy locality in central Hyderabad with a usual encounter story. There was a writ petition against the police story in the state High Court. The bench which included the then Chief Justice P S Mishra, in its judgment on August 14, 1995, directed that a criminal case should be registered and investigated in all such instances. The judgment said: "Do we have the law that a group of police personnel will report that they were making arrest of a person who attempted to evade the arrest and since in his attempt to evade the arrest he used force, they returned the force and caused his death and the law would accept the statement and sanctify the end of life in accordance with the procedure prescribed by law? We have already noticed that the guarantee under Article 21 of the Constitution of India and also the words 'procedure established by law' are not ineffective and lifeless but are expressions of the faith of the people who have sanctioned interference with the life of a person only by a procedure which is reasonable, fair and just."[6]

The "encounter" at Kopardang in which thirteen activists were killed is another incredible case of Andhra Pradesh police overstepping their jurisdiction in entering Orissa without even informing the local police. It is alleged that the police used helicopters and bombs to attack a meeting of the Naxalites in the deep forests of Rayagada district of Orissa. The attack took place on August 8, 1998 and it is reported that while some activists died on the spot, some others were apprehended and killed later.[7]

The "encounter" case of Nalla Adi Reddy, Arramreddy Santosh Reddy, Seelam Naresh, and Singam Lakshmirajam stands as a best (perhaps worst!) example of the State policy of elimination of Naxalites. The case has all the ingredients of covert operation, treachery, arrest, torture, cold-blooded murder, killing witness to tamper with evidence, false claims to receive gallantry awards, charges and counter charges by police officials themselves, etc. The three Central Committee members of the CPI (ML) (People's War) were arrested in the afternoon of December 1, 1999 in Bangalore and brought to Koyyur forest of Karimnagar district where an encounter was stage-managed. In order to show the encounter as a local affair, a local youth was also killed and accorded a posthumous distinction of being a Naxalite and given a *nom de guerre* as Arun. Later fact findings proved that the den keeper of the top leaders in Bangalore worked as a covert for the police and indulged in treachery. The friends and family members of the victims alleged that there were tell tale signs of torture on the dead bodies and post-mortem reports corroborated the allegation. At least three senior police officials claimed the credit for participating in the "encounter" of the top leaders and received *Shourya Chakra* gallantry awards in 2003. However, simmering discontent within the police department brought the facts to light and conclusively revealed that the three police officials were not at all involved in the incident.[8]

The encounter that is supposed to have taken place at Padmakshamma *gutta*, a hillock on the outskirts of Hanumakonda, part of Warangal on December 25, 2001, is another glaring example of how people are taken from their homes and workplaces and killed in so-called encounters. A popular singer Ilaiah, a teacher and activist of Democratic Teachers' Federation Chandrasekhar, an ambulance cleaner with Employees State Insurance Hospital Surendar and an autorickshaw driver Shankar were taken from their homes and work places while dozens of people were watching and killed them within hours. The victims were neither armed nor underground activists and at least two of them were public activists.[9]

The encounter that took place near Manala in Nizamabad district on March 7, 2005 presents a gruesome picture. Ten activists including three women were killed in this "encounter" and it was alleged that all of them were administered poisoned food through a covert operation and all of them were in drowsy state when they were attacked by police. A petition was moved in the High Court to get a proper post-mortem done to clarify on the allegations of poisoning. However the police officials hurried the medical personnel to finish off post-mortems before the judge visited the hospital. The police also forced the family members to cremate the bodies within no time to wipe out evidence. A petition seeking trial of concerned police officials with murder charge under Section 302 IPC was heard by the High Court and judgment is reserved.

The "encounter" in which Riaz (Ch Venkateswarlu) and three others were killed on July 1, 2005 is another bizarre case. Riaz was a well-known leader of the CPI (ML) Janasakthi and represented his party at the talks between the government and Naxalites. Along with other representatives at the talks, he stayed in the State guest house for over a week and participated in talks with the government delegation that included state home minister, other ministers and legislators. The talks were held in media glare and it would be impossible not to recognise him. However, he was killed and shown as "unidentified" person. While he was arrested during late evening on June 30, his friends alerted the press and home minister by midnight and almost all the newspapers published his arrest news the next day. After all this, police announced that four unidentified persons were killed in exchange of fire.

Impunity once allowed would have its own momentum and spreads fast and wide. After being allowed to kill Naxalite activists without questions for decades, the police started thinking that the same method could be applied universally according to their whims and fancies. Local vested interests started bribing police to get their opponents eliminated in the name of encounters. Gradually police realised that it would be easier to kill and justify it by describing it as encounter and the victims as Naxalites or their sympathisers.

In Medak district, police killed a farmer who had to go out in the night to water his fields since power is supplied during that time of the day, and termed it encounter. A folk artiste who was returning in the night after a performance at *Sri Ram Navami* festival was killed in Warangal district and the incident was justified as encounter. A couple of shepherds were killed in order to eliminate witnesses of the killing of Naxalites in Kadapa district. A physically challenged person who was running a public telephone booth was killed in Mahabubnagar district and he, who cannot use his hands properly, was shown as involved in exchange of fire. A police officer was also killed in this killing spree in Khammam district. He was waiting in a hotel room to apprehend some accused and another police officer knocked the door and shot at the police inspector when he opened it. The number of so-called dacoits, faction followers, ISI operatives, and suspicious persons killed in "encounters" runs into dozens. Dozens of innocent youth in Hyderabad were killed in so-called encounters just to terrorise old-city Muslims.

In a complaint filed by the APCLC before the National Human Rights Commission in 1994, it was mentioned that out of 496 deaths during the previous three years, only 204 (41.1 per cent) were Naxalite activists while 210 (42.3 per cent) were peasants. The list also included rural and small town poor, students and unemployed youth, persons involved in crimes other than Naxalite activity and elected representatives.

The recapitulation of this kind of incidents can go on and on. Even as some of these incidents provoked large-scale protests and subsequent enquiries, the state police and the powers that be ensured that nothing comes out of those enquiries. In fact it is customary to institute a magisterial enquiry into all encounter deaths and none of the enquiry reports were published till now. Of course, the local level magistrates need police help always and one cannot expect them to be so courageous to distance themselves from the local police. Even when a magistrate submitted a conscientious report, the state government saw to it that the report would gather dust in the corridors of power. In one of the incidents cited above, when a joint collector filed a report indicting some police officials and showing that there was no encounter and it was a cold-blooded murder, he and the collector who accepted the report, were shunted out of the district to some insignificant positions.[10] When the APCLC fought a case in Supreme Court, Government of Andhra Pradesh said this report was "improper".

Voices against the inhuman practice

As part of the democratic resurgence euphoria during the post-Emergency days, the practice of fake encounters as a public policy came to lime light and Jayaprakash Narayan set up a non-official fact finding committee under the chairmanship of V M Tarkunde to enquire into the encounters in Andhra Pradesh. The Tarkunde Committee which included Arun Shourie, B G Verghese, Nabakrishna Choudry, Kaloji Narayana Rao, K G Kannabiran, etc placed its reports before the nation. *Institutions in the Janata Phase* by Arun Shourie (1980) makes a detailed reference to the reports. The Tarkunde Committee findings and consequent concerns resulted in the appointment of Justice V Bhargava Commission in 1978. The commission went ahead earnestly in its effort to fathom the truth and its first round of enquiry into the killing of four Naxalites in Giraipalli forest conclusively proved that the victims were arrested, tortured and killed in cold-blood, demolishing the police story. The proceedings were widely reported and the people's suspicion that the encounters were simple killings by the police was confirmed. When the commission began its enquiry for the second round, the government created obstacles in its functioning by ordering in-camera proceedings. The civil liberties organisations opposed this move and boycotted the proceedings. The commission had to close down its enquiry abruptly.

Andhra Pradesh Civil Liberties Committee all through has been judiciously enquiring into each and every encounter case by sending fact finding committees and publishing the reports.[11] The APCLC also approached Supreme Court several times with regard to the extra judicial nature of the encounter killings. The first petition was filed in 1981 and Supreme Court in 1987 asked the petitioners to submit a memorandum to the state government and seek redress at local level. The APCLC's second petition, filed in 1985 was disposed in 1987 itself advising the friends and relatives of the encounter victims to file private complaints in the local magistrate courts. The Supreme Court's recent response, in March 2007, with regard to the encounter killings is even stranger. In a case questioning accelerated promotions to police officers involved in "encounters", the Supreme Court bench upheld the policy of offering accelerated and undue promotions to killer police officers.

In yet another attempt the APCLC approached the National Human Rights Commission (NHRC) and the latter directed the Government of Andhra Pradesh in November 1996 to investigate all cases of encounter deaths. The NHRC expressed its concern over the practice of registering a case under Section 307 (attempt to murder) against the deceased persons. The NHRC noted that in all these cases of killing by police by firing, prima facie, the ingredients of 299 IPC are satisfied and Section 157 of CrPC is attracted calling for investigation. The Commission made the following recommendations especially in regard to encounter deaths.

a) When the police officer in charge of a police station receives information about deaths in an encounter between the police party and others, he shall enter the information in the appropriate register.

Table
Number of 'Naxalites' killed in encounters

Year	Number of persons killed
1969-77	335 - 450
1978	-
1979	-
1980	7
1981	5
1982	4
1983	3
1984	-
1985	35
1986	20
1987	29
1988	61
1989	51
1990	20
1991	104
1992	256
1993	136
1994	109
1995	67
1996	161
1997	159
1998	275
1999	226
2000	245
2001	129
2002	107
2003	173
2004	46
2005	170
2006	135

Source: *Praja Swechcha*, Journal of AP Civil Liberties Committee, November – December 2006

Note: This list could be, in all probability, incomprehensive since even the police records show different figures for some years.

b) The information as received shall be regarded as sufficient to suspect the commission of a cognisable offence and immediate steps should be taken to investigate the facts and circumstances leading to the death to ascertain what, if any, offence was committed and by whom.

c) As the police officers belonging to the same police station are the members of the encounter party, it is appropriate that the cases are made over for investigation to some other independent investigation agency such as State CID.

d) Question of granting of compensation to the dependents of the deceased may be considered in cases ending in conviction if police officers are prosecuted on the basis of the results of the investigation.

These directions were considered to be of general applicability and accordingly were communicated by the NHRC in March 1997 to all Chief Ministers of states to be followed in all cases where deaths were caused in police encounters.[12]

There is no need to state that Government of Andhra Pradesh did not care to follow these directions and allowed its police department to function above law. It is already seen that the government did not heed the direction of the state High Court in registering cases under 302 IPC in each and every encounter.

Public response

While there have been sporadic and local protests at the way the encounter killings are taking place, various civil liberties organisations in the state have been consistently making it an issue of public concern. The major argument of the civil liberties bodies has been that even if one doesn't subscribe to or opposes the victims' political beliefs, there is a need to defend rule of law. No agency should be allowed to indulge in extra-judicial killings in the name of enforcing law. Besides the civil liberties organisations' efforts, at least twice there were state-wide organised public mobilisations against "encounters" in the last decade. For the first time 34 different mass organisations came together to form Joint Struggle Committee against Fake Encounters in 1999 and members of this committee suffered severe repression. Later the police started preventing family members of the victims to claim dead bodies and perform proper funeral with a fear that the dead bodies would reveal the way of killing. Consequently the Committee to Claim Dead Bodies was formed and the need to form such a committee itself is an indication of the pathetic state of affairs in the state. Even this committee was not allowed to function. The society at large is terrorised so as to not raise its voice against this patent violation of human rights and Constitutional right to life.

Conclusion

The case of Sohrabuddin Shaik and Kauser Bi rekindled hopes in hundreds of families of encounter victims in Andhra Pradesh and many of them are looking forward for an opportunity to make their agony public. Even as it may appear as vengeance, it is not vengeance at all. It is only a desire for rule of law and a wish for others whose kith and kin could not be killed with impunity by the law-enforcing agencies. A simple request that comes out of all those anguished family members and friends is that any person who killed another should be booked under Sec 302 IPC and if the culprit had done that in self-defence, it should be proved in a court of law. The culprit, even if he wears khaki, cannot take law into his own hands and cannot don the role of perpetrator of the crime, investigator, prosecutor, judge and jury rolled into one.

Notes:

1 Naxalite Conspiracy Case FIRs, Vol. V, p. C-142 – 2.

2 A large body of literature informed by this viewpoint appeared in the last three decades in Telugu and Varavara Rao (1990) – *Srjana Sampaadakeeyaalu*, a collection of editorials of Srjana, monthly, is a systematic chronicle of such criticism between 1970 and 1990.

3 Ilaiah K (1989) – The State and Repressive Culture, p. 82 and also OPDR (2003) – Rights on Gallows and Repression on People, pp. 159-162.

4 Balagopal K (1988) – Probings in the Political Economy of Agrarian Classes and Conflicts, pp.86-87.

5 APUWJ & APCLC (1994), *Rendosaari Rasool Hatya*, Hyderabad.

6 *Bootakapu Encounterla Vyatireka Aikya Porata Committee* (2000) – *Madhusudan Raj Encounter Caselo High Court Teerpu*, Hyderabad.

7 APCLC (1998) – *Sarihaddulu Cheripestunna* Encounter*lu*, Visakhapatnam.

8 Joint Fact Finding Committee of Organisations of Democratic Rights and Civil Liberties (2000) – Where the Dead Speaks Truth – A Report on Koyyuru Encounter, Vijayawada.

9 IAPL (2004) – Encounter – Face to Face with Victims of State Violence in AP, Mumbai; and N Venugopal, Padmakshammagutta Abaddhaalu, Prajatantra,

10 Balagopal K (1997) – *Kallola Kathaachitraalu*, p.60.

11 Some of these reports can be found in APCLC & OPDR (1991) – *Prajalapai Ukkupaadam;* APCLC & PUDR (1984) – NTR's One Year; APCLC (1989) – *Telugu Desam Paalanalo Encounterlu;* APCLC (1990) – State of Civil Liberties in AP; APCLC (1991) – *Tupaakiraajyam – Perugutunna Nirbandham meeda Nivedika;* APCLC (2000) – *Chandragirigutta* Encounter; as well as in its organ Praja Swechcha.

12 Committee of Concerned Citizens (2002) - A Note to the National Human Rights Commission on Human Rights Violations in the State in Third Report, pp. 43-51.

15

Singing about Dark Times

In one of his short poems Bertolt Brecht wondered if there would be singing in Dark Times, Yes, he wrote, there would be singing - about the Dark Times. This is a report of the Dark Times in Andhra Pradesh. Any report on the repression in the state, as a recent pamphlet noted, rapidly becomes outdated because the state is working round-the-clock to 'curb the Naxalite menace'. This report of events between September 3 and November 16, is based on clandestine pamphlets, posters, legal magazines and informal conversations with the people who are actually experiencing coercive atmosphere in Warangal and other places.

On the morning of September 3, Dr A Ramanatham, vice-president, APCLC was shot dead in his clinic by the police who were taking the dead body of N Yadagiri Reddy, sub-inspector, Kazipet police station. Reddy had been killed allegedly by Radicals on September 2. When the Andhra Pradesh Assembly, then in session, met to discuss the murder of Reddy all the members stood up to condemn Radicals and to pay tributes to the deceased SI, Of course, the most vociferous among them belonged to CPI (M), BJP, CPI, and MCPI. While Congress (I) tried to make capital out of the incident, TDP attempted to present its actual position *vis-a-vis* Naxalites. A BJP member from old city, Hyderabad, who is famous for his hand in communal violence, alleged that "the extremists were getting highly sophisticated weapons through the Nepal-Sikkim-West Bengal and Bangladesh-Assam routes". A Congress (I) member known for his involvement in faction-fights in Rayalaseema lamented the fate of law and order in the state. The CPI members offered

Published in Economic and Political Weekly, Vol XXI No.6, February 8, 1986.

their cooperation to the government on behalf of the opposition, and the CPI (M) member chided the police for using only brawn but not brain to crush the Naxalites. The mood of the house was urging the ban on all extremist organisations. But, in fact, by then a de-facto ban was clamped on all the democratic activity in the state, let alone, the so called extremist activity.

Even while these discussions were taking place, five young people were killed in the forest of Visakhapatnam-Lotha Rajeswari (17), Bukka Venkateswerlu (18), Santosh (18), Anand (19) and Kumar (20) all of whom belonged to an armed squad of CPI (ML) (People's War). They belonged to the Korukonda squad which consisted of nine members. They arrived at Burugupakala, a small village of 15 huts under the jurisdiction of Chintapalli Police Station 25 kms away, to hold a meeting there on the night of September 3, which went on up to midnight. After the meeting the squad went to sleep in the hut of a tribal. Just before day break, a police party of 20 descended on the village. According to a Sub-Inspector, they "were able to sorround the Naxalites as they were not alert". The police arrested five of them as the other four escaped. The arrested five were tied to a nearby tamarind tree and shot dead at point-blank range. Of these five, three were tribals, Lotha Rajesweri was a most backward *bagata* tribal girl, Venkateswarlu and Santosh were *valmikis*. These three youth had joined the squad only five months before, according to *Kranti,* the organ of PW.

Promptly the police came out with a statement that "the armed group consisting of eight persons including two women opened fire at the police who returned the fire in self-defence, resulting in the death of five extremists". The police identified only two persons. Post-mortems were ordered with unusual haste, but the concerned doctors did not comply with the order and conducted post-mortems only on the 5th.

Police officials openly bragged about this encounter-that it was a revenge for the killing of a police constable in September 1984. (That was the one real encounter in Andhra Pradesh in which a policeman was killed and some Naxalites were injured.) A Telugu daily reported that "there were several policemen and homeguards who were boasting of having killed the extremists and that they looked as heroic as a hunter who succeeded in killing 'a lion or a tiger'."

The APCLC refuted the fiction of an encounter on several counts. As the police said, the Naxalites were having only possessed muzzle-loaders, the effective firing range of which was 20 yards, while that of the .303 rifles carried by the police was 200 yards. The trees behind which the police claimed to have taken cover were at a distance of 50 yards from the hut in which the Naxalites slept. A muzzle-loader takes 15 to 20 minutes for reloading and firing, whereas the .303 rifles could be fired almost continuously. The APCLC report contrasted the post-mortem report with the police version and showed that the physical evidence of the postmortems was also against the latter. The police said that the bodies were cremated after the post-mortem was duly conducted. The APCLC questions the justifiability of the action arguing that it was *ultra vires* as the case was a medico-legal one.

Alumina, the small, two-page weekly newspaper of Narsipatnam, put forth another piece of evidence to counter the police version. It explained the topography of the hut and surrounding areas and argued that if at all a real encounter had taken place, the Naxalites could have been in a safer and more guarded area while the police would have had to fight in the open field.

A thorough combing operation in Chintapalli, Rampa-chodavaram, Addatigala, Maredumilli, Rajavommangi and Devipatnam forests in Visakhapatnam and East Godavari districts was initiated employing 500 men and 25 officers of AP Special Police. Special outposts were set up in all in addition to the existing four police stations. (Incidentally, these police stations were the targets of Alluri Sitarama Raju's raids in the 1920s). During this operation the police were given orders to ride roughshod over 118 tribal villages and adjoining forests. The aim of the State in the operation was to terrorise the tribals and the police wanted to demonstrate by capital punishment.

This incident was followed by the killing of a tribal in East Godavari district. According to the police, another encounter took place in Bodlanka under Rampachodavaram police limits on September 12. But one survivor of the so-called encounter Gorle Krishnaiah showed the fallacy of the police story. Krishnaiah, a tribal of Patha Kota wrote a letter to the press in which he stated that he, alongwith Gorle Pullaiah and Jidiguru Bangaraiah, were arrested and were asked to come to Bodlanka to meet the Superintendent of Police and the local moneylender. When they refused, they were forcibly taken there. On the outskirts of Bodlanka, Pullaiah was forced to stand against a tree and a rifle was aimed at Krishnaiah. Acting on the spur of the moment Krishnaiah pushed the constable aside and ran for his life. Firing ensued, but Krishnaiah escaped into the thick forest. Hidden in the bushes, he was a witness to the cold-blooded shooting down of Pullaiah.

The Sub-Inspector who is said to have taken part in the combing operations and the encounter denied Krishnaiah's version. This was the only occasion when a reaction came from the police's side. But, even that denial did not offer any concrete evidence to refute Krishnaiah.

Karimnagar was another battleground. Here four revolutionaries were killed on October 5-6. According to the police they reached Kondapur under Korutla police station (this is another Kondapur, it is not the same where five Naxalites were killed in April this year on October 5), after receiving information that three Naxalites were active on the outskirts of the village. The Naxalites started firing at the police from point-blank range. They tried to throw a powerful grenade on the cops, but it failed due to the drizzling rain. In self-defence the police returned the fire and three Naxalites were killed.

It is the same old story. For every killing the police give this formula fiction. In Kondapur once again it was a total falsification of truth. Rachamallu Madhava Reddy (27), Burra Lakshman (25), Gangaboina Gangaram (20) were shot at when they were trying to escape. When the police started firing on them, they were waiting in a maize field for the villagers. Of these three only the former two were the activists of PW, Gangaram was a poor peasant who brought them food.

The 'encounter' that is said to have taken place on October 6, was even more strange. When a group of Naxalites tried to attack (of course, with intention to kill) an ex- MLA, his police guard fired at them. One of them was killed and the others fled-that was the report which appeared in the press. This story of attack, counter attack and the death of the attacker was travesty of truth, to say the least. What actually happened on October 6 in Dumala under Gambhirraopet police station was, Chelimela Ramaswamy, an activist of PW and others arranged a meeting to discuss the grievances and solutions of the villagers.

During the meeting they came to know that Mohan Reddy, an ex-MLA and the landlord of Almaspet had come to the village. The people had two major grievances against Mohan Reddy. He had appropriated the Rs 7,000 given by Lambada tribals of Akkapalli for allocating community electric pumpsets. He had also cheated a woman of Gollapalli and deserted her. People assembled there wanted Ramaswamy to talk to Mohan Reddy on these two issues. When Ramaswamy and others were walking towards the car in which Mohan Reddy had arrived with his accomplices, the gunman-bodyguard Venkat Reddy suddenly started firing at Ramaswamy who died on the spot.

'Police Raj' in Warangal

These killings were just a culmination of the police raj in the state. Particularly Warangal at present can be easily compared to a ghetto. It has become a prohibited zone and inaccessible to vocal and freedom loving youth. The murder of Dr Ramanatham was only a prelude to the onslaught of the police. All the educational institutions and the hostels were raided. Everybody, who is suspected of having remote leanings towards revolutionary politics, was arrested. One of the important targets was the campus of the Regional Engineering College (REC). Denying the allegations of police high-handedness in the REC, Janak Raj Tiwari, DIG, Warangal range, alleged that the college had become a centre of extremist activity. But this was only an attempt to legitimise the excesses of the police in the college in particular and in the town and district in general.

Hundreds of students and mess workers of the college were interrogated and scores of them were kept in the lock-ups and tortured. Mess workers were forcibly taken to work at the last rites of the deceased SI. Many of the students and workers of the college were implicated in false cases. Friends and relatives of the students who were staying in the hostels at the time were also arrested and interrogated.

Sujata, a final year post-graduate student of the college was arrested at her home town Kakinada. Two top police officers of the district went all the way to the coastal town to arrest her. They stripped her and made her parade in the streets. She was kept in the lock-up of Kazipet police station for 10 days. She was tortured in order to force her to 'divulge' the 'conspiracy' hatched to kill the SI. A letter which expressed happiness over the death of the SI was attributed to her. Another girl Lakshmi belonging to the Radical Youth League of Jayagiri, was also arrested and stripped. She was also kept in the lock-up cells of Hasanparthi and Hanumakonda police stations. While Sujata was implicated in the criminal case after 10 days of illegal custody, Lakshmi was intimidated and let off.

The repression was not limited to the students and youth involved with revolutionary politics alone. Dr Prasada Rao, Medical Officer and B V Subba Rao, Assistant Professor of the REC were arrested and harassed-they were among the few who sided with the students' genuine demands, A Bobbili, a lecturer in History at Kakatiya University evening college was arrested and implicated in a false case.

After 'defeating' the institutions and hostels the police invaded different areas in the town and raided all the students' rooms. More than 100 youth were arrested in and around Kazipet. Several workers of South Central Railway at Kazipet were also arrested. The number of students and youth who were questioned and suspected of revolutionary leanings runs into hundreds in the whole of Warangal.

The attack on Kasibugga, Mill's Colony and Labour Colony reads like a page from Hitlerite encirclements and raids of Jewish localities. Dozens of vans encircled the area at the dead of the night sometime in the second week of September. All the males in the age group of 16-45, irrespective of their social and economic statures were bundled into the vans and taken to different police stations in the town. The police turned a deaf ear to the claims and protests of the arrested people. The scrutiny started the next morning only when the people who could prove their bonafides were escorted to their respective workplaces in vans. An officer of a local bank was also arrested and received abuses when he requested the police to let him off to go to work on time as the keys were with him. The people who could not prove any bonafides were illegally locked up for days together, while some were let off on recommendations from influential persons or on payment of bribes.

When the Radical Students Union and the Radical Youth League and other mass organisations gave a call for bandh in protest of Dr Ramanatham's murder on September 13, the police geared up all their energies to make it a failure. Section 144 Cr P C was promulgated in all the mandals. The police were given orders to 'shoot at sight' such persons carrying weapons in disturbed areas of the district. A fresh wave of arrests of students and youth in the town was undertaken. The police officials convened the Chamber of Commerce and threatened them with consequences, if they observed the call. In that explosive situation the organisations postponed the bundh call in Warangal giving the reason as the highly provocative mood and actions of the police and the mounting repression. Instead, they called upon the people to observe a protest day on September 16 as a part of state-wide call. On that day the people, including traders, the market committee and the picture houses voluntarily observed the bundh. Even the *Indian Express* remarked it as 'complete and peaceful'.

Repression in rural areas of Warangal district is even more inexorable. Hundreds of people were arrested and tortured in Parkal, Chityal, Jangaon, Ghanpur, Mulug and Etur Nagaram taluqs. Property worth thousands of rupees was destroyed. Memorial statues of Giraipalli martyrs (whose case became famous with the findings of Tarkunde Committee and the trial of Bhargava Commission) and Jannu Chinnalu, a peasant leader of Warangal district at Paidipalli were demolished. The police blasted them when the people refused to demolish the memorials themselves or even to help in the demolition. The repression in villages is a saddening and unending list of torture, illegal custody, destruction of property, false cases and unendurable mental strain. To put it briefly, the police are disturbing the life of rural people in social, economic and cultural realms.

To top it all, the police declared that they found two unidentified dead bodies in a decomposed state in the forests of Mulug. While no civil liberties organisations and revolutionary mass organisations are able to investigate the case, the police have hushed up the matter and even the press did not take it up. People of the area believe that these dead bodies were of two activists of CPI (ML) ROC. It seems they were arrested and beaten to death in the lockup.

In a cold blooded plan to crush the revolutionary movement in Warangal the students and youth were trampled upon. Their organisations were broken. Civil liberties movement was intimidated. The APCLC's district president was murdered. The secretary and the joint secretary of the district unit were forced to resign. The house of Dr K Balagopal, state general secretary, APCLC was raided in his absence and all his belongings, books and records of the organisation, clothes and typewriter were stolen. (It was a simple dacoity because they did not give any receipt for the articles). And finally another APCLC activist K Seetharama Rao, lecturer in Public Administration, Kakatiya University was beaten up seriously by plain clothes policemen. They left him unconscious thinking that he was dead. They humiliated his wife and manhandled his son.

Thus curtailing the free movement of revolutionary activists, denying any chance to democratic activity, the police started another campaign. They published a pamphlet urging the house owners in the town not to rent their houses to Naxalites. The owners were advised that nobody in the age group of 18-30 should be given a house. The full particulars of the tenants should be recorded. Identity cards and bonafides of the tenants should be checked. Suspicious persons should be reported to the police immediately.

This is nothing new, as the police of Karimnagar have announced the same things over the loudspeakers in the towns. But the Warangal police have gone a step ahead and threatened that, if any person with Naxalite connections or literature were to be found in any house the owner as well as the tenant would be punished!

The condition of other areas in the northern Telangana is equally bad. Of late Visakhapatnam, East Godavari and Chittoor districts are also being repressed with similar brutality. Revolutionary movement in the state capital is also under constant threat of illegal custody and torture. Day after day Telugu and English newspapers carry statements condemning the arrests and demanding the production of arrested people in the courts.

Arrests under the new Act

Recently the state government has adopted The Terrorist and Disruptive Activities (Prevention) Act, 1985 of the Centre. The police now imprison literally everybody under the Act. Nothing, neither shame nor 'self-respect' nor the 'regional autonomy against Centre' prevented N T Rama Rao from adopting the Act.

A worker and the manager of Peace Book Centre, a shop of revolutionary literature in Hyderabad were arrested and tortured for days together before being imprisoned under the Act. The shop was forced to close down. The office of *Kranti* in Hyderabad was raided and mailing lists and thousands of rupees worth literature were taken away.

Sagar, a poet and an executive member of *Virasam* (Revolutionary Writers' Association) was arrested on a false charge and tortured in Nizamabad; Ambika, an IFTU organiser and Jangaiah, president of the State Teachers' Union were arrested along with dozens of revolutionary students in a midnight swoop in Hyderabad. Houses of Nammu, convener, People's Writers' Federation and G Narsaiah, lone ML MLA, were raided. S S Venkateshwarlu, president RYL and lecturer in English at Anakapalli, Visakhapatnam was arrested under the Act. Benjamin and Sukhajeeven Reddy, RYL activists were arrested and not produced in any court even after 50 days. These are but a few instances from a long list of assaults on the movement.

Besides this, the indications of the government's vicious plans are more frightening. The authorities deputed 299 personnel from City Civil Police and 167 men from Central Armed Reserve for a 'week-long crash training programme' in November. These forces after receiving training in 'weaponry, firing and extremist ideology' would aid the existing civil and special police in seven districts, *i.e,* Adilabad, Nizamabad, Karimnagar, Warangal, Khammam, East Godavari and Visakhapatnam.

All this violence might be inevitable in the view of the State as the repressed are either those who have decided to 'overthrow the government established by law' or those who speak on behalf of them. But the repression once allowed would gain its own mementurn. Now in Andhra Pradesh, the police violence is directed against everybody who has a voice and who wishes to use it against injustice.

Katthi Padma Rao, leader of dalits and Rajashekar, another leader of dalits belonging to Congress (I) were arrested under the NSA and their meeting in Vijayawada was shamelessly disturbed. It was a Jallianwallah Bagh minus the firing. All the thirty thousand people were allowed to enter the Hindu High School grounds. It has just one small gate, When the first speaker finished his speech the audience were indiscriminately lathi-charged. Many people were injured in the stampede to get out of the grounds.

The press has been threatened with a proposed Press Bill against yellow journalism. In fact, purely yellow journals in AP are only 0.2 per cent of all the registered newspapers. But the proposed Bill was to become an intimidating weapon in the hands of the police to use against all the news papers. After widespread protests from all circles, the minister declared that he would reconsider it after convening a national seminar on the issue. But closely following this declaration came the news of Pingali Dasaratharam's murder. He was the editor of a yellow journal named *Encounter*. Local police are now trying to hush up the case in spite of protests from his family. The attitude of the police seems more dubious, when popular belief attributes the crime to the ruling party. Torture of a journalist of the *Indian Express* group by a police officer of ASP rank in a rural police station of Nalgonda district followed this.

A Police Bill is being pushed forward to provide magisterial powers to the commissioners of Vijayawada and Visakhapatnam. These powers would be extended to the police chiefs of other towns also. The Bill simply turns the police chief into a feudal lord and his town into his kingdom.

Throughout this depressing period, the voice of APCLC has been among the few sane voices raised against the Dark Times. Almost every incident reported above was investigated and condemned. Dr Balagopal took personal pains, that too under constant threat to life, to demand justice, in the process of mounting violence and continuous muffling of the dissenting voice. It is but logical and imperative for the State to curtail his movements and muffle his voice.

That is the raj. The promised raj of Lord Rama. Raj of the 'representative of the aspirations of Telugu nationality'. Raj of the 'restored democracy'. Raj of the 'fighter against the Centre'.

During the recently concluded training classes, Telugu Desam party activists were given some hints on public speaking. Adolf Hitler was quoted and respectfully put on the list of good speakers of the world. Of course, N T Rama Rao is also a good speaker. And he is following his predecessor. Hail Fuhrer NTR!

16

Attempt on Gaddar's Life : A Symptom of the Malaise

That the attempt on a famous poet-performer's life should bring so many other sinister things to light is in itself a dangerous portent of the things that are taking place in Andhra Pradesh. By now, the dastardly attack to kill Gaddar, the widespread protest it evoked and the miraculous escape of the singer from the jaws of death have become so popular that a recapitulation may be redundant.

However, what has been happening since January, if not for the last couple of years, in the state has to be taken into account to put the attack in the perspective. The assault on Gaddar bears a direct reference to the dramatic events of the last two months, comparable only to those in Latin America.

Most people might not be aware of the fact that Gaddar was the convener of the 'Committee to Claim Encounter Dead Bodies' when he was sought to be bumped off. The committee's name sounds very cynical and abominable but in the obtaining situation in the state, the committee grew as a natural outcome like the famous 'Mothers of Missing' in Latin America.

Since January 1997, several peace-loving individuals and organisations have started appealing to both the government and the Naxalites to initiate a dialogue to bring peace to the state. Reduction of hostilities and violence was the major demand from these forces. The organisations and individuals ranged from pro-RSS Krishna Patrika to the liberal Intellectuals Initiative comprising of civil libertarians like K G Kannabiran, retired civil servants like S R Sankaran, and academicians

---

Written in 1997. Unpublished.

like Prof G Haragopal and Prof D Narasimha Reddy. These forces started discussing the related issues to pave the way for a much needed dialogue.

As a response to these efforts, CPI (ML) (People's War) came out with seven proposals as a basis of the negotiations. Equal recognition, freedom of the parties involved and political handling were the minimum requirements for any such dialogue, said People's War in its statement.

Withdrawal of ban on People's War and its mass organisations, immediate stoppage of encounter killings, initiating criminal proceedings against the police officers involved in six specific encounter killings as directed by the National Human Rights Commission, unconditional release of Naxalite cadres who have been in jails for the last five years or more under the non-existent TADA, recognising the rights of poor over the lands they occupied, withdrawal of police camps and paramilitary forces from rural areas, immediate cessation of police attacks, destruction of property and illegal arrests and restraining from the proposals to bring in the Disturbed Areas Act or the Prevention of Left Extremism Act were the demands put forth by People's War.

"Without discussing these proposals and taking a favourable attitude, imposing preconditions on a banned party and blaming the party for not accepting the conditions is at best betrays innocence," the statement reminded the intellectuals.

The state government's reaction was ambivalent. On the one hand, A Madhava Reddy, the state Home Minister wanted to know "whether People's War was ready to surrender arms, join the mainstream and work democratically". He said the state government was already implementing most of the proposals put forth by the Naxalites. But on the other hand, within a week, a high level state police delegation led by the Home Minister himself left for Israel to acquire latest technology to suppress the Naxalites. The team's itinerary included discussions with 'anti-terrorist' (read anti-PLO) experts in Israel. The state government announced that it was going to purchase state-of-the-art unmanned helicopters which detect the "enemies" with the help of ultraviolet rays.

Consequently, there was a spurt in the encounter killings in the state beginning with an encounter in the Nallavelli forest near Narsapur in Medak district on February 16. The killed Naxalites were recognised as Gorantla Rameshwar, Secretary of the City Committee of People's

War and another City Committee member, Majjiga Raju. It was alleged that both of them were arrested in Hyderabad a day earlier and killed at point blank after torture.

Gaddar, along with the leaders of the All India People's Resistance Forum (AIPRF) and Andhra Pradesh Civil Liberties Committee (APCLC), immediately rushed to Narsapur and demanded a proper post-mortem and investigation.

In the thirty years of the infamous history of encounter killings in the state this kind of a questioning was unheard of. Usually, police used to arrest activists and kill them point blank and announce it as "encounter". In Andhra Pradesh, the term "encounter" lost its original meaning and came to mean killing unarmed activists. Immediately after each such killing police used to get nominal post-mortem done by a local civil surgeon. It was common to get the report written at gun point.

In fact, in some of the cases courts and democrats found out that there was no sufficient infrastructure to conduct post-mortem at the local hospitals. In most of the cases even the reports failed to take note of open wounds of bullets and tell tale marks of torture on the bodies. Then police used to cremate the dead bodies without informing their families or following the set procedure.

In the brutal case of Gulam Rasool, a journalist and Vijaya Prasad, his friend, the police initially stated that the dead were unidentified. When the journalists identified them through photographs and demanded the dead bodies, the then Congress-I Home Minister promised to hand over the bodies within half an hour. He engaged the journalists' delegation for some time to give time to the police to cremate the bodies and later fled from back door and left for Delhi.

However, after much persuasion, and particularly after the High Court's direction to hand over the dead body of Chintala Venkataswamy, Provincial Committee member of People's War to his family three years ago, the police slowly started giving the dead bodies to the families but would force the families to conduct last rites fast. Thus police used to get away in erasing whatever little evidence the dead bodies could produce in further investigations.

When Gaddar and others went to Narsapur on February 17 the slain Naxalites' bodies were about to be cremated by the police. Hoodwinking the team, the police have taken the dead bodies and put them on the pyre. Rameshwar's mother and brother demanded that his body be given to them. Gaddar physically scuttled the designs of the police to dispose off the bodies and launched an agitation to get a proper post-mortem done. A number of people from democratic and mass organisations joined the agitation.

The battle went to the High Court which ordered a re post-mortem. A team of forensic experts from Hyderabad went to Narsapur and conducted the second post-mortem. It was found out that the hospital in Narsapur did not have sufficient infrastructure to conduct a post-mortem. Finally, the High Court has directed that Rameshwar's body should be handed over to his mother and on February 20, thousands of people paid homage at his native village. In a situation where no public meetings are permitted in Telangana, the funeral of Rameshwar was turned into a large meeting.

Meanwhile, Gaddar went to the State Legislature which was in its Budget session and met the Speaker and asked him to prevail upon the government to hand over the dead bodies to the families and friends. The Home Minister also spoke to him in the Assembly and assured that justice would be done.

Closely on the heels of these developments, Maraiah, the Deputy Commander of Rachakonda squad was killed in Rachakonda hills of Nalgonda district on February 20. Gaddar immediately went to Nalgonda to demand that the dead body be given to Maraiah's family. The Nalgonda police arrested Gaddar and seven APCLC activists on February 22 and charged them with "obstructing public servants from discharge of their duties, supporting a banned organisation and spreading hatred against Chief Minister, Home Minister, Director General of Police and Inspector General (Grey Hounds)." In the mean time, Maraiah's body was handed over to his parents but they were forced to cremate the body immediately.

Imprisoned Gaddar refused to seek bail and instead preferred to stay in jail. A wide spread protest against this arrest made the state government bow down and withdraw the case releasing Gaddar and others after a week.

Then all the mass organisations which came together to fight the arrest of Gaddar decided to form into a body called "Committee to Claim Encounter Dead Bodies". Gaddar naturally became the convener of the committee comprising of 32 mass organisations. M T Khan, President of APCLC has become its co-convener. When the police claim an encounter, the dead bodies will help to verify whether that was a real or fake one and that is why the dead bodies should be preserved until a proper post-mortem is done, said Gaddar. The committee demanded that the procedures regarding the preservation of dead bodies and disposal of unidentified bodies should be followed.

After the formation of the committee, Gaddar went ahead with exposing the fake encounters and within three weeks, police machinery felt threatened to continue encounter killings.

A shocking encounter killing of seven naxalites took place again in Medak district on March 21. Jubilant after "wiping away the Gummadidala squad", the District Superintendent of Police threatened that the three more Naxalite squads operating in the district will also meet the same end. The local reports say that this encounter is also a fake one. The dead included M Damodar Reddy, a State Committee member, Siddi Ramulu, Trade Union squad area committee commander and three female and two male activists. The activists hailed from Medak, Ranga Reddy, Nalgonda, Warangal, Mahabubnagar and Nizamabad districts. Again, a lengthy fight for the second post-mortem and handing over the dead bodies has taken place. At the end, this long drawn legal battle and funerals-turned meetings at a number of places in remote Telangana resulted in quite opposite of what the police anticipated. People could not be terrorised as expected but attended in thousands in the funeral meetings. Encounter killings have started exposing themselves.

But the powers that be have become so insensitive and audacious that two encounter killings in Warangal and Medak districts followed in which two and four activists were killed respectively.

Thus, on the whole the police have killed 37 activists in the first three months of 1997. They wanted to continue the tempo and hence wanted to do away with the "nuisance" Gaddar and the committee was creating.

The police brought a bus load of people claiming to be "Naxalite victims" from Nizamabad to Hyderabad on April 1 to give a memorandum to the Chief Justice of the High Court. The same gang, consisting of several plain clothes policemen, went to K G Kannabiran, the famous civil libertarian and threatened him. After that they went to Gaddar's house and in his absence abused his wife, Vimala.

The attack might be a rehearsal to the real attack on April 6. Vimala even says some of the goons of April 6 resemble those who came on April 1. They came into his house on an apparent enquiry about a land deal and one of them flashed a revolver and fired six rounds. Four of the bullets passed through narrowly away from the vital parts like heart, lungs and spinal chord. Being a diabetic, Gaddar's survival has become very difficult.

Apart from the immediate reason of the exposure of encounter killings, there is the long-time wrath of the state against Gaddar. Born in 1948 into a poor dalit family of Toopran in Medak district, Gummadi Vithal Rao, left engineering studies due to poverty and joined a bank as a clerk. A talented singer-performer, he used to perform for information and public relations department before 1972. Art Lovers, an organisation of artists and writers inspired by the Naxalite politics spotted the star singer in him and by 1973, he became one of the key figures of Jana Natya Mandali, a cultural organisation formed in 1972 to propagate revolutionary politics.

His songs started getting published in 1973 and by 1975 his collection of songs went into several editions. During the Emergency he was arrested for some time and went underground after his release.

In the post-Emergency period, when the peasant struggles broke out in Karimnagar and Adilabad districts, Gaddar drew his inspiration from the struggles and in turn inspired thousands of people to join the movement. Gradually, he developed and improvised a number of folk tunes and art forms and revolutionised them. Voggu katha, burra katha, ballet, veedhi bhagotham, drama and song – whatever form he attempted, each became a weapon in his hands. JNM (Jana Natya Mandali) has become a household name and its collection of songs, with more than ten editions, had a combined sales of more than a million copies.

From 1983 to 1986 he toured all over India and gave performances in several cities and towns. His tour was a part of an all India propaganda mission about the repression on people's movements in Telangana organised by All India League for Revolutionary Culture. While the team was in tour, the repression in Telangana turned from bad to worse and Dr Ramanatham, Vice President of APCLC was killed by police in the broad day light in September 1985 in Warangal. There were enough indications that the police was targeting Gaddar also.

Then, Gaddar chose to go underground in 1986. On February 18, 1990 he came over ground and gave his performance on February 20 before three lakhs of people in Hyderabad. In the subsequent period, the mass organisations have held a number of meetings which were attended by lakhs of people. The largest of the meetings was a state level conference of Raithu Cooli Sangham in May 1990 at Warangal which was attended by at least 12 lakhs people. All these meetings witnessed flowering of people's culture of which Gaddar was recognised as a high water mark.

Thus the attempt on Gaddar's life was essentially an effort by the powers that be to cut off the pointing finger. It was an attempt to erase people's revolutionary culture. Everybody feels that the heinous act was nothing but a handiwork of top police officials and politicians with the help of Grey Hounds, a special anti-Naxalite police force.

Even as the protest gains wider base all over the state and the country, the police try to put the blame on somebody else. A new organisation called Green Tigers has been floated and statements owning up the murderous attack and further threats to kill K G Kannabiran, K Balagopal and Varavara Rao have been issued. A high drama of red alerts and enquiry commissions and computer pictures to "nab the culprits" is being enacted.

Whatever the government does to hoodwink the people, the truth is on everybody's lips. The bullets not only could not erase the song from the lips of Gaddar, but also gave birth to the truth that no tyrant can scuttle a people's voice.

❖ ❖ ❖

17

Vakapalli : Impunity of the Grey Hounds

Anger and despair are palpable in the otherwise cool and pleasant weather of Eastern Ghats. The eyes and gestures of the Khond tribals of the village seem to ask the visitors whether any other community would have tolerated such a crime with such impunity. The questions, the disappointment, and the anger are quite striking, particularly among women. Contrary to the popular image, the tribal women are outspoken and they are not exhausted to repeat for the umpteenth time the story of their humiliation suffered in the hands of custodians of our democracy.

The place is Vakapalli. The women are eleven victims raped by Andhra Pradesh's special anti-Naxalite police force named not so surprisingly Grey Hounds. The incident happened seven weeks ago and still the shock and disbelief are visible on the faces of women, not only for the agony they have undergone, but also for the government's apathy.

From Visakhapatnam, the district headquarters touted as "the most happening city", you reach the village after a harsh drive of 150 kms, more than a third in the ghat section, a feast to the eye with hills and valleys, but a stomach-turning journey. After passing Paderu, headquarters of Integrated Tribal Development Authority, G Madugula, mandal headquarters and Nurmati, somewhat big village by tribal standards, you have to stop your vehicle on the road to get down the hill. You have to scale up and down another hill and valley to reach the village Vakapalli, a very nondescript village that came to limelight thanks to the appalling episode of gang rape of tribal women.

Publisehd in Tehelka Magazine, Vol IV, Issue 45, Nov 24, 2007.

I visited the village seven weeks after the incident, yet the painful mood of the villagers in general and the women in particular has not had any soothing effect. Not only they haven't still got any justice, but the culprits have neither been booked nor even named, though the government and the police higher-ups very well know which party visited that village on that fateful day.

For Pangi Barso (30), Pangi Sittai (26), Korra Harsamma (28), Pangi Ande (30), Vanthaala Rendo (25), Korra Kumari (22), Pangi Lakshmi (22), Korra Janakamma (20), Pangi Sridevi (20), Korra Chilakamma (38), and Vanthaala Chittemma (45) it was like any other day. They did not know that jungle fatigues and T-shirts clad Grey Hounds would descend on the village in the early hours when all the men go out to work. "We generally go out to fields around 3-4 in the morning and come back around 9-10," says an elderly person of the village explaining their absence at the time of the offence. But he was very clear on who the culprits could be: *"Machchala machchala battalu vesukunedi vaallekada"* (it's only them who wear that kind of dress). "We live peacefully with snakes, tigers and bears, but these hounds came to our village for the first time and did this," he adds.

The ostensible reason for the raid of the Grey Hounds was search for the Maoists. Incidentally, the area is a known stronghold of the Maoists, but that day the Grey Hounds did not even do a search operation in the village. It appears that they wanted to terrorise or teach a lesson to the tribals in general as to what happens if they support the Maoists.

By all accounts, the Grey Hounds team had 20 or 21 men and they at once dragged 11 women out of their huts, from their hearths and usual morning chores. Some of them were even chased into the fields and all of them were raped.

Even as mass rape of tribal women itself is a heinous crime, the subsequent developments make one further shameful for living in this democratic country of impunity for uniformed rapists. The Grey Hounds do not even have uniforms, they do not wear badges, they do not travel in numbered vehicles, their sojourns are never recorded. Unless the official who sent the team comes out and tells who were there, nobody would be able to make out.

The incident happened on the morning of August 20 and the women immediately approached Gram Panchayat president of Nurmati and he along with elders of both the villages took the women to Paderu for reporting and booking a complaint with the officials there. The police tried to hush up the case even at that stage but the local MLA Lake Raja Rao belonging to Bahujan Samaj Party took up the case and he has been very active in the struggle of the victims and their families for justice. For taking up this cause Raja Rao is under constant threat from police.

Then the police tried to delay the process of medical examination so as to tamper with the tell-tale evidence. Knowing fully well that the hospital at the nearest town Anakapalli does not have proper facilities for examination, the victims were taken there. Several mass organisations forced the district authorities to bring the victims to Visakhapatnam Hospital. As a result, the examination could take place only on the early hours of August 21, after full 24 hours. Naturally the external examination did not suggest any rape. The report of the State Forensic Laboratory did not confirm rape on the basis of the collected samples. But the not-yet-released report of the tribal welfare commissioner is believed to have confirmed the rape. While the victims were going round the hospitals, the husband of one of the victims was taken away by police and he was threatened to force her to withdraw complaint.

Immediate reaction of the district Superintendent of Police Akun Sabharwal was a flat denial saying that his men did not go to the village at all. Later, he said policemen did go there but did not rape. Similar responses followed by the state Director General of Police and Home Minister. The DGP discovered a theory to rebut the rape charge: "The tribal women are raising this bogey of rape to prevent our men from combing operations. They are doing this to help Maoists and at their behest," he said. The government did not reveal the identity of the Grey Hounds that went to the village leave alone an identification parade before the victims to find out the real culprits.

As part of departmental enquiry from police, an additional SP came to the village and tried to lure the victims by offering Rs 5 lakh each. The women retorted by offering an equal amount on their part if they get justice.

After a lot of procrastination, the government heeded the High Court's direction to order a CID enquiry. However, the CID enquiry officials have not visited the village, the scene of offence, even after seven weeks of the incident. Anil Kumar Singhal, District Collector and Akun Sabharwal, SP visited the village for the first time on October 14 when this correspondent was there. “Now the case is being investigated by CID. They have to submit their report to the High Court and we will act accordingly. It is not our intention to protect any culprit,” said Singhal.

“You have every right to protest and fight. Anybody who feels wronged would fight. I came here to do justice only. But as it is my responsibility to do justice to you, in the process I cannot do injustice to others also. As you yourselves are saying there were 20 policemen and all of them were not culprits. Neither I nor you do not exactly know who the culprits are. We cannot punish those who are innocent. Let the court tell us who are responsible, and I will immediately see to it that they are punished,” Singhal told a group of men in the village. He did not speak to the victims and said, “since the women do not know Telugu I am not talking to them.”

However, at least six victims speak Telugu very well and poured out their anguish with this correspondent. Even as the collector was addressing the men at a distance, the victims were expressing their views clearly and loudly. One of them said, “this government and police have neither eyes nor ears”. Another said, “this fellow comes and goes, that fellow comes and goes, but no body is interested in doing justice. We may not be having voice, but don’t we have modesty?” Their common refrain was “we are telling what happened to us, why would we tell if it hasn’t happened?”

“We want justice. Unless justice is done we are not going to take their relief also. We are even ready to get killed in the process but we won’t rest till we get justice,” said Pangi Sridevi, a victim. “Punishment to the culprits is what we want, that is how we see justice,” added Pangi Sittai.

The victims express disappointment over their Hyderabad experience. Within three days of the incident, some mass organisations affiliated to the CPI took them to Hyderabad to register complaints with authorities. “We met Chief Minister, he did not even say three full sentences with us. We went to Home Minister and he promised to take action depending upon forensic reports and directions of SHRC, High

Court, Tribal Welfare Department." The victims also met Justice B Subhashan Reddy, Chairman, State Human Rights Commission.

When the victims were undergoing harrowing experiences in hospitals and state capital, the rape was seen as pollution by the tribe and there was a customary prescription of making them pure. On September 2, a ceremony of sacrificing cows, goat and chicken took place to bring them back into the tribal fold.

From the next day onwards the victims and several mass organisations, under the banner of Adivasi Ikya Porata Samithi, set up a hunger strike camp in Paderu demanding immediate action. The relay hunger strike went on and marking one month of the incident, the hunger strike was extended to become indefinite. The indefinite hunger strike was withdrawn after one week when the CID enquiry was ordered. While the hunger strike was on, four tribal youth were killed in a fake encounter at Amidelu, four kms from Vakapalli, on September 28.

However, the public response to the horrible incident was somewhat relieving. The entire agency area observed bandh immediately and dozens of mass organisations and all the opposition political parties visited the village and offered solace to the victims. The common demand was to book and arrest the entire team of Grey Hounds that went to Vakapalli on that day under the charges of rape and the SC, ST Atrocities (Prevention) Act among others. It was also demanded that all the Grey Hounds members of that team should be paraded in front of the victims to identify the culprits. They also demanded that all the police officials to be charged with tampering the evidence. The SHRC, High Court and the SC/ST Commission have also responded immediately and positively. The SC/ST Commission was one of the first to visit the village. High Court went further ahead and issued a notice to the DGP to furnish his evidence for denying even before investigation.

The eternal enquiry, investigation, examination process goes on while the tribals once again realise they are at the receiving end. "If the victims were not tribal women, would their FIR go uninvestigated even after so many days? At least wouldn't they record the testimonies of the victims? Would the High Court and SHRC remain silent after making some noises?" asks K Balagopal of Human Rights Forum. "The path to this killing of goats and raping girls by the marauding hounds is laid by society which has been silent in case of fake encounters for the last 38 years, and unquestionable atrocities by Grey Hounds for the last 21 years," says Varavara Rao, revolutionary writer.

One aspect that comes out strikingly is that another Manipur is in the making in the forest areas of Visakhapatnam and unless it is prevented before hand, Manoramas of Vakapalli might turn more violent.

Update on Vakapalli

No definitive action, not even a fair trial, was initiated into the rape incident even after 12 weeks, in spite of protests from all quarters. In the meanwhile, the High Court directed the government to make the report of the Secretary (Tribal Welfare) public. The report, popularly known as Nagi Reddy Report was believed to have indicted the police and it was alleged that the government was dilly dallying to publish it since it approved the tribal women's version. It was also alleged by mass organisations that the government was attempting to tamper with the report. It was also pointed out that the government did not even care to send the complete report to the national SC and ST Commission.

Ultimately the report was submitted to the High Court and thought it did not categorically support the victims' version, its implied conclusions were obvious.

The reports observations include, "the grass presents a disturbed look as if a person lied down there", "the turmeric plants in an area of nearly 10 sq feet were disturbed. There were a few bangle pieces at the site" and "the repeated exhortation of rape by the 11 tribal women cannot be ignored".

The major breakthrough of the report is that it has listed the suspects for the first time, while all the authorities have been closely guarding the names. The report has given the names of all the 21 police personnel and their versions. According to the report A Ravi Kumar, Sub Inspector of Police, Paderu, who headed the team of 20 police personnel who visited the village said that while eight constables were assigned the duty of watching, the remaining personnel followed him for picking up a tribal suspect as per the orders. When the police party wanted to apprehend the tribal, about 30 women attacked the police party.

❖ ❖ ❖

18

Where Writing Becomes Unlawful: Ban on Virasam

Many times in the history of humanity, creative writing has been perceived as a potential threat by the powers that be and writers have been subjected to persecution, harassment, restrictions on liberty and right to express, attempts on life, physical elimination, and more perilously forcing the writers to denounce their own writings. It may now be the first time that an association of writers has been declared unlawful and for all practical purposes banned from conducting its business. Andhra Pradesh claims this dubious distinction and the writers' organisation that is subjected to this unenviable predicament is the 35-year old 'Viplava Rachayitala Sangham' (Revolutionary Writers' Association), popularly known as 'Virasam', its acronym in Telugu.

K Jana Reddy, home minister of Andhra Pradesh, at a press conference on August 17, announced that his government was reimposing the ban that existed till July 22, 2004 on the then CPI (ML) (People's War) – which subsequently became the CPI (Maoist) – and its seven "front organisations" under the Andhra Pradesh Public Security (APPS) Act, 1992. All the seven organisations could not have been bundled as "front organisations" of a political party when at least one organisation – Virasam – has its own independent manifesto and constitution and has been operating in the public domain, particularly in the fields of art and literature for over three decades. Virasam has been refuting the same allegation by the police – of allegiance to the Naxalite party – consistently time and again.

Published in Economic and Political Weekly, Vol XL, No. 40, October 1, 2005.

Government Orders

On August 19, the government published its notification with regard to the supposed ban on Virasam, along with other six notifications, in a Telugu newspaper. The GO Ms No 373 mentioned that the government received a letter from the director-general of police on August 17, 2005 and within hours, the government decided to impose a ban on Virasam along with other organisations (of course, with separate GO Ms Nos). The notification lists nine "offences" of Virasam and argues about the need to declare it as "unlawful".

In fact, there lies a fine line between banning an organisation and declaring it as unlawful. The APPS Act, indeed, doesn't talk about a ban or prohibition or proscription. It only provides the government an authority to declare an organisation unlawful and take necessary action. However, while Section 3 provides the power of the government and Section 8 talks about penalties on the persons associated with the organisation, Sections 4 to 7 elaborate on the procedure that spreads over to three months to confirm the notification. Even after that period, Section 12 of the act provides scope for the association to move a court of law. Though the act is ambiguous on whether the process is concurrent or sequential, there is ample room to interpret it as sequential. For, there are provisions, in Sections 4, 6, and 12, for the office-bearers of the organisation to represent to the government, to seek a personal hearing before the advisory panel constituted by the government, and to move the court during the process and hence one can interpret that the representatives of the association cannot be arrested during the process. Arresting them during the process amounts to the denial of their right to represent themselves.

But even before the official gazette notification declaring Virasam as unlawful was published in newspapers, police swooped down on Virasam leaders and began arresting and intimidating them. In the early hours of August 19, mufti policemen descended on revolutionary poet Varavara Rao's house and tried to take him away without any warrant. His family immediately alerted the media and after two hours uniformed policemen arrested him. Even then, he was not served a warrant despite his protests and the only piece of paper from which the inspector of police read out was a photocopy of Section 8 of the APPS Act. On the same day Virasam held a press conference to denounce the notification and give a rebuttal to the nine offences charged against the association as well as to condemn the arrest of Varavara Rao. In fact, Virasam pointed out the legal implications and argued that they cannot be arrested until the advisory panel gives a verdict in favour of the government. However, Virasam's president and popular novelist G Kalyana Rao was taken into custody from the gates of the Press Club, where he addressed the press meet. Needless to say, he was also not served any warrant.

Killings and Encounters

It is generally believed that a gruesome incident in which 10 persons lost their lives at the hands of the Naxalites was the immediate reason for the ban. Two days prior to the ban, an armed squad of the CPI (Maoist) killed C Narsi Reddy, a sitting ruling party MLA, his son and eight other persons at a meeting on Independence Day at Narayanpet in Mahabubnagar district. The Narayanpet killing was condemned by all political parties, mass organisations and intellectuals. In an edit-page article in *Andhra Jyothi*, Varavara Rao criticised the killings for its indiscriminate nature and the snatching away of lives of some innocent people.

Given the prevalent feelings against Naxalites in the wake of Narayanpet killings, the police establishment of the state seems to have thought that it was the right time to launch an onslaught on Naxalites. That's why the SIB prepared a note asking the government to ban the CPI (Maoist) and its alleged front organisations and the government acceded the demand at once.

In fact, if at all a major killing were to be shown as a provocation to ban, the Narayanpet killing is not the first such violent incident in the history of the Naxalite movement in the state. Earlier also the CPI (Maoist) had caused at least two major incidents of violence, in Vempenta where eight people were done to death and in Chilakaluripet where two policemen and four civilians were killed. In contrast, the police are also credited with equal and brutal incidents where they killed 10 activists in Manala in Nizamabad district and killed Riyaz, a representative of the CPI (ML) Janashakti at the talks, and three others along with him in fake encounters. On the whole, during the eight-month resurgence of violence and counter-violence, both police and Naxalites have killed over 100 persons each.

This spiral of violence-counter violence stands in contrast to the relative peace that existed between June and December 2004. Not even a single death on account of Naxalite-police-informer-landlord conflict was reported during that time, after a nine year period of unabated violence. (Contrarily, there were more than 100 killings of Telugu Desam Party activists by Congress activists in Anantapur district alone in three months during the same period.) That was the time when Naxalites announced a unilateral ceasefire for the first two months which was followed by a bilateral ceasefire for the next three months.

That was the time when the first round of talks between the CPI (Maoist) and the CPI (ML) Janashakti on one hand and the state government on the other took place. That was the time when Naxalites were treated as State guests with all paraphernalia and police and politicians were freely visiting the countryside. That was the time when people's democratic spirit blossomed with over two dozen public meetings across the state and a number of publications and writings in newspapers.

But, that relaxation was short-lived. Within three months of the Naxalites leaving Manjeera Guest House on October 18, 2004, both sides began accusing each other of violating the ceasefire agreement. The first loss of life came in the form of a fake encounter in Warangal district on January 6, 2005, after a respite of seven months, followed by a spate of such fake encounters killing more than 100 activists and sympathisers. The state and police were to be blamed more for these violations of the ceasefire agreement, but for the want of a neutral agency that monitors and tabulates respective violations, people had their own assessments. Though the government had created a monitoring committee with 20 prominent intellectuals and public personalities just before the first round of talks, it could not take up any monitoring activity.

The spate of encounter killings put an end to the idea of talks. After a series of encounters in which more than 10 cadres were killed within a week, the CPI (Maoist) announced that it was pulling out of the peace talks process. Its statement said it would not consider a second round unless the government stuck to the ceasefire agreement and stops encounter killings immediately. The government did not respond and the Naxalites began "retaliation" in their own way.

Thus the political atmosphere in the state has turned into one of apprehension, mistrust, intolerance and violence from that of peace, talks, and democratic expression within no time. The state police machinery, which has been enjoying unlimited and unquestioned power in the name of anti-Naxalite operations for a couple of decades did not want to lose that position. In fact, the Telugu press widely reported the loss of money and power on the part of the police during the so-called relaxation period between June and October 2005. Thus the police top brass has again managed to humble the political class in the state by reversing the peace process.

However, this can only explain the ban on the CPI (Maoist) and its supposed, or basically non-existent, "front organisations" like Radical Students Union (RSU), Radical Youth League (RYL), Raithu Cooli Sangham (RCS), Singareni Karmika Samakhya (SiKaSa), Viplava Karmika Samakhya (ViKaSa), and All India Revolutionary Students' Federation (AIRSF). The question that still seeks an answer would be why should a writers' association be declared unlawful. The police would have everyone believe that Virasam is not a writers' association and only a front organisation of the CPI (Maoist). This allegation is being repeated *ad nauseam* by the state police for the last 35 years, but they could not prove the charge in any court till now after foisting more than two dozen criminal cases against Virasam members and inflicting punishment before trial and considerable harassment.

Writers in Conflicts

The police cite the functioning of Varavara Rao and Kalyana Rao as emissaries of the CPI (Maoist) during the talks between the state government and the Naxalite parties in 2004 as a proof of Virasam's relations with the Naxalites. Even a cursory look at the history of civil conflicts all over the world shows what role writers played in finding a solution to those conflicts. In tune with that tradition, Varavara Rao, Kalyana Rao and Gaddar were chosen as emissaries by the CPI (Maoist) since the former were in the public life and renowned intellectuals and cultural personalities for the last couple of decades. In any negotiations, it is common that the contending parties choose their own emissaries to settle any dispute. In fact, the duty assigned to these emissaries was evolving modalities of the talks only. Though it is common knowledge that these three individuals share a common political belief with the Naxalites, that does not amount to their being a party to all the activities of the Naxalites. For that matter, there are thousands of organisations and lakhs of individuals who share a common belief in Gandhian principles in India and elsewhere, but that doesn't make them part of a single party or somebody doesn't become a front for somebody else.

History of Virasam

Here, it would not be out of place to recount the history of Virasam as given by the association as part of its representation to the government: Virasam was founded on July 4, 1970 in Hyderabad. The great Telugu poet of 20th century *Mahakavi* Sri Sri was its founder president and Kodavatiganti Kutumba Rao (a novelist, short story writer and literary critic) and Rachakonda Viswanatha Shastri (a novelist and short story writer) were its founder vice presidents. Noted literary critic and poet K V Ramana Reddy was its first general secretary.

Along with these doyens of Telugu literature, a number of renowned as well as budding writers, poets and cultural activists joined the organisation. Its first conference was held in Khammam in October 1970. Since then, till the state-level literary workshop held in Visakhapatnam in January 2005, the organisation held its conferences or state-level literary workshops every year, except for the two years during the Emergency, legally and openly. Apart from these state-level annual programmes, Virasam has been conducting meetings, seminars, conferences, workshops and orientation classes both at state and local level for discussing various literary forms and contemporary social and literary developments.

In Virasam's 35-year old history of meetings, conferences and seminars, one cannot find even a single theme that was accused by the police for breaking the law. Moreover, the issues discussed at the meetings pertained to literature, culture, history, philosophy, political economy and ideology. Between 1970 and 1978, Virasam had used its own annual numbers and fraternal literary magazines to propagate its literature. In 1978, Virasam had launched *Arunatara* as its official literary and cultural quarterly and converted it into a monthly in 1980. *Arunatara* is an open and legal literary and cultural magazine.

During the last 35 years Virasam has published hundreds of books averaging 20 per year in various literary forms. These books are published openly and legally and sold in all the bookstalls in the state.

All lovers of Telugu literature regard the achievements of Virasam in book publication and literary forms as highly remarkable. Virasam had published the collected works of Sri Sri, in 20 volumes spread over 5,000 pages, Kodavatiganti Kutumba Rao's non-fiction writings – ranging over 6,000 pages in eight volumes, launched the five-volume project of Cherabanda Raju's collected works and has already published four volumes. Virasam's founder general secretary K V Ramana Reddy had written over 20,000 pages of poetry, literary criticism, biography, history and socio-political commentary.

Virasam's first poetry anthology *Jhanjha* (1970) carried the poem '*Narudo Bhaskaruda*' and it was a pathbreaking attempt in Telugu poetry. This attempt paved the way for reviving the due respect for song and oral art forms in Telugu literature. Virasam members have penned more than a thousand short stories and portrayed almost all facets of Telugu social life. Virasam writers have mastered the form of novel and presented the richness of life and ups and downs in the struggle of life in most realistic, reliable, creative and emotional way.

Literary criticism in Telugu had a strong tradition even before Virasam's formation. But Virasam has placed literary criticism on a solid foundation of philosophical, historical, and political economy perspective. It is a recognised fact that Virasam's literary criticism is far ahead in the analysis of relationship between society and literature, form and content as well as making this relation intelligible in a dialectical way. Another achievement of Virasam has been developing speech into an art form and a powerful tool of analysis. A number of Virasam members have become popular and famous public speakers through their oration and analysis.

Any literary critic would agree that it is impossible to write the history of Telugu literature of the 20th century without any reference to Virasam. The reason for this prominence and this recognition is because of Virasam's consistent adherence to peoples' literary and cultural traditions and creation of literature with highest standards, but not due to its association with some political party as the police allege.

Wrath from Powers

Virasam had also earned a great deal of wrath from the powers that be and received more than its share of prosecution and harassment. The government proscribed Virasam's poetry anthologies *Jhanjha* (1970) and *Le* (1972), but the Andhra Pradesh High Court had quashed the ban orders. Varavara Rao's poetry collection *Bhavishyathu Chitrapatam* (1987) was banned by the government, but later that ban was revoked. In 1971 Virasam members M V Ramana Reddy, Jwalamukhi, Nikhileshwar and Cherabandaraju were arrested under the Preventive Detention Act, but it was quashed by the Andhra Pradesh High Court. The historical judgment said, "nobody should be arrested for political beliefs. Political beliefs cannot be curbed by arrest." In 1973 Virasam members Varavara Rao, Cherabandaraju and M T Khan were arrested under the Maintenance of Internal Security Act (MISA). But they were released by a high court order which said writers cannot be arrested for giving expression to their imagination unless there is a direct link between a piece of art and an armed action.

In 1974, police foisted the Secunderabad Conspiracy Case on Virasam members K V Ramana Reddy, T Madhusudana Rao, Cherabandaraju, M T Khan, Varavara Rao, and Ranganatham who were implicated in the case along with some political activists. This case was under trial for over 15 years and in 1989 all the writers were acquitted as not guilty. The government had wasted lakhs of rupees of public money on this case but could not prove even a single charge against any Virasam member. Cherabandaraju died during the trial of this case. In 1979, the Chittoor Conspiracy Case was foisted against Virasam members T Madhusudana Rao, Jyothi and Samvarta under the same charges. However, Chittoor Sessions Court acquitted all the writers in 1985. In 1986, the same charges were foisted against Virasam member Varavara Rao as part of Ramnagar Conspiracy Case but the prosecution could not establish even a single charge. After 17 years of trial Varavara Rao was acquitted as not guilty in 2003. Apart from these infamous and big cases Virasam members all over the state were implicated in about two dozen cases and charged with the same accusations.

This recapitulation shows that there is no case for declaring Virasam unlawful. Indeed, reinforcing this point, there was a widespread protest from a cross section of Telugu society. Almost all political parties condemned the action. Ironically enough the president of Pradesh

Congress Committee and the chief minister himself, in their personal capacity, said they did not like the ban on Virasam.

Role of Mafia Groups

Virasam began its legal efforts to oppose the notification and has already filed a number of petitions and representations with several authorities including the government, the AP High Court, the State Human Rights Commission, etc. However, within weeks of the notification, things have become worse with three mafia groups – calling themselves Narsa Cobras, Kakatiya Cobras and Nallamala Cobras – raising their ugly head. It is not new to have this sort of vigilante groups and mafia in Andhra Pradesh. During the last two decades at least a dozen such groups, formed basically from the surrendered Naxalites, have emerged and their single-point programme is to threaten and kill the Naxalite sympathisers and leaders of mass organisations. The killer gangs include Fear Vikas, Praja Bandhu, Green Tigers, Red Tigers, Kranti Sena, Nalla Dandu, Nallamala Tigers, Tirumala Tigers, Palnadu Tigers, etc. The mafia dons have amassed hundreds of crores of property through unaccounted money siphoned from anti-Naxalite operations as well as settling property disputes and extortions.

As part of the two-pronged onslaught on the revolutionary movement, the police have managed to impose a ban on Virasam's activity on one hand and made use of these mafia to create terror among those who question government and police on the other. That's how these killer gangs were used to liquidate Kanakachary, a teacher and a former co-convenor of Telangana Jana Sabha in Mahabubnagar on August 24 and Manne Daivaprasad, district secretary of Kula Nirmoolana Porata Samithi in Singarayakonda, Prakasam district on September 10. While Narsa Cobras claimed responsibility for the first killing, it was Nallamala Cobras for the second one. In both cases the killer gangs announced their killing lists beforehand, but neither the police nor the intelligence department had taken any preventive action, exhibiting their complicity in the crime. As of writing this, at least 30 names including G Haragopal, K Balagopal, Varavara Rao, Kalyana Rao, Gaddar, Pinakapani, Punna Rao, Padmakumari – all of them leaders of different mass organisations in the state and prominent personalities in exposing anti-people policies of the state government and extra-judicial killings of the police, are on these lists. To put it in other words, the killer's sword dangles above the heads of all those who have a voice and are willing to lend it to the people's cause. The state government which acted so swiftly within hours to follow up a letter from the police in banning some mass organisations has shown no desire to initiate any action on these killer gangs. In fact, the DGP, in a typical Modi way described the actions of the killer gangs as a proof of Newton's Third Law!

❖ ❖ ❖

19

Dilemma between Carrot and Stick

There are quite a few pointers to suggest that the Naxalite movement is attracting more and more attention and has almost become a highly saleable commodity. At the same time it is also true that an authentic, informative, objective, reliable and well-argued history of the movement would not be found in the market. This is the scenario of a huge demand-supply gap and perhaps that's why a shoddy and ill-informed book like *The Naxalite Movement in India* by Prakash Singh goes to print twice, gets translated into French to become a bestseller and also gets a revised edition. Of course, the revised, second edition not only retains the factual mistakes and flawed arguments but also adds newer mistakes. In fact, by his own admission, the author's interest in the subject was on the decline and 'destiny had charted a different course' and he had to renew his interest in the subject resulting in revising and substantially expanding the book.

Whatever may be the shortcomings of the book, it deserves a keen and critical reading on several counts. It is an interesting contribution to the existing literature on the history of one of the important social and political movements in modern India. It is also unique in the sense that it is written by a police officer who had an 'opportunity to see movement from close quarters and even interact with some of its top leaders including Charu Mazumdar himself'. Besides a couple of books by police officers like Amiya K Samantha and K Aravinda Rao as well as a few articles by officers like Ranajit

---

*Review of **The Naxalite Movement in India** by Prakash Singh; Rupa & Co, New Delhi, 2006; pp. 318 + xiv. This is a 2006 revised version of the review on the first edition of the book, A Police Account of the Naxalite Movement published in Frontier, July 20, 1996*

Gupta and S Venugopal Rao, the police officers' point of view has not come to light as clearly.

Before going into analysing the book properly, it should be mentioned that Prakash Singh's book has become a casualty between two different, if not mutually exclusive, perspectives – that of a liberal and of a police officer. The liberal in him tries to recognise poverty and misgovernance and gives scope to comprehend the movement on a sympathetic note as well as prescribing carrots, but more often than not, the police officer in him comes out with the stick and starts beating the movement. In this scenario of neither here nor there, reader is left confused with official versions full of lies, half-truths and obfuscations.

The book contains eight chapters: The Spark is a general introduction on the initial stirrings in Naxalbari. The Flame goes on to explain the Naxalbari uprising, the birth of the CPI (ML) and the spread of the struggle. The Fire recapitulates the expansion of the movement into Andhra Pradesh, West Bengal, Bihar and Uttar Pradesh, besides other parts of the country. The Blaze gives a bird's eye view of the movement and tries to make generalisations on the foregoing narrative. The Flicker gives an account of dissensions in the party and the events after Charu Mazumdar's death. The Embers tries to present the revived movement in Andhra Pradesh, Madhya Pradesh, and Maharashtra under "Peoples War Group", and Bihar under the "New Left".

An addition in the revised edition, The Fire Rekindles has three sub-chapters with self-explanatory titles: Expanding Arc of Violence (2000-2005), Unity Moves and Extra-territorial Links, and Maoist Movement in Nepal.

The final chapter, Retrospect and Prospect attempts an analysis of the movement on the whole with a vision for the future.

The book also consists of four appendices dealing with *Peoples Daily*'s famous editorial welcoming the Naxalbari uprising, Biographical sketches of some Naxalite leaders, Joint statement of the Maoist parties and organisations of South Asia, and Chronology of events.

The Naxalite movement, whatever may be its successes and failures, strengths and weaknesses, rights and wrongs, and stagnations and expansions, is a great social and political movement inspired by revolutionary optimism on the one hand and grew inevitably out of an unbearable oppression and exploitation people suffered on the other.

Indeed the movement instilled hope in lakhs, if not crores, of toiling masses that there was a way out of their suffering. It did, indeed, achieve a certain amount of prestige and self-respect, for the underdog. It awakened the Indian communist movement from the slumber and brought people's politics and militant struggles on to the agenda as an alternative to self-seeking parliamentary path. It inspired middleclass youth to selflessly lay their lives in the cause of the masses. It signalled an unstoppable struggle where one or the other group has been continuing on the militancy without losing mass base. With all its mistakes, failures, and blunders, the movement, one has to accept, has also thrown up a number of positive aspects. So, in order to evaluate the movement one should not lose sight of this comprehensive stock taking of merits and demerits.

As Justice M N Rao of the Andhra Pradesh High Court observed in 1996, 'while leftwing extremism is viewed as a problem by the administration, it is increasingly being perceived as a solution to their problems by the alienated masses.'

Thus, there is a possibility of having two extreme positions of considering the movement either as a problem or as a solution. Of course, there may be shades of opinion within each perspective of understanding it as a socio-economic problem or a law and order problem or as a problem arising out of various social ills or a final solution or a partial solution.

At places, Singh, the liberal, seems to have understood the positive elements of the movement but the police officer in him quite often objects. As a result, the book is at a loss.

Liberals generally consider the movement as a reflection of genuine aspirations of the masses as well as their grievances. Thus they always quote population figures below the poverty line, hunger, illiteracy, unemployment, underdevelopment, oppression and exploitation. They also imply that there would be no need for the movement if these issues were properly addressed and suggest remedies to the powers that be. However, as it were, the problems, if they are essentially socioeconomic, can neither be wished away nor can be removed through a patch-work as long as the society is managed in a particular way which benefits the same powers that be. In fact, the rulers never take the suggestions of the liberals seriously. The experience of the last 38 years with dozens of commissions, committees, expert groups, task forces, etc speak volumes on this, with voluminous reports gathering dust in the corridors of power, both literally and figuratively. The movement has been saying that the real hitch lies in transforming the particular social order and bringing about a change where the present rulers are thrown out of power. The attempt to do that, a 'protracted process' in the understanding of the movement, becomes an 'incident' or 'violence' and gradually the liberal recedes into background and the administrator or the police officer replaces him, to tackle the 'crime'.

The book under review is a glaring example of this transformation.

In fact, there is a serious rupture between the perspectives of a liberal and an administrator. The liberal's construction of causes of a movement almost justifies the latter and demonstrates the inevitability of the flare-up, may be inadvertently. But then, for the administrator, the causes are of no consequence and any defiance on the part of the masses is seen as a mere law and order problem to be tackled by using force, whether it is sanctioned under law of the land or not. Then in a compromise with the administrator, the liberal treads into an eternal debate on violence and non-violence and starts preaching altruisms. Suddenly he forgets the structural violence of the landlords and indifference of the State he was talking about a short while ago and begins condemning the movement for its 'violence'. Then the liberal and the administrator sing in unison about the 'brutality' of the movement.

The same kind of violence and non-violence paradigm informs Singh's narrative. He does not even try to separate both socioeconomic and law and order paradigms neatly. Each page speaks in both languages confusing the reader about the author's position.

Administrators in general and IPS officers in particular have developed a particular theory of uprisings. This is true for the entire colonial period where each episode of our national movement was presented in the same language. Since the police officers cannot afford to explain a movement in terms of the State's failure to deliver goods and meet people's aspirations, they treat the uprising as either a 'plan' or a 'conspiracy'. Singh also falls into this theorisation quite often or maybe he was easily influenced by the police documents which he referred extensively.

While the liberal in him says, "Naxalism arose from certain basic factors – social injustice, economic inequality and the failure of the system to redress the grievances of large sections of people who suffered and continues to suffer – as a result therefrom", the police officer uses a language like "intimidating and even coercing the unwilling *kisans* to become members", "incited violence", "violent incidents", "instigated to commit various acts of violence", "terrorist acts", "senseless terrorism", "lethal punch", and "gory phase". He even goes to the extent of calling Naxalites "hired killers."

Even a non-serious reader can find this kind of contrasting expressions peacefully coexisting at dozens of places.

At least in one area, the police officer had gained upper hand and there is almost a deafening silence about police repression. But for a couple of instances (where Satyanarayan Singh was quoted as alleging "massive police repression" and where a figure of Naxalites "liquidated" was given), there is no mention of repression on the movement. Any cursory look at the last 38 years of the movement cannot ignore to find out the large scale onslaught on the part of the State. The number of activists, sympathisers and people killed might touch a 10,000 figure with those arrested and harassed accounting to at least half a million. Singh, being an insider, must be well aware of the growing coercive and unquestioned power of the police. How the strength of the police force has been on the rise, how many a special force have been organised, how much free hand (unnumbered vehicles, fuel and money without accountability) is being given, what kind of rewards are being offered to 'liquidate' Naxalites, etc. are everybody's knowledge. The number of draconian Acts that have been brought into force is an open history. As far as Andhra Pradesh government's policy is concerned, police officers get cash incentives and auxiliary promotions for killing Naxalites. This policy has led to making the police mercenaries and on several occasions, unconcerned innocents were also killed to claim cash prizes and promotions.

Even if one thinks that the thousands of young men and women who were killed were 'misguided', surely they deserve to be remembered, particularly in a book on the movement they built with their blood.

The repression on the movement manifested in a myriad ways: burning of villages, evacuating villages, rapes and molestations of women, damaging houses and property, mixing kerosene in foodgrains, burning crops, illegal custody, torture, missing, implicating in false cases, killing in cold blood describing them as encounters...Singh would never look at this tragic saga. Even at a couple of places where he referred to the 'liquidation' of Naxalites, it is only as a matter of fact packed in one sentence or a half. The repression was never looked at as a deliberate policy. In contrast, he spent a lot of space to give tables and explain Naxalites' violence and lists of persons killed by Naxalites.

Though the author has an enviable access to a wide range of sources, his comprehension of information is not commensurate with the task he had undertaken. Most of the information is carefully chosen with a clear perspective, the author being a police officer. The information includes misinformation, disinformation, half-truths, lies propagated by police and vested interests, presenting one part to conceal other parts, etc.

Even as there are a number of mistakes of facts and figures, misquotations, improper expressions, it would suffice to mention a few. Singh always mentions the CPI (ML) (People's War) as PWG and states that it became Peoples War after its merger with CPI (ML) Party Unity in 1998! Even after stating this, he continues describing it as PWG! In fact, there was never such a thing called PWG either before 1998 or later. The CPI (ML) (People's War) was formed on April 22, 1980 (not on April 20 as Singh mentioned), and the police propagated the term "PWG" to denigrate it as a mere group and not a party. The press has gulped this in its thirst for short forms. Whether one treats a political formation as a party or a group is a different matter, but one cannot afford to change a proper name as one wishes.

Indravelli massacre that killed at least 13 Gond tribals took place on April 20, but not on May 20 as the author mentions. Here also Singh repeats the police version of firing and lathi charge, as "inevitable"! In explaining Indravelli firing, he mentions the tensions between the Lambadas and the Gonds, a partial truth made out of proportions by the police.

His naivete and patriarchal understanding comes out when he says, "the girls were not to be left behind and there were small groups of Marxist-Leninists in Indraprastha College, Miranda House, and Lady Shri Ram College. It has been said that some of them were drawn to the ideology because their boy friends were Naxalites".

While all these mistakes, including printer's devils, continue to exist in the revised edition, the latter add some more. In the expanded edition, the author unnecessarily dwells at length on the developments in Nepal and China.

In a symbolic gesture, the author quotes Lord Krishna from the Bhagavad Gita at the beginning of the book. The quote goes as, "I am the terrible time. The destroyer of people, and am here proceeding to destroy them; Even without you, all these warriors in every division shall cease to be. Therefore, arise and attain fame, and conquering your enemies, enjoy a flourishing kingdom. By Me alone have these been killed already. O Savyasachin, you be merely an instrument".

What does the author want to convey through this quote? Whom does the author treat as a 'mere instrument' to the eternal and inevitable dance of death? Is it the Naxalites or the police?

The Naxalite movement of the first phase has produced more than a dozen good informative and insightful histories. Even as the movement in the post-Emergency period has been growing from strength to strength, though confined to a couple of states till the early 1990s and extending to some more states of late, there is a lack of studies that match the expansion and growing interest. Singh's attempt glaringly points at the work that is yet to be done.

❖ ❖ ❖

IV

Culture

In Andhra Pradesh and Telugu society the influence of Naxalite movement is most visibly present in the cultural and literary spheres. The Naxalite movement polarised the literary class in 1970s and the next four decades have seen a vibrant revolutionary literary and cultural movement. This section, in four essays, tries to capture various facets of the history of revolutionary cultural and literary movements. While the first essay is a portrayal of Gaddar, the last gives an account of Telugu revolutionary literary movement. The other two essays deal with the new genre – underground literature – developed by Telugu revolutionary literary movement, as well as the movement's extended influence on Dandakaranya literature.

20

Revolutionary Rhapsodies

'Hold on, O cartman,
I'll come with the cart
O cart man, stop
I'll come with you'

sang Gaddar, eighteen years ago. Since then he is never tired of going along with the cartman. In fact he himself became the cartman. Gradually the lone cart turned into a caravan and the cartman a helmsman of the cultural movement, not only in Andhra Pradesh but also else where in India.

The song of the cartman is said to be his first song after his transformation from a DAVP propagandist to Jana Natya Mandali activist. Is it odd to see the transformation from a government publicist to an anti-establishment provocateur? He has woven his songs bringing experiences of his childhood and sufferings in his school life. He brought an admixture of form and content, which he learnt throughout his childhood.

His success lies in the fact that he depended completely on the source of people's knowledge and wisdom in the areas of song and music. He started performing in his schooldays itself. Born as Gummadi Vittal Rao in 1949 into a poor dalit family at Toopran, a small village of Medak district, he keenly observed the songs and all other art forms of peasant castes and nomadic tribes.

Published in Deccan Chronicle, February 24, 1990, following Gaddar appearing overground after four years of underground life.

He chose *burrakatha* as his form in high school days and within no time he became famous for it. Studentship with reservations and scholarships brought him humiliation form upper caste schoolmates but talents in performing 'Alluri Sitarama Raju' and 'Ambedkar' brought him wider acclaim.

He joined Osmania Engineering College during the early 70s but could not complete his studies due to financial troubles. At that time DAVP approached him to give performances on family planning and other themes. He divided his time to give government performances on the one hand and his favourites, 'Alluri Sitarama Raju', and 'Ambedkar' on the other.

As he became famous for his *burrakatha* on Alluri Sitarama Raju, he was invited to perform in a seminar organised by Art Lovers in Secunderabad in early 1972. Art Lovers was an organisation committed vaguely to people's culture but it was groping in the dark to pin point the people's culture.

The members of Art Lovers used to go to villages and recite free verses written about people at that time. But the effort did not get expected results. As the group was influenced by the people's struggles, it tried to evolve a more simple way to reach the masses. The seminar was a step in the direction. Gummadi Vittal Rao came to the seminar to perform Alluri Sitarama Raju and the friendship that started between Vittal and revolutionary politics was a lasting one and it turned Vittal into V B Gaddar and didactic looking politics into attractive popular songs.

Slowly Art Lovers faded out to give way to Jana Natya Mandali. Gaddar with his team, started performing *burrakatha's*, singing songs and enacting plays. His first book of songs came out in October 1973. A single book among them, *Jana Natya Mandali Patalu* published by Kranti Prachuranalu went into more than ten editions and the total print order is above 1,50,000. Combined with other collections at different times and places, more than 10 lakhs copies might have been published. Gradually Gaddar became a symbol and an ideal for hundreds of lyricists and singers. At present amongst the 1,000 or more songs of JNM, Gaddar has penned only 200. Though Gaddar has travelled widely all over AP, his performances are about only 10 per cent of the total JNM performances.

He is looked upon as a leader and guide by revolutionary cultural activists from Tamilnadu, Karnataka, West Bengal, Maharashtra, Gujarat, Bihar, Madhya Pradesh to name a few.

JNM really went to masses and found a gold mine of folk forms. With these developments JNM has become 'the cultural organisation of the masses' by 1980s. Since 1983 Gaddar started touring other states to introduce the techniques of revolutionary cultural movement to the activists there.

This ever growing popularity of the singer earned him wrath. As the people's movement he was supporting was subjected by Telugu Desam government to severe repression, Gaddar became a target.

Thanks to the change of government, today the atmosphere is turning in favour of Gaddar.

Though there are many other artists who braved the wrath of the TDP, one distinct feature which separates Gaddar from others is his multifaceted talent. He sings melodiously that even the opponents of his ideology commend his voice. He collects such beautiful folk tunes that almost all the political parties have imitated him. More over, Gaddar, the political propagandist and Gaddar, the artiste are so well united that they cannot be separated. That's why Gaddar, the rebel has become a legend.

❖ ❖ ❖

21

Literature from Underground: *The Poetry of Earthy Passions*

In the history of politics and literature, Andhra Pradesh has a notable place by virtue of its predominantly revolutionary trends. It was in Andhra Pradesh that a writers' organisation, openly championing the cause of Naxalites, was formed, way back in 1970, giving voice to their struggle. It is in this state that these Naxalites are braving severe repression as well the ban imposed recently on them by the government. It is here that a remarkable poet - singer - performer, Gaddar, and his Jana Natya Mandali took root in the oral traditions of the rural and tribal areas of Andhra Pradesh. It is here that the revolutionary literature and practice have grown into a force to be reckoned with.

However, a less known fact is that, in Andhra Pradesh, there is a long tradition of poets and writers who compose poems and literary pieces from a self imposed underground existence. They are basically activists who organise landless and small peasants in the plains and forests of the state. In a sense, they are the equivalents of the bards of the decades past, who were involved in agricultural activities as well as literary creation.

The Telangana Armed Peasant Struggle of 1946-51, in fact, gave birth to the practice of mixing revolution and poetry. Poets like Yadagiri (an illiterate composer of the famous song, *Bandenuka Bandi Gatti* later used in the film *Maa Bhoomi*), Suddala Hanumanthu, T. Ramanjaneyulu, Maqdoom Mohiuddin and others emerged from the struggle.

Published in The Economic Times, August 11, 1992.

During the Srikakulam tribal struggle (1968-72) the leader, Vempatapu Satyanarayana himself wrote a number of songs to voice the woes of the tribals and to win over more people to participate in the struggle. Many of the poems may appear prosaic to an aesthete but, at the time that inspired them, they served a particular purpose, like any other piece of art. They rallied thousands of Savara and Jatapu tribals around the banner of the movement.

A major poet whose name is associated with the Srikakulam struggle is Subba Rao Panigrahi. He has been by now, translated into almost all the Indian languages and stands as an ideal for the litterature concerned with the people. Panigrahi was born into a poor Brahmin family in the early '30s in Sompeta in Srikakulam district. Although his mother tongue was Oriya and he was well-versed in Bengali, Hindi, Assamese and English, Panigrahi wrote all his songs in Telugu alone. Influenced by communist ideology in the '50s, he started performing the *Harikatha* (a popular art form of devotion) and gradually drifted towards a more popular folk form *Jamukula Katha.*

When a meeting of tribals was fired upon by landlords and two tribals were killed on October 31, 1967, Panigrahi's indignation led him to write a lengthy *Jamukula Katha* based on the incident. Later he took to fulltime activism and even became the taluqa secretary of the CPI (ML).

In a poem titled *Erupu (Redness)*, Panigrahi writes,

Redness strikes
Some with fear
Kids are far
Better than them
First flush of the Sun
Is full of redness
The gladness of the red
Is ravishing...
Mark in us
There is redness
Red is our blood
To reckon...

In another song, he says:

We have raised the flag aloft
With the life blood of toilers
And we shall march forward
With the aspirations of heroic martyrs.
You can't obstruct the people's might
By arresting them
You just can't stop bright sunlight
By raising your palm against it

A book of his poems was published while he was alive. Another collection of poems and the *Jamukula Katha* were published posthumously.

Subba Rao Panigrahi was killed by the police on December 22, 1969, and his 'martyrdom' became a touchstone in Telugu literature, a kind of literary polarisation between those on the side of the people and those against. The formation of the Revolutionary Writers' Association (*Viplava Rachaytala Sangham - Virasam*) was a direct outcome of Panigrahi's influence on Telugu literature.

Another poet-revolutionary after Panigrahi and in his mould was *Samudrudu* (Kanakaraju). He was an activist of the People's War operating in Medak district. A book of his poems was published while he was alive and three books have come out since he was killed on September 1, 1991.

Some time ago, the state government announced various amounts as the 'head-price' for the underground cadre of the Naxalites. This was grist for *Samudrudu*'s mills. He immediately published a book titled *The earth is my head, Decide its price.* In an elegy to one of his comrades who was killed in a fake encounter, he wrote

How can I believe the fact that you are no more?
I have not yet forgotten the warm feeling of your intense handshake
The enemy says that he killed you

How do I digest the news?
He also claims that he killed the wind, the light, and the dawn

How do I trust..?
He decides the prices of our heads
He won't stop beheading us
We chose this path quite knowingly.

In yet another poem, *Samudrudu* says

When the moon was wounded by the rifle shots in the night and appeared red
I understand that the enemy was digging another grave to the truth
With a burning stink the wind sadly wiped the tears from my cheek...
The grass crushed in the night weeps in the morning...
My children, please open your eyes at least once...!
Just now
A seat fell vacant
My wound blossomed like a flower
A comrade fell down
Another rises from his injuries
I am invincible
I disintegrate and explode
It is my heart that breaks
But not my weapons and wishes
My death becomes a song and rests
But the struggle continues to flow.

Samudrudu was arrested on September 1, 1991 at Toopran, taken to a remote village Pambanda, and killed there with a usual encounter Story. Incidentally, Pambanda was the village where PW cadres exchanged kidnapped Congress (I) MLA Sudhir Kumar with four of their arrested comrades. One of the four released activists, N. Bhaskara Rao, himself a poet, writes under the pseudonym *Ajnata Sureedu* (Exiled Sun). He has published two collections of poetry and was rated one of the most sensitive poets of his generation.

Another important poet-revolutionary is Sivasagar (K.G. Satya Murthy), who came overground in January 1990. He had three collections of poems and a jail diary to his credit while he was underground. Another volume of poetry followed. A respected poet, he is regarded as a trend setter in revolutionary romanticist poetry.

Rikkala Sahadeva Reddy was an activist of the CPI (ML) under the leadership of C.P. Reddy, and has a corpus of memorable poems.

There is no spring in our lives
Like in autumn
Our existence always falls down
This naturalness of poverty invaded us like inertia
Until this pest is away
There will be no spring in our lives
In our desert way of life
We forever love the monsoon
If only our lives became oases
We allow dream of a spring

He was arrested on September 25, 1988 and shot dead three days later.

In the recent spate of 'encounters', the police have killed at least three artists-revolutionaries - Amar Jyothi and Noothan, both poets and Shankar an artist. It is all too likely that many more such talents have died early, unsung deaths, both literally and metaphorically.

Revolutionary activity has always been a kind of catalyst for a flurry of literary activity and has proved fecund for poets, novelists and essayists where earlier there might have been few. *Arunatara,* the official organ of the Revolutionary Writers' Association, and *Srjana,* a forum for modern literature in Telugu, regularly publish a number or writings of the exiled. Both the journals published novels by members of an underground cadre based on the struggles in Dandakaranya.

The writers get their pieces published under pseudonyms in almost all the journals in the state. Recently, two poetry collections by underground activists - *Raktasikta Sopanalu (*Blood -soaked staircase*)* by Chandrahasa, and *Aavaahana (*Embracing*)* by Goutham - have been published.

Life in the underground is far from comfortable, but then comfort has never been the best friend of revolutionary literature. What is, at best, missing is the wherewithal to record impressions as and when they come and the paraphernalia with which to record them with. And while fame might neither be aspired to or, for that matter, readily forthcoming, underground literary creativity could have its own hidden benefits. Frenchman Regis Debray started his novel, *Undesirable Alien,* by saying that "the underground has its own aristocracy". May be one should add that "the underground has its own aesthetics."

As poet Moleena put it :

How great a pleasure it is
To write poetry in the battlefield
Here poetry loses its artificial delicacy..
Here even flowers and moonlit nights are blood soaked
For these there is no place in the poetry encyclopedia of the civilised.

❖ ❖ ❖

22

Literature from Dandakaranya Revolutionary Movement

Sad and nostalgic memories overwhelm me at this moment when we meet here in memory of C V Subba Rao, my friend, guide and comrade in arms and letters for over twenty years. Our first meeting was in 1975, a couple of months before the Emergency. The post-Emergency upsurge of democratic movements and his presence in Delhi at that time strengthened his bonds with the revolutionary movement in Andhra Pradesh. He was one of the early propagators of the rural mass upsurge in Karimnagar and Adilabad. As one of the driving forces behind *Sahitimitrulu*, the group that ran ***Srjana***, forum for modern literature in Telugu and a member of *Viplava Rachayitala Sangham* (*Virasam* – Revolutionary Writers' Association), Subba Rao became an indivisible part of our lives. I think it is true of anybody who came into contact with him.

He used to spend every summer in Warangal and he and I might have spent hundreds of sleepless nights filled with conversation, poetry and literature every summer between 1979 and 1984. As lovers of literature and students of social sciences both of us seem to have accepted the Baconian axiom that all knowledge is our province. There is – simply – nothing on earth that he did not expose me to and nothing we shared our views on. We dreamed and worked together on several projects, published and unpublished.

C V Subba Rao Memorial Lecture, organised by People's Union for Democratic Rights, New Delhi, 1999.

He introduced me to Peoples' Union for Democratic Rights (PUDR) way back in the early 1980s and I had several occasions to meet with the organisation and make friends with many of its activists. The theme of today's meeting is a fitting tribute to the living memory of Subba Rao. He was a person who integrated literature, social activity, political mobilisation and democratic rights movement into a single organic whole and inspired quite a few across the length and breadth of this country to follow his example. A voracious reader and lover of all that is best in literature, he attempted to blend democratic rights movement with literature. He was amongst the first who reflected on the beginnings of Dandakaranya movement. Thus I feel privileged to speak on Literature from Dandakaranya Revolutionary Movement on the occasion of commemoration of Subba Rao. I thank friends of PUDR for giving me this opportunity.

Before going into the literature that is coming out of Dandakaranya Revolutionary Movement, let me first attempt to introduce what the movement is about, how did it originate and how did it reach its current stage.

Dandakaranya is that part of the forest in the central India spreading towards south and east. It comprises of 12 districts in four states — Garchiroli, Chandrapur and Bhandara in Maharashtra, Balaghat, Rajnandgaon and Bastar in Madhya Pradesh, Malkangiri and Koraput in Orissa and Adilabad, Khammam, East Godavari and Srikakulam in Andhra Pradesh.[1] Roughly between the Narmada and the Godavari, Dandakaranya is the land of rich flora and fauna. Much larger than many states in the country, the area has plenty of arable land and water resources. Besides providing rich timber, the land has large reserves of minerals like iron ore, bauxite, tin, granite, limestone and carborundum.

The rich and powerful not only from the neighbouring four states, but also from whole of India, amassed wealth from these natural resources leaving the tribals in abject poverty. This forest is the home of a number of tribal groups that speak at least 20 languages. The tribal languages are losing their separate identities due to the overbearing influence of Telugu, Hindi, Marathi and Oriya. The prominent existing languages are Gondi, Madia, Kolam, Muria, Alfi, Gowali, Baiga, Samanta, and Chattisgarhi.

What is the significance of Dandakaranya and why did the movement choose Dandakaranya as its area of operation? The revolutionary party, which is spearheading the movement, had formulated its Guerilla Zone Perspective in 1980, and decided to work amongst the tribals in Dandakaranya so as to develop the area into a Guerilla Zone.[2] Thus the spark ignited by a couple of cadres from Telangana, Dandakaranya adivasis' struggles spread like a wildfire and within two decades, the number of cadres went up to thousands spread over 2,500 villages and more than 8 million people. The movement, with a network of the party organisation, armed squads, revolutionary mass organisations, people's militia, revolutionary grassroots democratic state organs and cultural propaganda teams, has been undertaking a number of political, military, social, economic and cultural functions.

Revolutionary agrarian – welfare development activities like constructing tanks and check dams, fishing, growing vegetables, distributing pulses and oilseeds and protecting forest have been taken up. Setting up schools and educational institutions, people's health centres, encouraging people to organise themselves into cooperatives include the other activities of the movement.

All these activities certainly do not lose themselves in the primary goal of establishing State power in the hands of people, thus giving prominence to the military activity of the movement. Naturally, these real and sincere pro-people development activities backed by a political ideology for State power have been earning the wrath of the powers that be. More than 300 people's activists have been killed in fake encounters in Dandakaranya.

It can be seen from the foregoing brief account of the movement that it has a multi-faceted character encompassing revolutionary changes in all walks of life. Needless to say that those momentous changes will get reflected in art and literature and the interaction is mutually complementary.

Since the revolutionary movement spread from Karimnagar – Adilabad to the Dandakaranya forest, early literature was an extension of Telugu revolutionary literature. However, as the movement spread into new areas, it had to make its entry into other languages. The first language of expansion was Gondi, into which Telugu songs were translated in the beginning.

As the revolutionary activists mingled more and more with local tribals, they explored the local traditions of song, dance, musical instruments, dance forms that go on whole night, and theatrical forms like *khel*, *dhemsa* and *juluva*. Gradually, the natural composers from the tribals started demonstrating their talents. The first set of dozens of songs blossomed from the forest. This is the confluence of two mighty streams of people's art traditions. One was an experienced revolutionary stream that has more than four decades of people's struggles behind it and the other was a natural stream which was an expression of misery and struggling to find a way out from that oppression. The tribal activists started to read and write and entered the exclusively literate zone of free verse also.

Dandakaranya writers have also tried their hand at short story. The short stories read like anthropological studies, social histories and explorations in political and military mobilisation. Jwala's story *Dorla Bidda* (Son of Koya doras) revolves around the theme of an adivasi becoming an efficient guerilla and speaks about technical modalities of people's militia. *Thupaakulatho Thunikaakulu Thempaleru* (You cannot pluck tendu leaves with guns), a story on tendu leaf struggles and repression by Kaadi is an impressive portrayal of the struggle and in turn the title of the story became a popular slogan in all the areas. There are at least two dozen short stories that have come from cadres or tribal activists, like Jwala, Kaadi, Swathi, Chinna, Thoorpu, Indravati, Vekuva, Pravin, Ramesh, Ajad, Janam and Devanna. Each of these stories throws light on a different facet of tribal life and struggle.

Dandakaranya literature has achieved significant results in novel, if one puts it in the proper perspective of such a young literary tradition comprehending the complexity of the genre. While the first decade of Dandakaranya literature witnessed two novels being written from outside, the second decade saw two novels coming from the activist-writer Sadhana.

Komuram Bheem, the first novel based on the area, is about the historical figure who fought against the Nizam's autocratic rule. Sahu, one of the first activists who entered the Adilabad part of Dandakaranya and translated Telugu songs into Gondi, had co-authored this novel with Allam Rajaiah.[3] The novel is an inspiring account of the Gond hero of 1940s and his mobilisation methods, his representations to the Nizam's government and his ultimate armed struggles.

The second novel, *Vasantageetham* by Puli Anandamohan, came in the late 1980s, is a very complex story of the development of an activist. Following the protagonist's emotional ups and downs, the novel described the military line of the movement and its implementation at the ground level in a very artistic presentation.

Sadhana's *Sarihaddu* and *Rago* are the perfect examples of Dandakaranya literature as the protagonists in the novels are Adivasis, ambience is Dandakaranya proper and the writer is an armed activist working amongst the Adivasis. While *Sarihaddu* speaks about the close relationship between the party cadres and Adivasis in Dandakaranya, *Rago* is the story of a Madia woman transforming into a guerilla.

The movement in Dandakaranya is also bringing out a cyclostyled literary journal, ***Jhankar***, regularly. The journal is a forum for budding and experienced writers and offers a variety of genres – poetry, songs, short stories, essays, reviews and reports. The journal, usually more than 100 pages without a fixed periodicity, presents writings in Telugu, Gondi, Marathi, Hindi and Oriya, composed in Telugu and Hindi scripts.

The editorial of ***Jhankar*** – 5 (1996) says, "in the last 16 years more than 230 comrades have laid down their lives in the course of building the people's movement. Continuing the legacy of Subbarao Panigrahi, Cherabandaraju and Paritala Sriramulu in building up revolutionary literary movement, they fought the enemy heroically on one hand and giving expressions to their feelings worked as literary soldiers in the field of arts, on the other. Capturing the dance and music of people, these children of people honed up people's art with right mix of pen and gun. They revolutionised people's song and added song to people's dance. Dolu, dappu, kundudu, keekur, sonnai, kommu, ulludi - not one but all the musical instruments in the forest and the song became armed. People's guerillas dedicating themselves to serving the people have been recording people's history on the path of the struggle."

Jhankar – 5 wrote about Bayyakka, an adivasi girl who joined the movement as an illiterate and became an accomplished writer, singer and a guerilla by the time she was killed by the police in Balaghat. There must be hundreds of Bayyakkas, alive and writing in the movement.

Jhankar reports a kavisabha that was held in February 1996. The event was organised with the slogan that "everybody is a writer." It was reported that every participant read out at least one poem in Telugu or Hindi or Marathi or Gondi. The guerillas and Adivasis have also experimented with *odur pata*, a popular narrative form in Madia society. Traditionally *odur pata* is sung by Patodi (singers) for two to three nights continuously.

Though Dandakaranya writers are in the midst of a thick forest and in the thick of a struggle, they seem to be up-to-date of the happenings in the literary and cultural fields outside. The editorial in one of the issues of ***Jhankar*** mentions about the anti-revolutionary trends in Telugu literature and says, "as Dandakaranya writers we should counter these attacks. We have to fight out their distortions, and falsehoods with a scientific theory. Similarly, it is our duty to counter the wrong theoretical formulations coming out in the garb of Dalit and feminist perspectives. In that direction we have to intensify our literary effort in both form and content. We have to overcome our weaknesses. In the last issues, a majority of writings was poems. Songs and short stories followed. Even amongst the poems, songs and short stories, most were elegies. It is also our weakness to find lesser number of women comrades who are taking up literary effort."

"Our writings should have the diversity of content. Deepening imperialist exploitation, immanent danger of communalism, the drama of reforms, woman question, problems of Dalits and Adivasis, repression, national and international issues – all these need our attention. The last 16 years of Dandakaranya revolutionary movement has impacted a number of changes in social, cultural, economic, and political life of adivasis. We have to record those changes in various literary forms."

"Correcting all our weaknesses, we have to develop ourselves in different genres like story, short story, full-length drama, play, novel, novella, skit, sketch, essay, book review, introduction, review article, memories and experiences."

Jhankar – 6 carried a review article on 'Bastar Struggle Songs' by Narkator. The writer says there were about 70 songs that emerged in Bastar between 1980s and 1997. The song forms came out of Bastar are Muria, Dorla, Madia people's songs, peetos (with chorus) and vesods. The writer classified the songs into four broad divisions. 1. Songs that speak of various forms of exploitation and oppression. 2. Reformist songs. 3. Women's songs, and 4. Elegies. The essay also mentions about the songs on other themes like the policies of Rajiv Gandhi, beauty contest and international women's day. However, he talks about the problems faced by writers in Bastar area and points out that catching local tunes and further exploration of nuances of local language need to be done rigorously.

Interestingly, ***Jhankar*** 6 also carried *Song in North Telangana – My Experiences* by Savyasachi, a self-made song writer's speech at a cultural forum in Dandakaranya. The speech reads very interesting and inspiring account of a budding writer and the process in which he gained confidence as a writer.

The most striking aspect of Dandakaranya literature is its wide variety. Though the writers are either armed squad members or Adivasi militants, the issues and themes covered in their writings are as varied as in mainstream literature that we know of.

There is a general conception that this kind of literature is either straitjacketed or eulogises martyrs only. But even a glimpse at Dandakaranya literature shows that it is a gross misconception. Of course, as in any other struggle, the fighters would gain inspiration from those who laid down their lives before. Thus it is natural to have a majority of writings about martyrs.

But the themes that found expression in the writings of Dandakaranya writers include all social issues. Displacements due to "development" projects, elections and election boycott, forest landscape, repression, problems of RTC workers, remunerative prices for farmers, anti-people policies of Chandrababu Naidu government, anti-smoking campaign, tribal problems, international issues like Palestine, woman question are some of the themes in their writings. When a brothel owner left the dead body of a hapless prostitute on the road and that was reported in the press, a Dandakaranya poet picked up the theme to write a touching poem.

This exposition of Dandakaranya literature can go on and on. I would like to quote from the preface to one of the poetry anthologies from Dandakaranya.

"In a review meeting amidst the war, during the recess, they want to look at themselves and the emotional expressions in their hearts in a mirror called literature. This is when they are involved in the critical battle. They also wanted to show us the large hill in this small mirror."

"During these times poets – no, fighters – have to compose poetry, write. While composing the strategy of the struggle with one hand, they have to compose their imagination also in words with another hand. The greatest advantage they have is that the distance of line of control between strategy and imagination is too short. They write their strategies relying totally on soil, new idiom and forest. As well they write their imaginations. They do not fight leaving the ground, neither they produce literature leaving the land. They do not have separate compartments for involvement and commitment. For them there is no difference between a bayonet and a pen. From the tip of the bayonet and under the shadows of spread moonlight cut by tree leaves, they write with the blood of martyrs and their own warm blood."

"Thus unless we grasp the war, we cannot comprehend its literary reflections. Unless we enter Dandakaranya, we will not be able to take in the fragrance of flowers, music of waterfalls, secrets hidden in the hearts of valleys and the proud songs concealed in the wounds of those who climbed up the summits."

To conclude, I would urge you to make an attempt to understand the movement. One may differ with the goals or methods of the movement, but it is an undeniable fact that the movement is facilitating one of the most creative upsurges in the history of our land. It is giving expression to those kept unlettered and mute for thousands of years.

Publications that helped in writing this paper:

Adivasi Peasant Movement of Maharashtra – Repression and Resistance, 1994, Dandakaranya Adivasi Kisan Mazdoor Sanghatan.

Dandakarany Amar Shahid – Amar Shahidonka Jeevan Charitr, 1994, Janata Book Trust, Kalimela.

Dandakaranya Amaraveerula Jeevitha Charitralu, 1994, Janata Book Trust, Kalimela.

Dandakaranya Revolutionary Movement – Government's repression and people's resistance, 1994, Dandakaranya Forest Committee, CPI (M-L)(People's War)

Dandakaranya Sahityodyamam – Pariseelana, 1993, Dandakaranya Rachayitalu.

Dandakaranya Thunikaku Sekarana Cooleelu – Samasyalu – Poratalu, 1997, Krantikari Adivasi Mahila Sangham

Jhankar, cyclostyled journals, 1996 and 1997.

Kamalapur Baatalu Moosi Kranthini Arikattagalara? 1984, Kranti Prachuranalu, Secunderabad.

Kondagogulu, an anthology of poetry from Dandakaranya, 1997, Diksuchi Prachuranalu, Srikakulam.

Netthuti Godari, poetry anthology, 1997.

Sadhana – *Rago*, novel, 1993, Srjana Prachuranalu.

Sadhana – *Sarihaddu*, novel, 1993, Virasam.

Saghrshrath Mahila, Hindi organ of Krantikari Adivasi Mahila Sanghatan and its Telugu organ, *Poru Mahila*

Toorpu Kanuma, Sahiti Sanskritika Vedika, Organ of Andhra Pradesh Jana Natya Mandali.

Notes:

1 The revolutionary movement in Dandakaranya has been redefining its area of operation from time to time based on its requirements and challenges. The area has changed from 12 districts in four states to six districts in three states over the years. Further, some of the districts were administratively divided and I am sticking to the entire area for this paper.

2 K Aravinda Rao, the infamous police officer of Grey Hounds writes, in his book *Naxalite Terrorism – Social and Legal Issues*, "these areas are strategically suited for guerilla type of attack on government agencies. All these areas have vast forest stretches where the armed squads can move freely. Dandakaranya was the abode of demons according to Ramayana, where the demons freely moved about, desecrated the *Yagna*s and killed the saints. It is a queer irony of history that the present day revolutionaries have chosen the same name…" Of course, it is not at all ironical for a police officer to compare the coercive State and exploiters with Aryan invader Rama, exploitation and oppression with the *Yagna*s and those fighting against the exploitation and oppression with demons!!

3 Incidentally, Subba Rao was the first literary critic to analyse this novel from a social science perspective.

23

Telugu Revolutionary Literature: Growth and Pattenrs

Introduction

Any study of the history of Revolutionary[1] Literary Movement (RLM) in Telugu has inevitably to be a multi-disciplinary exploration since the RLM encompasses a number of different dimensions like social dynamics, literary experiments as well as literary reflection of society, politics of the ruling classes as well as the ruled, economic developments that have a direct bearing on the lives of the people, individual writers' efforts, differences within and influences from outside, repression by the state and pressures from other forces, so on and so forth. Each of these varied dimensions needs a detailed exposition taking into account quite a bit of factual developments. Similarly the RLM covers a wide period of more than four decades, beginning with 1967[2] when a new path was broken by people's movement in Andhra Pradesh when poets and writers began supporting and spreading its message, and to the emergence of the first consolidated organisation of the RLM – *Viplava Rachayitala Sangham* (popularly known with its acronym *Virasam*) on July 4, 1970 till writing of this essay. This time period of about forty years as well as the large span of activities undertaken by the RLM in writing, public speaking, analysis of contemporary events, rewriting history, joining and expressing solidarity with people's struggles in general and giving voice to Naxalite struggle in particular, facing State repression, debating with other streams of writing, are tumultuous in

---

Commissioned chapter for the forthcoming Vol. VIII of Comprehensive History and Culture of Andhra Pradesh to be published by Andhra Pradesh History Congress in 2012

various ways and comprehending all that momentous history in a single and brief essay would be near impossible. An attempt is made here to present a bird's eye view of the historic developments, origin, growth and identifiable patterns of the RLM, with pointers to future study and analysis.

Progressive trends in Telugu literature

Modern Telugu literature is known for its close relationship with social movements and progressive ideology ever since the ideas of modernism entered Telugu society. While colonial administration and education in parts of present-day Andhra Pradesh exposed Telugu society to modern ideas of life, and the irrigation facilities created by the British during the mid-19th century led to prosperity in agriculture bringing in its wake dispensable surplus flowing into arts and culture. That's why modern trends and questioning of tradition based on the newly acquired value system can be traced in Telugu literature from 1850s onwards. Though there were other voices that expressed this mood of the times, Kandukuri Veeresalingam (1848-1919) is regarded as the pioneer of modern literature in Telugu, because of his powerful expression and multifarious social reform activity. Veeresalingam's major writings span three decades beginning 1880s and during the same time his efforts were complimented by other writers and thinkers like Gurajada Appa Rao (1862-1915) and Gidugu Rammurthy (1863-1940) among others. The path-breaking efforts of these three scholars inspired several subsequent writers and the progressive, socially relevant and concerned writing tradition continued through national movement, anti-Brahmin movement, rationalist and women's liberation ideas, romantic poetry and progressive writers' movement, during the first half of the 20th century. The other part of the present-day Andhra Pradesh, which was not under the British rule also witnessed spread of modern and socialist ideas during the early part of the 20th century, some of them leading to Telangana Peasant Armed Struggle (1946-51) and associated literature, with a particular stress on song and other oral and folk forms.

However, there was a break in this tradition of social relevance of literature with transfer of power and some of the leaders of national movement occupying the positions of government. Till 1947, the British colonial rulers or their supporters were holding the establishment and progressive ideas in literature flourished because of anti-establishment character of the literature. But post-1947, the establishment seems to have changed and literature started losing its anti-establishment nature and began to be co-opted, resulting in going down in its popular appeal.

Post-1947 aspirations and disappointment

But exactly at a time when literature was losing its popular appeal, people started getting agitated as their aspirations for a better life in free India began fading away. Since it is literature that leads people in forming their outlook and inspiring them to find solutions to their problems, people were in search of such literature and found themselves at a loss. Thus the period of about two decades from 1947, Telugu literature has seen a lull. Writers subscribing to nationalist and romantic dispensations joined the establishment and lost their capacity to be socially relevant and inspire people, while those of *Abhyudaya Rachayitala Sangham*[3] (*Arasam* - Progressive Writers' Association) attached to the Communist Party of India, also started seeing people's progress through parliamentary path and thus joined mainstream. Poets who hitherto voiced the concerns of the people and wrote about people's struggles joined commercial fields like cinema or media and lost touch with masses, and began talking about peaceful transformation and collaboration. A popular example is that of Arudra (1925-98), a poet who published *Tvamevaaham* poems in support of Telangana Peasants' Armed Struggle in 1948, changed so much that he wrote "rebellion is a mistake" in 1962[4]. And this change of heart seemed to be general phenomena. Of course, Telugu literature witnessed some of the best prose writings – short story and novel – during the period, but they were either middle class sentimental or nostalgic in character and mostly away from the pressing problems of people around and their struggles. Thus, historians of modern Telugu literature termed this period as a period of stagnation[5] and arrival of *Digambara* poets was a shock treatment to wake up Telugu literature from its slumber and put it back on socially relevant mode.

Emergence of alternative people's movements

Even as *Digambara* poets were questioning the existing modes of thinking, writing and action among the literate middle classes, some sections of the same class were responding positively to the calls of people's struggles erupting all over. Failure of the powers that be in addressing the problems of unequal agrarian relations, widening gap between rich and poor, illiteracy and unemployment resulted in large scale resentment among people and for a decade beginning the late 1950s the state witnessed various agitations[6]. Indeed it was the time of world wide churning with Great Proletarian Cultural Revolution in China, Students revolts in France, Mexico and the US, Black and civil rights movements in the US, protests against the US role in Vietnam War, nationality struggles in Indo-China and Africa, and back home in India, tribals of Naxalbari paved the way for a new revolutionary thinking. The call of Naxalbari soon reverberated in Srikakulam in Andhra Pradesh, where Savara and Jatapu tribals fighting against exploitation and oppression for over a decade then joined their forces with the Naxalite movement. This movement needed oral and written forms of literature to spread its message and thus born revolutionary literary stream in Telugu. It is not surprising to see the leaders of the tribal peasant movement themselves becoming writers to spread their message.

Early signs of Revolutionary literature

If one looks at it chronologically, the credit of launching revolutionary literature in Telugu, at least three years before the formal organisational structure took shape, goes to Subbarao Panigrahi (1933-69) and Vempatapu Satyanarayana (?-1970). The earliest genre of revolutionary literature seems to be song and folk forms, used to inspire the tribal struggles that began during the late 1950s in Srikakulam. Subbarao Panigrahi's collection of songs *Agnikanaalu* (Embers) was published in 1968[7]. In fact, he began writing songs much earlier and his first book of songs *Arunakiranalu* (Red rays) came out in 1964[8], as part of Srikakulam tribal struggle prior to the Naxalite upsurge. The tribal struggle identified itself more with the Naxalbari line after the attack and killing of two tribals by landlords at a tribal conference on October 31, 1967. Subbarao Panigrahi's *Jamukula Katha*[9] about the incident is another example of early revolutionary literature. The leader of Srikakulam struggle Vempatapu Satyanarayana also wrote songs, which used to be sung at all the tribal meetings, and these songs were collected and published posthumously in 1973, in *Srikakula Satyam*, published by *Virasam*.

Towards the formation of a structure

However, these early signs of revolutionary literature were only rudimentary and confined to a few areas in a remote district. A powerful organisational form that would consolidate and extend the new literary school to the entire state had to emerge on the scene. The emergence of *Virasam,* the first of its kind organisation within the Naxalite politics[10], is an attempt to address that felt need and considered to be a historic inevitability. Indeed, there are a number of immediate and long-drawn causes that led to the formation of the organisation.

The major influence, quite naturally, was of the tribal struggle in Srikakulam district. Long suffered under the yoke of exploitation and oppression by migrant-merchants and landlords from plains, police, revenue and forest officials, apathy from all political parties including the parliamentary left, the *Savara* and *Jatapu* tribals of the district launched an agitation against landlords, police and forest officials under the leadership of Vempatapu Satynarayana, a teacher, way back in the early sixties. The tribal agitation turned violent with the killing of two tribals by the landlords at a meeting of the tribals' association in 1967. The leadership of the struggle looked up to a similar struggle that was blossoming in Naxalbari and soon the relationship became symbiotic. Charu Mazumdar (1918-72), the theoretician-founder of the Naxalite movement in West Bengal visited Srikakulam and hailed it as "India's Yenan" (the latter being the base area of Chinese communists before liberation).

The Srikakulam struggle attracted the imagination of many an intellectual from all over Andhra Pradesh - Guntur and Warangal being major centers affected. Laudatory poetry was written about the struggle. Students from lucrative fields like medicine, engineering, and law left their studies to join the movement. Many of them were later killed in fake encounters and Subba Rao Panigrahi was one among those killed.

On the other hand, the Telugu literary scene had witnessed a movement by six angry young men who called themselves *Digambara Kavulu* (Naked Poets) during 1965 to 69. They were rebels against the existing stagnation in literature. They wanted to break the hypocritical and indifferent attitude of the littérateurs towards the problems of the masses. Through sensationalism bordering on publicity mania they created a storm in the literary field by their novel expression and shocking treatment in writing poetry and making it public. They published three collections of poetry in 1965, 68 and 69.

Close on the heels of *Digambara Kavulu* came *Tirugabadu Kavulu* (Rebel Poets), another group of young poets from Warangal, the hot bed of peasant movement inspired by the Naxalites. The group got its name through its anthology of poems named *Tirugabadu* (Rebel, 1969) which avowedly supported the cause of the Naxalites and called on people to join the movement.

The celebrations at Visakhapatnam of sixtieth birthday[11] of Sri Sri[12] (1910-83), the legendary revolutionary poet who inspired virtually every poet in Telugu (indeed Telugus' admiration for him can be seen in their unfading qualification *Mahakavi* – great poet – before his name), gave a chance to blend these three channels flowing differently till then. At a meeting organised on the occasion in February 1970 a pamphlet was distributed by *Visakha Vidyarthulu* (students of Visakhapatnam). The pamphlet, titled *Rachayitalaku Savaal* (A Challenge to Writers) asked the assembled litterateurs to decide which side they would take in the ongoing struggle between the masses and the powers that be. The pamphlet cited the examples of the Spanish Civil War[13] and Subba Rao Panigrahi's martyrdom and urged the poets and writers to join hands with the Naxalite movement. Most speakers in the meeting reacted favourably.

Formation of *Virasam*

This formal polarisation in Visakhapatnam was taken very seriously by both the camps and each tried to consolidate its position by winning over big names in literature to their side. The government and the literary establishment wanted to prevent Sri Sri from lending his substantial support to the youngsters. Literary organisations and individuals owing allegiance to the parliamentary left parties also joined in the move against the Naxalite sympathisers. Thus the pro-establishment writers prepared to hold a two-day 'seminar on progressive literature' in Hyderabad during July 3-4, 1970, and felicitate Sri Sri with a money purse to be given by Chief Minister. The meeting was organised under the auspices of Seven Star Syndicate, a literary forum in Hyderabad, supported by Progressive Writers' Association and film stars. Kodavatiganti Kutumba Rao (1909-1980), *Digambara* poets, and *Tirugabadu Kavulu* opposed this conclave as a ploy of establishment to buy and co-opt progressive writers and asked the writers to boycott the meeting. "Is it proper for animal-lovers running to the seminar on non-violence organised by the butchers," asked Kutumba Rao in his appeal to boycott.

The previous night, the night of July 3, Sri Sri, in his own personal capacity as well as along with Rachakonda Viswanatha Sastry (1922-93) and K V Ramana Reddy (1927-98) announced that they were boycotting the bait and in the same breath proposed the need to have a new organisation for revolutionary literature. The same night, to be precise at 1.07 AM of July 4, 1970 Sri Sri along with 14 other writers[14] announced the formation of *Viplava Rachayitala Sangham.* The signatories included some of the *Digambara Kavulu, Tirugabadu Kavulu* and a couple of old guard from the *Arasam.*

Sri Sri was *Virasam*'s founder president and Kodavatiganti Kutumba Rao, a novelist, short story writer and literary critic and Rachakonda Viswanatha Shastri, a novelist and short story writer were its founder vice presidents. Noted literary critic and poet K V Ramana Reddy was its first general secretary. Along with these doyens of Telugu literature, a number of renowned as well as budding writers, poets and cultural activists joined the organisation. Its first conference was held in Khammam in October 1970. Since then, till its bi-annual conference and Sri Sri centenary in Visakhapatnam in April-May 2010, the organisation held its conferences or state-level literary workshops every year, except for the two years during the Emergency. Apart from these state-level annual programmes, *Virasam* has been conducting meetings, seminars, conferences, workshops and orientation classes both at state and local level for discussing various literary forms and contemporary social and literary developments.

The initial manifesto of *Virasam* released on July 4, 1970 was a brief statement of objectives. It reads:

"Reformism is outdated and there is stagnation in cultural affairs around us. Even the progressive writers' movement appears dead. Revolutionary Writers' Association is being formed to remove this doom and to take the nation towards a comprehensive liberation.

Every sincere writer has to take an uncompromising attitude towards today's exploitative system. Writers have to shed their fear and doubt to speak out the truth and stand by the people. They have to transform their pens into swords and torch lights. Revolutionary Writers' Association dedicates itself to cultural awakening and plans to make literature an important part of national life.

1. Marxian socialism is the objective of all of us.
2. Writers who recognise and support people's protracted liberation struggle are its members.
3. We support people's class struggles in whatever form they take.
4. Comprehensive independence of the country is our aim.
5. Removal of all the vestiges of colonial, feudal and capitalist nature and helping establishment of new democratic system is our aim.
6. Proletarian internationalism is our standpoint.
7. We whole-heartedly support people's liberation struggle in all the countries." (Arunatara: January 1990, p. 15-16)

This initial manifesto, however, was changed several times to add, delete and revise according to the times and improvisations in ideological perspective and the key portions of the current manifesto, which was finalised at the 20th conference of the organisation in Hyderabad in June 2006, reads like:

"Naxalbari armed peasant struggle has introduced the line of protracted people's war in the political agenda of India. It has given the objective of New Democratic Revolution with agrarian revolution as its axis, to the oppressed masses of India. Marxism – Leninism - Mao Tse Tung Thought has rejected revisionism in Indian communist movement both in theory and practice. It drew a clear-cut demarcating line and came to be a beacon light in the hands of struggling masses.

Srikakulam armed peasant struggle has also taken the line of Naxalbari struggle. Panigrahi who held both pen and gun became a guide and model for cultural activists. That is the historical context of Revolutionary Writers' Association. Marxism – Leninism - Mao Tse Tung Thought is the world outlook of the Revolutionary Writers' Association. Building up new democratic culture in the process of eliminating feudal and imperialist literature, culture, arts, theoretical trends and ideology, is the primary aim of the Revolutionary Writers' Association."

The manifesto also talks about its support to various nationality struggles in India, its solidarity with Adivasi struggles, its support to local and native languages, its opposition to religious fundamentalism and particularly Hindu communalism, its support to anti-caste democratic movements, struggles against patriarchy, and struggles to protect environment against imperialist greed. The manifesto also talks about the degenerated values promoted by the ruling classes and commercial interests particularly in the areas of sex and violence. "Opposing all these trends in literary, cultural, art, educational and other fields in the light of Marxism – Leninism – Mao Tse Tung Thought, Revolutionary Writers' Association takes it as its aim to constantly revolutionising culture, arts and value system through creation of people's literature and arts."

The manifesto also talks about its opposition to all the existing unequal and dominant relationships. It mentions the contradictions between manual labor and mental labor, town and country side, literate and illiterate, and those who can express and those who can't.

The manifesto respectfully lists its legacy from the role of writers and intellectuals in Bolshevik revolution and Chinese revolution, theories of Marx, Engels and Lenin on arts and culture and revolutionary mass line proposed by Mao in his Yenan talk, writings of Gorky and Lu Hsun, cultural revolution in China, as well as the progressive trends in Indian literature and arts with a particular mention of Premchand, Panigrahi, Kabir, Vemana, Phule and Joshua.

"The Revolutionary Writers' Association accords membership to creative writers, artists, cultural activists and people working on history, philosophy, education, natural sciences, and social sciences who accept this manifesto."

Virasam's contributions to literature, people's movements and middle class activism

The Revolutionary Writers' Association held 22 annual (later changed to bi-annual) conferences and 16 state-level literary classes in its history of 40 years. These events of the organisation were held in almost all the districts of Andhra Pradesh and thousands of people participated in these programmes. The strength of the organisation varied over time with over 250 at the highest and 60 at the lowest. The organisational structure also changed in the course of time. While the ad-hoc body set up on July 4, 1970, had a president, two vice presidents, a general secretary, assisted by a couple of secretaries, and an executive committee, the structure remained more or less same till the promulgation of Emergency in 1975. In the post-Emergency reorganisation, the structure became simpler with a secretary and an executive committee. Again in 1998, the structure was expanded to include a president, a vice president, a general secretary, a joint secretary and an executive committee and this extended structure was replaced by a secretary and an executive committee in 2006. Those who served as secretaries of the organisation were: K V Ramana Reddy, Cheabandaraju, Nikhileswar, Kalipatnam Rama Rao, T Madhusudana Rao, P Varavara Rao, Chalasani Prasad, V Chenchaiah, G Kalyana Rao, T Krishna Bai and G Pinakapani, all important names in Telugu literature while Sri Sri, K V Ramana Reddy, Chalasani Prasad, C S R Prasad and G Kalyana Rao served as presidents when that position exised.

The organisation did not have a regular organ till 1977 and during that time it used to bring out an annual special issue for its conferences, some times named Erupu (Red) while *Srjana*, monthly forum for modern literature and a very popular literary magazine at that time became an unofficial organ of the organisation. However, *Virsam* began its own organ *Arunatara* (Red Star) in 1977 as a quarterly, changed it into monthly in 1980 and bringing out consistently.

Virasam's first poetry anthology *Jhanjha* (Whirlwind, 1970) carried the poem '*Narudo Bhaskaruda*' (O Man, O Bhaskara, 1970) and it is considered to be a path-breaking attempt in Telugu poetry. This attempt paved the way for reviving the due respect for song and oral art forms in Telugu literature. Thousands of poems and songs, more than a thousand short stories, more than thirty novels, about twenty plays and quite a bit of literary criticism are the contributions of *Virasam* to the body of literature in Telugu. These numbers pertain to the writings of *Virasam* members only and there are many more writers who were influenced by the ideology and wrote revolutionary literature, even though they were not technically part of the organisation. *Virasam* writers have mastered the forms of short story and novel and presented the richness of life and ups and downs in the struggle of life in most realistic, reliable, creative and emotional way. Besides, *Virasam* members mastered the art of public speaking and influenced millions of people through their speeches ranging anywhere between five thousand and ten thousand. Not only as creative writers and analysts but also as social commentators and catalysts for and bards of a revolutionary social change, the influence of *Virasam* members is far and wide. A number of *Virasam* members have become popular and famous public speakers through their oration and analysis.

Literary criticism in Telugu had a strong tradition even before *Virasam*'s formation. But *Virasam* has placed literary criticism on a solid foundation of philosophical, historical, and political economy perspective. It is a recognised fact that *Virasam*'s literary criticism is far ahead in the analysis of relationship between society and literature, form and content as well as making this relation intelligible in a dialectical way.

During the last 40 years *Virasam* has published hundreds of books averaging 20 per year in various literary forms. All lovers of Telugu literature regard the achievements of *Virasam* in book production and literary forms as highly remarkable. *Virasam* had published the collected works of Sri Sri, in 20 volumes spread over 5,000 pages, Kodavatiganti Kutumba Rao's non-fiction writings – ranging over 6,000 pages in eight volumes, five-volume collected works of Cherabanda Raju (1944-82) and currently going on with 16-volume complete works of Kutumba Rao. *Virasam*'s founder general secretary K V Ramana Reddy alone had written over 20,000 pages of poetry, literary criticism, biography, history and socio-political commentary.

Any literary critic would agree that it is impossible to write the history of Telugu literature of the 20th century without any reference to *Virasam*. The reason for this prominence and this recognition is because of *Virasam*'s consistent adherence to peoples' literary and cultural traditions and creation of literature with highest standards.

Associating with other mass organisations

Post-1970s Andhra Pradesh has seen the growth of several students, youth, women, working class, teachers and peasants organisations and the credit, at least partly, should go to *Virasam*, since it was the writings and public speeches of *Virasam* members that inculcated the idea of "it's right to rebel" among people at large and middle classes particularly. One cannot find a serious meeting on contemporary literary, social and political issues without speakers from *Virasam*. In fact, during the 1970s and 80s, *Virasam* had contributed leadership to some of the mass organisations and thus *Virasam*'s role in Telugu society is varied and rich.

Repression on Virasam

Their role in society has naturally driven *Virasam* writers into a camp that is inimical to the rulers of all the hues. *Virasam* earned a great deal of wrath from the powers that be and received more than its share of prosecution and harassment. More than fifty of its members were arrested and implicated in all kinds of cases ranging from "unlawful assembly" to "conspiring and waging war against the state". About two dozens of its books have been proscribed by successive governments. A couple of its members who were also activists in the peasant and workers struggles were killed by police and vested interests.

The government proscribed *Virasam*'s poetry anthologies *Jhanjha* and *Le* (Rise Up, 1972), but the Andhra Pradesh High Court had quashed the ban order. Varavara Rao's poetry collection *Bhavishyathu Chitrapatam* (Portrait of the Future, 1987) was banned by the government, but later that ban was revoked. There are at least ten other publications, including *Ippudu Veestunna Gaali* (The Wind That is Blowing Now, 1971), a short story collection, and several issues of *Srjana*, monthly forum for modern literature, on which the government's ban orders exist as on today.

In 1971 Virasam members M V Ramana Reddy, Jwalamukhi, Nikhileshwar and Cherabandaraju were arrested under the Preventive Detention Act, but it was quashed by the Andhra Pradesh High Court. The historical judgment said, "nobody should be arrested for political beliefs. Political beliefs cannot be curbed by imprisonment." In 1973 *Virasam* members Varavara Rao, Cherabandaraju and M T Khan were arrested under the Maintenance of Internal Security Act (MISA). But they were released by a High Court order which said writers cannot be arrested for giving expression to their imagination unless there is a direct link between a piece of art and a criminal action. In 1974, police foisted the Secunderabad Conspiracy Case on *Virasam* members. K V Ramana Reddy, T Madhusudana Rao, Cherabandaraju, M T Khan, Varavara Rao, and M Ranganatham were implicated in the case along with some political activists. This case was under trial for over 15 years and in 1989 all the writers were acquitted as not guilty. Cherabandaraju died during the trial of this case.

When the Emergency was promulgated it was *Virasam* which bore the brunt of repression heavily. Outof less than seventy of its members, thirty five were arrested and most of them were kept in jail for the complete nineteen months period of Emergency.

In 1979, the Chittoor Conspiracy Case was foisted against *Virasam* members T Madhusudana Rao, Jyothi and Samvarta under the same charges. However, Chittoor Sessions Court acquitted all the writers in 1985. In 1986, the same charges were foisted against *Virasam* member Varavara Rao as part of Ramnagar Conspiracy Case but the prosecution could not establish even a single charge. After 17 years of trial Varavara Rao was acquitted as not guilty in 2003. Again in 2005, four members of *Virasam* – V Chenchaiah, G Pinakapani, S Ravikumar and N Venugopal – were charged under Aurangabad Conspiracy Case along with two other political activists and all of them were acquitted in 2010. Apart from these infamous and big cases *Virasam* members all over the state were implicated in about two dozen cases and charged with the same accusations.

The government also imposed ban on *Virsam* in August 2005 under the Andhra Pradesh Public Security Act and the statutory advisory panel struck down this order in November 2005 after listening to the arguments of the organisation why it should not be banned.

Differences within *Virasam* and emergence of other trends

Virasam, even in its heyday was not devoid of differences among its members on the questions of writing styles, relative significance of genres, relationship with political parties that lead people's struggles and the correct path of Indian revolution. Thanks to these differences, *Virasam* witnessed acrimonious debates within and outside. Even as the pro-establishment and anti-Naxalite forces in literature were denouncing *Virasam*'s writings and activities, members of its own ranks were raising all kinds of questions on commitment, role of writers in new democratic revolution, and left and right deviations within people's struggles. Beginning with May 1973 when Volga presented a paper on "Cultural Revolution and Our Tasks" at an emergency general body meeting at Tenali, a debate on the role of writers in New Democratic Revolution and the propriety of keeping Marxism – Leninism – Mao Tse Tung Thought as a criterion for membership in the manifesto raged. This debate finally led to split in the organisation in 1975, while the organisation said it expelled 14 members including Jwalamukhi, Nikhileswar and Volga, the latter said that they left the organisation against its politics of "left-adventurism" and "individual terrorism". Thus born a new organisation *Janasahiti Samskrutika Samakhya* (*Janasahiti*) in 1977 under the leadership of Jwalamukhi and Nikhileswar, among others. However, whether this organisation treats itself as a part of revolutionary literary movement is questionable since it talks about a broad-based united front against feudal and imperialist cultural forces in contrast to revolutionary trends in politics and literature. But it is true that *Janasahiti* could not attract any non "revolutionary" writers just because it did not have Marxism – Leninism – Mao Tse Tung Thought in its manifesto and had to be content with writers and artists supporting a particular revolutionary party only.

Similarly, there was another split in *Virsam* in 1984 when a group of writers under the leadership of Nammu, a poet, left the organisation after a debate on the manifesto and formed *Praja Rachayitala Samaakhya* (*Prajarasa*) which can be treated as revolutionary because it had writers and artists owning allegiance to a particular revolutionary party as its members, but the organisation did not continue for long. During the 1980s and 90s there arose different trends in Telugu literature like Feminism, Dalit literature, minority literature, Bahujan literature, and regional literature and almost all these trends levelled criticism against revolutionary literary movement for the latter's failures and inadequacies.

What did revolutionary literature achieve?

It's not very easy to briefly sum up the successes and failures of an organisation that has so much history with a lot of complexity. It would be worthwhile to quote from the organisation's own assessment of its successes and failures presented openly in its organ *Arunatara* at the time of 25 years of its existence. The assessment titled "Revolutionary Literary Movement and the Role of *Virasam*" (Arunatara: January 2006, p. 1-19) is a detailed presentation of the context in which the organisation has emerged and the constraints under which it had been developing. Based on this, the review listed out social context, capturing the concrete reality, creativity, democratisation, commitment, optimism, literature as a means of class struggle, iconoclastic attitude, and variety of literary forms and it also discussed failures of the organisation in all these areas.

Realisation of social consciousness of literature can be termed as a major contribution of *Virasam*. It has become difficult to talk about severing relationship between society and literature in post-*Virasam* days. Similarly in terms of understanding and capturing society literature always discussed whether it should be concrete or abstract. More often than not, writers and artists thought that abstraction enhances the artistic value of literature. But, it was *Virasam* which brought down literature to space and time specific concrete social reality. At the same time it never put aside the need to conceptualise and understand abstract concepts.

Virasam's another success was in demonstrating that creativity was not the exclusive prerogative of a few rich and powerful or a few upper castes. *Virasam* showed that the real creativity lies in the working masses and downtrodden. And it is only the duty of the middle class literate intelligentsia to support and highlight the literary traditions of the lower classes. This stress on the origin of the creativity led *Virasam* to democratise Telugu literature. Post-*Virasam* more and more writers and readers have come up to be connoisseurs of literature. The masses who did not have any contact with literacy and literary activity hitherto have started seeing revolutionary literature as their own and themselves began to write. Another aspect of democratisation of literature was that there was a manifold increase in the forms of expression with new dialects and new idiom coming into literature.

Virasam also contributed the idea of commitment of writers and artists to social cause. Post-*Virasam* writers and artists began not only to speak and write about the struggling masses, but also engage themselves in the day to day struggles of the oppressed masses. Another aspect of *Virasam*'s contribution is that it always imbibed a sense of optimism among its readers and followers. Strongly fighting against pessimist tendencies, *Virasam* writers inspired people to look ahead for a bright future and to never lose hope.

The last but not the least aspect of *Virasam*'s role in literature and society was that it identified the class struggle that is being waged in society and reflected it in literature. It always stood with the forces of future and always propagated the idea that literature can be a powerful means in supporting and spreading class struggle. The paper also made self criticism in terms of its failures in achieving the goal of revolutionising society. It listed out where it faltered and what could have been done to arrive at better results.

Conclusion

Revolutionary literary movement and revolutionary literature in general, and *Virasam* or other organisations in particular, are products of cumulative history of Telugu people and in turn they made history and became part of making history. It is impossible to separate *Virasam* from the history of Telugu literature and one cannot have a comprehensive history of Telugu society or literature of the 20th century without recognising the remarkable role played by this organisation. *Virasam* in particular and the Revolutionary Literary Movement in general are the products of history and they played very significant role in making history.

Bibliography

Anantam – *Telugu Sahityamlo Kallola Ksheena Dasaabdaalu 1965 – 1985*, Vikaasini Prachuranalu, Visakhapatnam, 1988.

B Sivarami Reddy, *Mahattara Srikakula Poratam*, Chaganti Bhasakara Rao Prachuranalu, Singarayakonda, 2006.

D Mohan Rao – *Repati Kavitvam – Jwalamukhi Siddhanta Gandaragolam*, Socialist Pubications, Vijayawada, 1973.

Jwalamukhi – *Abhyudaya, Viplavodyamaala Vaaradhigaa Digambara Kavitvam* in S V Satyanarayana (ed) *Adhunika Telugu Sahityamlo Prakriyalu, Dhoranulu*, Telugu Akademi, Hyderabad, 2005.

Jwalamukhi and Nikhileswar – *Virasamlo Vichchinnakula Kutralni Bhagnam Cheyandi*, n.p, 1975.

K K Ranganathacharyulu – *Saamayika Vyaasaalu*, Author, Hyderabad, 2000.

K Mutyam, *Srikakula Udyama Sahityam*, Drishti Prachurana, Hyderabad, 1993.

K V Ramana Reddy – *Aadhunikandhra Sahitya Charitra*, Virsam, Hyderabad, 1992.

K V Ramana Reddy – *Abhyudaya Rachayitala Sanghaniki Kayakalpa Chikitsa?*, Viplava Rachayitala Sangham, Hyderabad, 1972.

K V Ramana Reddy (ed.) – Sri Sri Miscellany – A Collection of English Writings, Sri Sri Shashtipurti Sangham, Visakhapatnam, 1970.

K V Ramana Reddy, T Madhusudana Rao and Varavara Rao – *Nannekkanivvandi Bonu*, Virasam, Visakhapatnam, 1986.

Kadiyala Ramamohan Roy – *Telugu Kavita Vikasam*, AP Sahitya Akademi, Hyderabad 1982.

Kethavarapu Ramakoti Sastry – *Abhyudayavaada Sahitya Vimarshana Drukpatham,* Visalandhra Publishing House, Hyderabad, 2004.

Kethavarapu Ramakoti Sastry – *Adhunika Telugu Samajika Kavitva Udyamalu*, Jijnasa Prachurana, Warangal, 2002.

Kethavarapu Ramakoti Sastry – *Sangharshana – Samvaadam*, Jijnasa Prachuranalu, Warangal, 2004.

Kotthapalli Ravibabu – *Aankshaloo Nishedhaalu*, Janasahiti, Vijayawada, 1998.

M Gangadhar – *Adhunika Telugu Kavitvamlo Viplava Dhoranulu – Oka Visleshana*, Pranahita Prachuranalu, Dharmasagar, 1994.

Rachamallu Ramachandra Reddy – *Saraswata Vivechana*, Visalandhra Publishing House, Hyderabad, 1989.

Subbarao Panigrahi, *Kalalu – Kavitvam*, Viplava Rachayitala Sangham, Visakhapatnam, 2004.

Tripuraneni Madhusudana Rao – *Kavitvam – Chaitanyam*, Virasam, Visakhapatnam, 2006.

Tripuraneni Mahdusudana Rao – *Sahityamlo Vastu Silpaalu*, Perspectives, Hyderabad, 1997.

Vempatapu Satyanarayana, *Srikakula Satyam*, Vipalva Rachayitala Sangham, Warangal, 1973.

Viplava Rachayitala Sangham – *Pranaalika – Nibandhanaavali*, n.d.

Viplava Rachayitalu – *Virasamlo Marxist Vyatireka Dhoranulanu Pratighatinchandi*, Aruna Sahiti, Hyderabad, 1973.

Various issues of Srjana, Arunatara and Erupu.

Notes:

1 This mode of writing is characterised as "Revolutionary" from 1970 onwards with the emergence of Revolutionary Writers' Association (RWA) which differentiated itself from the earlier trends of socially concerned literature. Particularly, the RWA called its literature "revolutionary" as against "progressive" literature of the Progressive Writers' Association, began in 1943 and affiliated to the Communist Party of India.

2 Generally the RLM is considered to have begun with the formation of the Revolutionary Writers' Association in 1970, but available data show that revolutionary literature was in existence for at least three years prior to that.

3 The PWA, *Arasam* in Telugu, began in 1943, enjoyed its heyday till the early 1950s, gone into oblivion following the 20th Congress of the CPSU (1956) and class-collaborationist policies. It was sought to be revived several times before 1970s. After the split in the CPI in 1964, the writers' organisation sailed with the CPI.

4 In the preface to Kesava Rao's *Udayinchani Udayaalu*,

5 See K V Ramana Reddy, K K Ranganathacharyulu, K V Ramakoti Sastry and T Madhusudana Rao.

6 The people's agitations during this period included land struggles, movements against price-rise, movement for setting up steel plant in Visakhapatnam.

7 Socialist Publications, Vijayawada.

8 Published by Srikakulam District Communist Committee.

9 Publiched by Virasam, Guntur in 1973.

10 The Naxalbari line in its earlier days was opposed to form any mass organisations, with an apprehension that mass organisations would breed revisionism as happened in the earlier history of the communist movement in India.

11 In Indian tradition it is customary to celebrate sixtieth birthday, called *shashtipoorthi* with fanfare. In Telugu tradition, years are named and sixty years make a cycle. With sixtieth birthday, one begins the cycle again. Though Sri Sri was a symbol of modernity and against tradition, Telugu literary circles wanted to observe this traditional custom, which ended up on a different note.

12 Srirangam Srinivasa Rao became popular with his acronym – pen name Sri Sri.

13 The democratic struggle against dictator Franco during 1936-39 inspired many a writer in Telugu, as it had done elsewhere. Almost all writers belonging to Progressive Writers' movement had fond memories of Spanish Civil War and the international solidarity it generated.

14 Sri Sri put his signature first and wrote time as 1.07 AM. The other signatories were: K V Ramana Reddy, Varavara Rao, Jwalamukhi, Rachakonda Viswanatha Sastry, Nikhileshwar, Ranganatham, Sripati, Nagnamuni, Umamaheswara Rao, Kesava Rao, Srinivasa Rao, S Hari Purushotham Rao, Pinakapani and C Prasad.

❖ ❖ ❖

V

Departed Friends

As mentioned elsewhere, I always grieve at the passing away of hundreds of close friends in the course of the movement. In Telugu I tried to write elegies on as many friends as possible to keep their memory alive. But when it comes to English their unfamiliarity with English readers becomes a major hurdle even though many of them had fantastic lives deserving to be written. Here are presented the tributes to six of my departed friends, who have become popular all over the country and contributed a lot in their own fields to people's culture and struggles as well as to the revoulutionary movement.

24

Cherabandaraju:
A Poet Who Questioned August 15

The day I do not spell out

The betrayal of August 15

I don't feel I earned my meal

said Cherabandaraju, a revolutionary poet, some twenty five years ago.

Though he did not live to see the current euphoria of golden jubilee celebrations of independent India, he was very much in the thick of the affairs and expressed his anger against silver jubilee celebrations in 1972.

In a satirical lyric on the silver jubilee celebrations he wrote,

It is a silver jubilee, they say,

Of execution ground?

Jails are the homes of masses, isn't it?

In a serious poem after some time, he said

I was 25 in 47

That day my mind was a

full blossomed lake with slogans of freedom

I was the edge of a generation

A ray that cannot be humbled by any weapon

I was the dawn that walked through

Upright over the history

... ...

Published in Andhra Pradesh Times, 1997.

But, now you know what is my age
This senility is not mine
But a symbol of failure of
Parliamentary democracy that
Destroyed me and my generation
No, this legacy should not continue

Cherabandaraju was an unmistakable powerful rustic voice who started composing free verse during the mid 1960s. He began as a poet through the group of six poets who called themselves *Digambara Kavulu* (Naked Poets). The poets' group was, in fact, a shock treatment like reaction to the stagnation and hypocrisy existing in society and literature at that time. They questioned every accepted value in society and literary establishment. A number of parallels could be drawn between them and angry young men like Beatniks, Black Panthers, *Bhooki Peedi*, etc. who raised their voice all over the world during the same period. The poets started as nihilists and publicised their poetry through sensational means. Starting from a confused philosophical state, four of them slowly moved towards Marxism and Naxalite politics.

During the transformation, Cherabandaraju wrote a memorable controversial poem *Vandemataram* in 1968:

O my dear motherland
You are the mother, the father and the god
Yours is the chastity that flirts with thugs
Yours is the beauty whose every limb is pawned in the world market
Yours is the forgotten youth that sleeps in the rich man's embrace,
Your intoxication is unruffled though spat at or denounced
You, dear mother, are the Bharati who stands resigned
To rats and bandicoots that burrough in the ripe fields
You are the lush prosperous land that feeds no mouth

Vandemataram Vandemataram
Yours is the courage that has got flags stitched
Out of the cloth on your body and goes naked
Yours is the wretchedness that moves restless
In the mansions built with borrowed money
Yours is the woe that fails to comfort
Children crawling over your milkless breasts
Yours is the famished coquetry that has taken
To the streets, decked in borrowed trinkets
Mother Bharati!
What is your destination?
Vandemataram Vandemataram

This poem stands at the cross roads of Cherabandaraju's life in letters. It contains both the hangover from *Digambara* diction and sensational elements as well as an anguish for motherland and a hoarse cry in search of a way-out from the predicament. That search led Cherabandaraju into his open sympathy for Naxalite politics. He became one of the key figures in the formation of *Viplava Rachayithala Sangham* (*Virasam* - Revolutionary Writers' Association) in July 1970 and he served as its secretary for some time as well as on its executive body.

Cherabandaraju was one of the first few who realised the need to popularise the message in song form. With a reed-like voice he used to sing the songs written based on lyrical metre and folk tunes. One of his early songs, *Kolimantukunnadi thithi ninda gali pothamga vunnadi nippari poniku ramanna poddekki poniku levanna* (The furnace is lit and the bellows are full with air, let not the fire go off, let not the time slip off) was an instant success in the period when Gaddar and Jana Natya Mandali had not entered the scene. People would ask Cherabandaraju to sing again and again his satirical song on Indira Gandhi: *Ammamma Indiramma sesindi saalu pomma nee nakili socialism maakasale vaddamma* (Enough is enough, we do not want your fake socialism).

Though very soft spoken, gregarious and emotional Cherabandaraju became the source of wrath for the powers that be as he wrote,

They erase with swords
The wetness on the children's cheeks
When I kiss them

His opposition to the establishment led him to prosecution and persecution, detentions, legal and illegal, implicating in cases and dismissal from his job as a teacher. Due to continuous imprisonment for more than three years during 1971 to 77 his health started deteriorating. But his determination was unflinching:

I will sprinkle my blood drop by drop
As the seed for the liberation of this land
Though I am in prison, I am not a slave
If I am shaken or slashed
I will rise like a wave again and again.

What began as a chronic head ache when he was in jail turned into brain cancer and Cherabandaraju had to undergo surgery for thrice between 1977 and 81. Even while he was on the death bed, the government dismissed him from his job which was later revoked after a widespread protest.

Two years before his death, in 1980, he wrote,

I'll ridicule death
And defy the enemy
I suffer from a disease
A warrior I am nevertheless
Even if the hand is cut
My fist will not let loose the sword

Of course, his sword was not a sword of a blood-thirsty person. As he himself admitted,

This soil fostered me by feeding my daily morsel
I will repay the debt by
Delivering her from the demoniac feudal oppression.

❖ ❖ ❖

25

KVR : A Multi-faceted Revolutionary Writer

The sheer volume of his work alone would have earned him the distinction and respect he commanded over more than two generations of scholars and progressive and radical activists of Andhra Pradesh. Indeed, it would not be a cliche to say that the death of KVR, on the morning of January 15, leaves a void in the field of letters in Telugu, as he had written restless for about five decades. About a hundred books and thousands of pages of published material both in Telugu and English - of poetry, drama, literary criticism, literary history, translation, letters, memoirs, court statements - stand testimony to his wide reading, perceptive thought and insightful analysis.

K V Ramana Reddy, KVR as he would like to be called without his caste suffix, was a historian and political scientist by training and profession. He worked as a lecturer both in history and political science. But he was more popular as a poet, literary critic, commentator, journalist, public speaker, and especially an organiser.

Starting from his student days in Student Congress and Students' Federation the flaming urge in him to organise for a cause made him the force behind *Abhyudaya Rachayitala Sangham* (*Arasam* - Progressive Writers' Association), *Viplava Rachayitala Sangham* (*Virasam* - Revolutionary Writers' Association), AP Civil Liberties Committee, India-China Friendship Association, and All India League for Revolutionary Culture, either in their formation or functioning.

Published in Economic and Political Weekly, Vol XXXIII, No. 10, March 7, 1998.

Born into a middle class peasant family in Nellore district in 1927, K V Ramana Reddy got educated in Nellore and Visakhapatnam. Nellore gave birth to a rich tradition of literature from mostly non-Brahmin castes and the Reddys produced some of the finest of the poets in the last part of the 19th and throughout the 20th century. The Reddys of Nellore were among the first non-Brahmins to enter education in a big way. KVR imbibed both the educational and literary zeal of his native land and his community and started writing poetry at an early age.

During his student days at Nellore KVR became a nationalist and joined Student Congress. He ran a written magazine *Kshatravani* for Student Congress. His disillusionment with the Student Congress came when his article on militant women Kalpana Dutt and Dr Achchamamba in their journal *Azad Hind* made the leaders angry. He was asked to leave the organisation and by then he started leaning towards Students' Federation. Gradually it was the radical intellectual atmosphere of 1940s at Andhra University that made him a communist. He joined Students' Federation and later the then fledgling *Arasam* in 1948.

Since then his first love was radical activity amongst literary circles, even as he maintained close contact with revolutionary politics in all walks of life. *Arasam*, IPTA and all other organisations associated with the then CPI have gone into slumber after 1955 in Andhra due to several historical and political reasons. It was KVR, along with a couple of colleagues, who tried to revive the organisation during the stagnant decade of 1955-65.

However, his attempts proved to be in vain since the guiding party itself was not interested in propagating radical politics. But then, he did not relapse into despair and inactivity as was in vogue then and tried to enliven the spirit alone. He went on writing poetry and literary criticism. In fact, he is one of the less than half a dozen souls credited with keeping the revolutionary spirit alive during that decade.

During the initial days of Naxalbari uprising, KVR opposed it along with his comrades in the CPI (M). But, he got a rude shock when his poetic outburst against the "encounter" killing of Subbarao Panigrahi was rejected and suppressed by *Janashakti*, the party's mouth piece then. Subbarao Panigrahi left an indelible impression on progressive intellectuals of the decade which finally resulted in the formation of *Viplava Rachayitala Sangham* in 1970. KVR edited six-volume collected works of Sri Sri published on the occasion of his Sixtieth birthday in February 1970. The celebration witnessed a polarisation amongst Telugu writers and led to the formation of *Virasam* on July 4.

KVR was the force behind the formation of the new organisation and he became its founder general secretary. He edited *Jhanjha*, the first collection of revolutionary poetry in Telugu for the first conference of *Virasam* in October 1970.

By that time he was an accomplished poet and literary critic with more than a dozen books to his credit. The most important of his publications was a literary biography on Gurajada, the pioneer of modern Telugu literature. The book, after more than three decades, still is a masterpiece on the renaissance in Telugu. His other major works include a literary biography of a peasant-poet Duvvuri Rami Reddy and edited anthology of modern Telugu poetry. He had also published three poetry collections, *Adavi, Angaaravallari* and *Bhuvanaghosha*, by then.

The post-1970 era enhanced the scope of KVR's work and he himself said that he got a youthful fervour again in those days. He published a number of books in quick succession, edited and translated a number of works and wrote prefaces to more than a hundred books. He started contributing to scores of journals in Telugu besides editing *Aruna Tara* and Spring Thunder, the organs of *Virasam* and AILRC, respectively. The *Virasam* leaders were instrumental in the formation of various mass organisations like AP Civil Liberties Committee (1973 December) and Indo-China Friendship Association (1974) and KVR had become the executive committee member and the General Secretary of the organisations respectively.

The activities of *Virasam* in general attracted the wrath of the powers that be and *Jhanjha*, which went into second edition within three months, was banned immediately. Arrests, searches, foisting false cases and tortures have become the order of the day to terrorise the revolutionary writers and sympathisers. As a culmination of these attempts there was the Secunderabad Conspiracy Case in 1974 against more than 40 revolutionary activists and five revolutionary writers. KVR was one of the accused in the case and he had to be in jail for three months before the Emergency. Ultimately the case was struck down by the court in 1989.

Besides Secunderabad Conspiracy Case, KVR was also implicated in two other "sedition" cases. The first one was for editing *Jhanjha* and the second was for supporting nationality struggles. As the General Secretary of the AILRC, KVR addressed a press conference in Goa in 1985 wherein he supported the right of nationalities to self determination. The government of Goa had initiated prosecution against him for sedition, which is still going on. In fact, KVR was in the process of preparing a court statement to read out during the trial.

The government imprisoned 35 members of *Virasam* during the Emergency and KVR also had to be in jail for about 21 months. In the post-Emergency phase, *Virasam* started coordinating with the like-minded organisations throughout the country and KVR was a key person in these efforts. As a result, All India League for Revolutionary Culture (AILRC) was formed in 1983 to which KVR had become the founder General Secretary. He relinquished his caste suffix from the AILRC conference dais in New Delhi. In the *Virasam* era, KVR published three poetry collections, *Erra Pidikili*, *Jailu Kokila* and *Suridu Mavodu*, and half-a-dozen major works in literary criticism and history. Starting from mid 1970s, KVR has been regularly contributing to Frontier, under the pseudonym Sudarshan, on various developments in the revolutionary movement in Andhra Pradesh. He enjoyed such a wide acceptability that there were dozens of journals which would solicit articles from him. He never failed any journal and it was estimated that he wrote about 7,000 pages under at least 50 different names.

KVR helped the PUDR's fact finding committee on Indravelli massacre in which several Gond tribals were killed by police in Adilabad district in 1981. He went round the tribal hamlets along with the team and helped in preparing the report. He also distributed the relief fund to the victims' families. Similarly, when tribal hamlets in Chintapalli were burnt by police in 1986, KVR wrote a book, Forests are Aflame, and formed a committee to help the tribal victims. On behalf of the committee he deposed before the Indian Peoples Human Rights Tribunal, which inquired the case.

KVR is always remembered for his early debates and analyses on woman question (1981), communalism (1984) and caste and class (1986). His was one of the earliest clear voices in Telugu over these pressing questions. He is also remembered for his principled stands in life. He never aspired for any positions from the establishment and shunned in unequivocal terms when he got them.

When the state government tried to give him honorary doctorate for his work on Gurajada, he declined to accept it. Even while appreciating and favourably assessing Pablo Neruda's work, KVR levelled serious criticism against the Chilean poet for accepting Nobel Prize.

Virasam had its 16th conference at Srikakulam during January 11 and 12 this year. As the organisation's association with the place is historic, KVR did not want to miss the opportunity to visit Srikakulam. In fact, he has been collecting information to write a history of Srikakulam struggle. He had already interviewed hundreds of surviving activists. He took an active part in the meeting and spoke in the public meeting on January 12. He complained of pain in the abdomen two days after reaching home and he succumbed to that after a couple of hours, as he was ailing from diabetes, hypertension and neurotic problems for quite some time.

In KVR's death, not only the revolutionary literary movement of India in general and Andhra Pradesh in particular, but also Indian peoples' literary tradition itself has lost a great contributor and activist. He lives in the memory of all those who cherish the organic relationship between society and literature.

❖ ❖ ❖

26

K G Kannabiran : A Humane Philospher

In the first week of November, a couple of days before he entered his 82nd year, Kannabiran told me that he was thinking of writing 'A Requiem to the Lost Leg'. He was convalescing after one of his legs, infected by diabetic gangrene, was amputated up to knee, and not allowing anybody to know that he was suffering. "I don't want people see me in this bed-ridden condition, image of Kannabiran in their minds should always be an active fighter for their rights," he said adding "but I want to write this obituary and make it public to thank this amputated leg that took me to so many places and allowed me to wage those battles for people." Except that he was lying down in bed covered up to chest, he looked brilliant and talked and joked and shared anecdotes as always. His "waiting in the departure lounge", as he was quite often describing his status for some years now, has ended at 5 p.m. on December 30, 2010.

The time has come to complete that unfinished requiem to the leg that took the person all over the country questioning the violations of democratic rights and challenging impunity of the powers that be. May be this time, the requiem has to be to the multi-faceted person, who was indeed a humane philosopher with social concerns.

It's a cliché to describe the death of a person as a void that cannot be filled, but in the death of K G Kannabiran, the renowned civil liberties advocate, "prosecutor of prosecutors" and a person highly

Published in Economic and Political Weekly, Vol XLVI, No. 4, January 22, 2011.

respected and loved by almost all the struggling communities in India, it is no longer a cliché and true to the core. Indeed Kannabiran was a passionate person who touched the hearts of almost everybody who was in suffering and made some effort to help them break out of that suffering. The multitude that he lent his hand was so large that it includes adivasis, landless dalit labourers, small peasants, industrial workers, miners, and the families of those killed in fake encounters and subjected to police brutalities as well as middle class poets and writers in Andhra Pradesh, adivasis of Central India, revolutionary activists all over the country, riot-victims in Delhi or Gujarat or Coimbatore or Bombay, alleged accomplices of Veerappan in Karnataka, arrested Tamil refugees from Sri Lanka, Muslims from Kashmir, the small Sikh community that was subjected to terror in Bidar, displaced persons in several "development" projects, victims from North East, miners from Chattisgarh…the list is unending. In one word, he used all his legal, personal and organisational skills to help all those who were subjected to the high-handedness of State machinery.

Being the scribe who sat with him for hundreds of hours and went through his papers, the legal documents he cited and innumerable literary and theoretical texts he quoted just from memory, this author feels privileged to know at least some parts of the gigantic personality with such a rich diversity in life, yet continuing to be unassumingly simple in committing himself unflinchingly to the cause of democratic rights of people. Our association produced *24 Gantalu* (24 Hours), a personalised social history, memoirs of K G Kannabiran, serialised in Telugu weekly *Prajatantra* for 27 months during 2006-08 and came out as a book in 2010 (Devulapalli Publications, Hyderabad). In the beginning it was thought to be an autobiography that he would recollect his life and dictate to me, but ended up as a social history of Andhra Pradesh in particular and democratic movements in the country in general seen through the eyes of a very sensitive and involved participant.

"It is so tedious to write about lived life. It is also very difficult to recapture the events, which led to your making. Fortunately what I am attempting is not my biography but about my response to militant radical movements in the state as a lawyer, as their defender in courts and my evolution as a human rights activist," he said. In the same vein, he wrote in his afterword to *24 Gantalu*, "…the brutalities I was witness to –

when I say witness to – very often refers to the deeds done before we get to the spot, the wreckage, the destruction wrought tell us how it was done. Meticulous recording of evidence enables us to reconstruct the scene as it happened. Exposure of these brutalities never did have any effect. Every visit of the fact finding team was followed by the Intelligence visiting the area and thrashing the people who spoke to us. The human rights defender who visits these places, in course of time gets dehumanised precisely for the reason these have had no effect. It becomes a duty to be painfully performed and later on it assumes the character of a pilgrimage. That was the reason why I was averse to writing my biography. A witness can at best record what he has seen or witnessed. Neither Tiresios of the Greek legend nor Sanjaya of the Hindu legend has anything to say about themselves. Their experience is limited to what they have witnessed…"

The fact that less than 10 pages in the 500-page memoirs cover his personal life is an indication of Kannabiran's philosophy of life. May be because of that modesty, simplicity, thirst for justice and self-less activity, details of his life are not very well known to people.

Kandadai Gopalaswamy Kannabiran (KGK in legal community, Kanna in his personal circle, *saar* and various altered and distorted forms of his name, filled with affection and respect used by thousands of his clients and admirers), was born on November 9, 1929. His father K G Iyengar was an ophthalmologist in Secunderabad's King Edward Memorial Hospital and mother Pankajam along with children left her husband after his second marriage. Thus Kannabiran had to live his early life in Nellore, declining from a well-to-do, "England-returned" doctor's family to a small-town poor family. Nellore in 1940s was a veritable laboratory of working class politics with P Sundarayya's early activities influencing every walk of life there. Kannabiran's elder brothers, already in their teens were influenced by these politics. Coming from an orthodox Vaishnavite family, K Seshadri (later to become political scientist) led dalit scavengers in Safai Karmachari Union and K G Ramanathan was to become a trade unionist in insurance sector. Admittedly, introduction to books through Seshadri and the political atmosphere in Nellore were Kannabiran's first leads in life. Anti-Brahmin movement of Dravida Kazhagam in Madras in the late 1940s and early 50s where he studied his Intermediate in Pachaiyappa's College and B. A. (Hons.) in Vivekananda College, and LLB in Madras

University exposed him to the need to fight the oppressive social structure based on caste discrimination. These influences of Marxism, struggle for the downtrodden and fighting against the injustice of social hierarchy informed Kannabiran's life for the next six decades.

Kannabiran joined Madras High Court in late 1954 and one of the first cases he fought successfully to force an amendment to the Indian Citizenship Act was based on the plight of a poor Muslim woman, Asia Begum, who went to newly formed Pakistan in search of livelihood, thrown out and sent back to India, with a paper in her hand. She did not know that the paper was called a Passport and that made her a Pakistani citizen, resulting in deportation notices from Government of India. This case, as he explained in detail in his memoirs, made him realise the fate of poor and illiterate in the hands of laws and governments. The humble childhood, reading, elder brother's ideas, political atmosphere in Madras, and the case of Asia Begum were key influences by the time Kannabiran was developing into a lawyer. "Much of my own understanding and clarity has come from what I have read (voraciously) through the years," he said in the preface to the collection of his essays, The Wages of Impunity – Power, Justice and Human Rights (Orient Longman, 2004).

Unable to maintain his cousin's successful legal office after the latter's sudden demise, failed attempt to join Mohan Kumaramangalam's office as well as the job his companion Vasanth Kannabiran got in Hyderabad led him to look at moving to Hyderabad as an option. Beginning in 1960, life in Hyderabad transformed the young lawyer into not only a much sought-after popular advocate, but also a receptive and insightful public intellectual. Thousands of cases he fought in law courts, hundreds of places he visited to document police atrocities, thousands of public meetings he addressed, thousands of thought-provoking articles and immediate responses to injustices show how versatile workaholic he had become.

Following his connections with trade unionists elsewhere, he began taking up the case of Singareni coal miners and that led to his entry into Communist circles in Hyderabad. Thus he was part of the attempts of the would-be CPI (M) leaders to form Andhra Pradesh Civil Liberties Association in 1964, but the split in the CPI distanced him from the efforts. His involvement with civil liberties activity earnestly began in 1969-70 when there was severe repression on Srikakulam tribal peasant struggle. Killing the tribal leaders and activists in fake encounters, arresting and implicating hundreds of people in false cases led to formation of Defence Committees by lawyers and democrats to expose the State policies and defend the victims.

Besides the Defence Committee activities, another major event that brought Kannabiran closer to the emerging Naxalite movement in the state was his appearance as defence advocate in the cases against ban on revolutionary literature and arrest of writers under the Preventive Detention Act in 1971. Three poetry collections of revolutionary writers, *March, Jhanjha* and *Le* were banned and Kannabiran argued against the ban on *March* and *Le*. He was successful in getting the ban order on *Le* struck down by court. Similarly when revolutionary poets Jwalamukhi, Nikhileswar and Cherabandaraju, were arrested under the PD Act, Kannabiran appeared for them and the act was set aside, with a famous judgement — "nobody can be detained for having political beliefs and giving expression to them" – delivered by Justice Chinnapa Reddy and Justice ADV Reddy.

The efforts to commute the death sentence of Bhoomaiah and Kishtagoud during 1974-75 made Kannabiran a real activist advocate. The two peasant activists were sentenced to death in 1972 and the sentence was ratified by AP High Court. Pending the President's clemency appeal, democrats all over the country, including Bhupesh Gupta, George Fernandes, K A Abbas, Mrinal Sen, initiated a movement against death sentence. The clemency petition was rejected and execution was to take place in November 1974. The defence lawyers used a technical ground to stay the execution but the hanging was again scheduled in May 1975, when the court was in vacation. Kannabiran moved a house motion and secured stay on execution. Finally, under the Emergency, they were executed on December 1, 1975.

It was during the Emergency that Kannabiran's judicial activism came to the fore. Since P Venkateswarlu, the then secretary of Andhra Pradesh Civil Liberties Committee (APCLC) was arrested along with several other defenders of civil liberties, Kannabiran had to take up the cases of arrested, illegally detained and tortured during Emergency. He used to file writ petitions almost on daily basis and during those 19 months he became a single source of challenge for the detainees belonging to different political views from Rashtriya Swayamsevak Sangh to Naxalite activists.

With democratic upsurge after the Emergency, almost all people's organisations became popular and broad-based and it was natural that Kannabiran, as a popular fighter for democratic rights in the Emergency, be in the forefront. He became the president of APCLC at its state conference in Warangal in April 1978. He continued in that position through the most repressive and crisis-ridden times till 1993 becoming the longest served president of the 36-year old organisation. It was during this time that the organisation spread its influence all over the state; became the real opposition to the powers that be; subjected to most brutal repression including killing its activists Gopi Rajanna, Dr Ramanatham, Japa Lakshma Reddy and Narra Prabhakar Reddy; and attracted people like K Balagopal into its fold. He was also associated with Peoples Union for Civil Liberties since 1977 and served as its national president from 1995 to 2009.

Kannabiran stands as the only advocate who defended the accused in almost all the conspiracy cases in Andhra Pradesh. He became part of the defence committee set up to fight Parvatipuram Conspiracy Case and Hyderabad Conspiracy Case in 1971-72. By the time of Secunderabad Conspiracy Case (1974-1988) he became the major advocate and in subsequent Chittoor Conspiracy Case and Ramnagar Conspiracy Case (1986-2002) he made important contributions not only to the defence arguments but also to jurisprudence on conspiracy cases. He always used to maintain that Sec 120-A to 124-A in Indian Penal Code referring to criminal conspiracy, sedition and waging war against government were vestiges of colonial administration and are untenable in post-1947 India.

Exposing and challenging the extra-judicial killings in the name of encounters is one of Kannabiran's major contributions. He successfully proved that the "encounter" lost its original meaning and became a deliberate State policy and was against rule of law and Art. 21 of Constitution of India. The reports of the fact finding committees he led into several such encounter incidents, his counter affidavits ripping apart the police versions of encounters, his efforts as secretary to Tarkunde committee, his defence arguments before Justice Bhargava Commission, his arguments before Andhra Pradesh High Court in Madhusudan Raj's encounter case in particular and before Supreme Court and the National Human Rights Commission in general have made people disbelieve the cock-and-bull stories police put forth after each killing. He also contributed to the change in the attitude of courts resulting in verdicts to register each and every encounter death as a culpable homicide, putting the burden of proof on police since they claim the shoot out was in self-defence. Even though police in Andhra Pradesh and elsewhere do not follow any of these judgments and guidelines of the NHRC, the efforts of Kannabiran and his colleagues have not gone in vain, as nobody today believes police version of encounters.

Another major contribution of Kannabiran, as member of Committee of Concerned Citizens (CCC), was initiating talks between the Government of Andhra Pradesh and the Naxalites. Along with other members of the CCC he met the underground leaders of the CPI (ML) (Peoples War) several times to get their point of view and approached the government for negotiations. Though the efforts failed for the first time in 2001, Kannabiran played a crucial role when the talks took place in 2004.

A considerable portion of Kannabiran's career as human rights defender pertains his arguments in favour of dalits and religious minorities. He was involved in defence arguments of a number of cases of atrocities on dalits in Andhra Pradesh and Tamil Nadu.

Kannabiran's defence of fundamental rights of people including the right to fight injustice was not limited to Andhra Pradesh alone. He rose to the occasion whenever and wherever a gross violation of democratic rights occurred. In the process he appeared and argued in a number of cases including Shankar Guha Niyogi murder case (1992-97), Coimabatore blasts case (2005-06), Nalla Kaman case (2007), Gujarat genocide cases (2002), Srikrishna Commission on Bombay riots (1993-96), APDR's case on encounter killings in West Bengal (1998), Shyamsundar Commission on Bidar riots (1987-90), Bangalore Conspiracy case (1992-99), Uttar Pradesh Human Rights Commission case (2002), Sri Lankan Tamilians cases including Ilango Natarajan case (1995-97), Premananda case (1997-2002), and Melavalapu case (1997).

All through his life he was fighting for rule of law and against impunity. The rule of law was creatively interpreted by him as adherence to the preamble, fundamental rights and directive principles of Indian Constitution. The Constitution is not just a document, but a result of people's struggle for equality and justice. Partial suspension of rule of law would subvert the systems and ultimately the law enforcement machinery would become illegitimate, he used to argue.

As a person he was very sensitive, loving, jovial, courageous and concerned. He had a quick wit. When a judge asked him why should the Naxalites be given Constitutional protection when they do not believe in Constitution, Kannabiran answered: "It is a test for the Constitution, not to the Naxalites. The Constitution was not selective and did not say that it wouldn't apply to nonbelievers. It was meant to be universal. We have to decide whether Indian judiciary can protect the democratic value system proposed by the Constitution – whatever may be the beliefs of the accused." He quite often narrated an incident in the forests of Medak when he went there on a fact finding mission into an encounter killing. Kannabiran posed a question to a shepherd he met there: "The Naxalites killed a landlord and in turn police killed Naxalites. Why should we bother?" The shepherd asked Kannabiran, "then why do we have law?" Kannabiran narrated this in court hall and in several public meetings to conclude, "unfortunately judges and educated do not have the wisdom that the shepherd had."

Though he attained a powerful stature and rulers would be afraid of him, there were some stealthy attempts to threaten and dissuade him from his work. There were at least half a dozen attacks on him by police and threats to his family members. He was remarkably fearless both in courts and in public life. Being a top legal professional in the country, he could have amassed money, but he led a very simple life and as he himself expressed, he shunned making money.

He would always ask his juniors and peers to be rigorous in studying the cases and the law and precise in making arguments. His approach to cases was humane and he used to tell lawyers not just note down adjournment dates and Sections of IPC and CrPC on the vertically folded dockets without opening them. "Just open those dockets, there are people inside. They are waiting for your concern and empathy," he would say. This urge to help human beings in removing their suffering and fighting for their rights was his criterion and that flowed consistently for six decades from Asia Begum's case in 1955 to a statement three days before death against the rigorous life imprisonment sentence to Dr Binayak Sen.

❖ ❖ ❖

27

Killing Azad : Silencing the Voice of Revolution

In a deliberate attempt to suppress the most powerful and articulate voice of Indian revolutionary movement, the State has indulged in cold-blooded, brutal assassination of Cherukuri Rajkumar, popularly known as Azad, spokesperson of the Communist Party of India (Maoist), along with freelance journalist Hemchandra Pandey on July 2. Azad was supposed to meet a courier at Sitabardi in Nagpur, Maharashtra at 11 am on July 1, to go to Dandakaranya forest from there. The courier returned back to the forest after missing him at the appointed time and place. Thus Azad might have met Pandey before that and might have been picked up either before they reached the place or at the place before the courier reached there. Dead bodies of both of them were shown on a hillock in the forest between Jogapur and Sarkepalli villages in Adilabad district of Andhra Pradesh, about 250 kms from Nagpur, with a story of an encounter that took place in the early hours of July 2. Since the "encounter" stories are very common and Azad is a very important functionary in the Maoist movement, this killing raises several questions that remain unanswered.

Andhra Pradesh is a state with about a dozen television news channels and one gets information flashes within minutes of happening. Around 9 in the morning on July 2 the channels started flashing that there was an "encounter" in which two Maoists were killed. Slowly the news developed to identify the dead bodies of two "top leaders" in the

---

Posted on several websites including www.mrzine.com.

beginning and a "top leader" ("because there was one AK-47") and his courier later. Within the next few hours it was speculated that the deceased were Cherukuri Rajkumar alias Azad and Pulluri Prasada Rao alias Chandranna, secretary of North Telangana Special Zonal Committee. By afternoon Gudsa Usendi, spokesperson of Dandakaranya Special Zonal Committee came online and told the channels that the second person might be Sahadev, an adivasi courier sent to fetch Azad, after an appointment in Nagpur. By the next day Usendi came again online and told that Sahadev returned back safely after not finding Azad at the rendezvous. Almost at the same time, friends of Hemchandra Pandey recognised the picture of his dead body that appeared in New Delhi edition of Telugu daily Eenadu and Pandey's wife Babita announced that at a press conference in Delhi. Pandey was not identified for the first two days and passed off as a Maoist and once he was identified, police started denying that he was a journalist, implying that killing a Maoist cannot be an issue.

The official version of the incident goes like this: On the night of July 1 police got information that there was some movement of Maoists in Maharashtra – Andhra Pradesh border forests for the last 10-15 days and a combing party consisting of police from both the states went in search of them. Around 10.30 in the night the police party identified the Maoists and asked them to surrender, but the intransigent Maoists, numbering around 20, started firing at them. In order to defend themselves the police returned the fire and the exchange of fire continued till 2.30 in the morning. The police party could not search the area due to pitch darkness and came back next morning to find out two unidentified dead bodies, along with an AK-47, a 9 mm pistol, two kit bags and revolutionary literature.

However, newspaper readers in Andhra Pradesh are sick of this version that they have been reading the same sentences over and over again for the last forty years with changes in proper nouns alone. That nobody believed the version handed out by police and accepted Usendi's statement was a commentary on the credibility of State machinery.

There are a number of reasons even usual believers in police stories could not trust this time round: Azad is known for his vigilant and alert attitude so much that police do not even have his recent photograph and content with a 30-year old picture of him. Given the importance of Azad as a member of politbureau and central committee, he would not be alone and would be protected by a well-guarded team if he were in forests. He could have been unarmed and single only if he were in an urban area. Newspersons who visited the site where dead bodies were shown also said that it was difficult terrain and would have been impossible for police coming out without a bruise, if it were a real exchange of fire. More over, there were no tell-tale signs of exchange of fire at the place except two bullets and the nearby villagers did not hear any sounds of gun fire, even as police claim that cross firing lasted for four hours.

The ruling class' wrath against Rajkumar was so much that even his dead body was not allowed to be accorded due honour. Rajkumar's mother, an ailing 75-year old Cherukuri Karuna, pleaded with the High Court to direct the government to bring the body from the remote Jogapur forest to Hyderabad, instead of a nearby hospital that does not have necessary equipment to protect the body from decomposition. She told the court that her age and health would not permit her to go all the way to Adilabad district and hence her request should be considered sympathetically. The court directed the police to postpone the post-mortem till the mother sees the dead body of her son, as if it was benevolently granting permission to a mother to see her son's dead body. Even at the ill-equipped hospital at Mancherial, where hundreds of people gathered to pay their last respects to Azad, heavy police force was deployed and people were dispersed with lathicharge. Finally the police allowed mother and brothers only inside the hospital.

Azad is a very popular leader of the CPI (Maoist) and in his capacity as spokesperson of the central committee of the party he interacted with a number of media organisations, including EPW, as well as with important members of civil society during the lat couple of years. People who know Azad for a long time describe him as the personification of commitment, experience and expertise.

Cherukuri Rajkumar was born into a middle class family of Krishna district in May 1954. His father, an ex-service man, shifted to Hyderabad to run a small restaurant to raise a family of four sons and a daughter, Rajkumar being the second son. Rajkumar had his primary education in Hyderabad and secondary education at Sainik School, Korukonda in Vizianagaram district. He did his graduation in chemical engineering at Regional Engineering College (REC), Warangal and post graduation in marine engineering at Andhra University, Visakhapatnam. He was a brilliant student throughout and his mother remembers: "He suffered from eyesight problem when he was in class X and had to begin using contact lenses. Initially he could not adjust to the lenses and arranged a friend to read out the lessons to him. By just listening, he secured distinction in seven subjects that year." Even when he was an activist, his teachers and friends say, he was a meritorious student as well as a prize winner in elocution and essay writing contests.

Srikakulam struggle broke out when Rajkumar was in high school and several of his family members were influenced by the struggle. His maternal grandfather's family settled in Adilabad district and some of them were part of peasant struggles in that area along with Kondapalli Seetaramaiah, one of the founders of the Naxalite movement in Andhra Pradesh. Rajkumar used to spend his summer vacation in that area and was influenced by the revolutionary environment around.

By the time he joined REC in 1972, it was a hot bed of revolutionary student movement, inspired by peasant movements in Warangal district, and being a very sensitive and sharp person, he became a part of that fervour. He was two years junior to and follower of Surapaneni Janardhan, a very effective radical student leader. Not only the impact of Janardhan, but also the peasant and working class movements in and around Warangal in the pre-Emergency days made a lasting impression on Rajkumar. Students of REC were in the forefront in forming Andhra Pradesh Radical Students Union (RSU) at state level in October 1974 and Rajkumar was part of that group. While the RSU held its first conference in February 1975 in Hyderabad, it had to undergo severe repression within three months, with the imposition of Emergency. Several radical students went underground to avoid arrest as well as to organise peasants. Rajkumar was also arrested under the MISA and let off after a couple of months. Janardhan, along with three other student activists, were killed in a fake encounter in July 1975 in Giraipalli forest in Medak district.

Giraipalli killing, along with several other killings, created furore in post-Emergency period. Janardhan, like Rajan, another REC student from Calicut, became a symbol of democratic rights movement then. Jayaprakash Narayan set up a people's fact finding committee under the leadership of V M Tarkunde to enquire the fake encounters in Andhra Pradesh. It was Rajkumar who helped Tarkunde Committee in gathering the necessary information and protecting the witnesses in Giraipalli forest and surrounding villages. Tarkunde Committee's report led to the constitution of Justice V Bhargava Commission which held its enquiry during 1977-78. It was again Rajkumar who helped the defence team led by K G Kannabiran in arguing the case before the commission. K G Kannabiran fondly remembered the help and efficient assistance rendered by Rajkumar during those days, in his autobiography *24 Gantalu*, published in 2009.

Radical Students Union was revived after Emergency and held its second conference in Warangal in February 1978 and Rajkumar, by that time doing his M Tech in Visakhapatnam, became its state president. It was at this conference, RSU gave the famous call of "Go to Villages" to students. These village campaigns of students brought out a sea change in the outlook of participating students as well as spreading the revolutionary message at the grassroots. The campaign was a prelude to Karminagar – Adilabad peasant struggles and in turn RSU gained strength through the peasant movement. The 'Go to Villages' campaigns directly led to the formation of Radical Youth League in May 1978 and Raithu Cooli Sangham in 1981. During these historic years, Rajkumar was the president of RSU. He was re-elected twice at the third conference in Anantapur in February 1979 and fourth conference in Guntur in February 1981. However, by the time of Guntur conference he was being hunted by police and he could not even attend the public proceedings.

In the meanwhile, both as the president of RSU and as a student of M Tech at Andhra University he led a number of struggles in Visakhapatnam in particular and throughout the state in general. Struggle against private local transport system in Visakhapatnam, under his leadership, resulted in nationalisation of city buses. He was a powerful public speaker and addressed hundreds of meetings of students and others till 1981. All these activities made him a dangerous person in the eyes of State and he was implicated in a number of cases, beginning from his arrest under the MISA in 1975 till arrest in a case of exceeding permitted time of a public meeting in Narsapur and burning national flag in Visakhapatnam.

During the second half of 1980 itself he chose to become whole timer and began his underground life and there was no looking back. However, even working clandestinely he never lost touch with people and his activity spread far and wide. In August 1981, RSU organised an all India seminar on the nationality question in India in Madras. Rajkumar wrote an introductory pamphlet as well as a paper to be presented at the seminar on behalf of APRSU. This seminar connected various students' organisations of different nationality struggles as well as radical democratic movements. As a follow up of the seminar, Revolutionary Students' Organisations Co-ordination Committee (RSOCC) was formed and culminating four years of deliberations, All India Revolutionary Students' Federation (AIRSF) held its first conference in Hyderabad in 1985. Rajkumar was one of the major forces that coordinated all these efforts.

For the next 25 years, he worked in different areas like Karnataka, Tamilnadu, Kerala, Maharashtra, Gujarat and Dandakaranya, giving theoretical, political and organisational inputs to struggles in all these places. He guided party units and committees in all these states as well as South-western Regional Bureau. He is known to have acquired fluency in at least six languages during this time. It is learnt that he used different names at different points of time for the sake of camouflage or depending on the nature of the job. He was known as Uday, Madhu, Janardhan, Prakash, and Gangadhar at different points of time. Though he was part of a collective decision-making body of the party, his personal contribution in terms of vision, expertise in several fields and a sharp insight into different developing themes helped the movement quite a bit. He was a voracious reader and a prolific writer. Given the nature of his clandestine activity he wrote under different pseudonyms, and more often credited his writings to collective, but one could easily identify his style in numerous writings in Voice of the Vanguard, People's March, People's Truth, Maoist Information Bulletin, etc. His hand could be identified in various documents of the party also. It is reported that he began thinking of international activity and solidarity about 15 years ago, demonstrating that he looked much ahead. It is also reported that he was instrumental in setting up Co-ordination Committee of Maoist Parties in South Asia (CCOMPOSA) and addressed its meetings several times.

A couple of instances of his theoretical, political and organisational guidance and coordination are worth mentioning:

When K Balagopal raised some fundamental questions on the relevance of Marxism as an instrument of social transformation, even as accepting it as an efficient tool of analysis, in 1993, a number of revolutionary sympathisers felt disillusioned and a theoretical rebuttal was expected from the party. It was Rajkumar who wrote a critical essay in 1995 and another in 2001 answering all the philosophical questions of Balagopal. Despite being so critical on the questions of perspective, Azad paid rich tributes to Balagopal after the latter's demise. The condolence statement stands as a model in recording both positive and negative aspects – respecting the significance of Balagopal's contributions to people's movements as well as mentioning post-modernist tendencies in him.

Consistently exploring the importance of the nationality question in India, he was again part of the collective instrumental in holding an international seminar on nationality question, under the auspices of All India People's Resistance Forum (AIPRF) in February 1996. Participated by scholars like William Hinton, Ngugi wa Thiongo, Luis Jalandoni, Raymond Lotta, Jalil Andrabi, Manoranjan Mohanty, this seminar had more than 30 papers on various nationality movements in India and across the globe. The seminar led to the formation of the Committee for Co-ordination of Nationalities and Democratic Movements (CCNDM), an important milestone in the expansion of revolutionary people's movement in the country.

In 2002, the government of Andhra Pradesh accepted the proposal of some well-meaning intellectuals and Committee of Concerned Citizens (CCC) to hold talks with the then CPI (ML) (People's War) to bring about peace. It was Rajkumar who guided the efforts of peace negotiations on the part of the revolutionary party and he wrote a number of statements and gave interviews to newspapers clarifying the party's position. The talks could not go ahead at that time, except a preliminary round between the emissaries proposed by the party and the government representatives.

Rajkumar was also part of the collective that guided Mumbai Resistance 2004, an event organised parallel to World Social Forum, which attracted quite a few revolutionary organisations from various countries towards the people's movements in India under the leadership of the CPI (ML) (People's War).

Again in 2004, in Andhra Pradesh the Congress party made an election promise to hold talks with the revolutionary parties and came to power. This time round the talks moved a little forward till the first round of negotiations between the representatives of CPI (Maoist) and CPI (ML) Janasakthi on one hand and the representatives of the government on the other. Beginning in May 2004 when Congress acquired power till January 2005, when the party withdrew from the process after gross violations of cease-fire agreement and spate of encounters on the part of the government, it was again Rajkumar who guided and prepared a lot of statements and documents for the talks. In fact, the party was so well prepared for the effort that it wrote the agenda, it prepared background papers on the three issues that were discussed and it circulated a number of documents and met with different sections of people to share the party's point of view, while the government, with its mammoth machinery and all resources at its disposal, could not even prepare a single sheet of information throughout and the government representatives did not do any home work.

Then again beginning with 2007 when the Prime Minister described the Maoist movement as the biggest internal threat, Rajkumar consistently exposed the real intentions of mining mafia behind the onslaught, including Operation Greenhunt. Through various writings and interviews in several media, he elaborated the party's positions on various issues including the peace process. Indeed, a number of statements given by him, an 18-page interview along with audio sent to press in October 2009, his 12,262-word interview given to the Hindu in April 2010 and his letter of May 31, 2010 in response to Home Minister P Chidambaram's letter of May 10 to Swami Agnivesh are crystal clear expositions of what the CPI (Maoist) thinks and does right now.

Azad's killing is an integral part of the Operation Greenhunt and by killing him the government wanted to scuttle the voice of resistance and revolution. The Operation Greenhunt is a mission of the Indian ruling classes to surrender rich resources of Indian people to MNCs and their Indian junior partners. Rajkumar was also a great resource of Indian people and the ruling classes have eliminated this resource since he was a powerful expression among those obstructing the outright plunder of people's natural resources.

❖ ❖ ❖

28

R S Rao : An Intellectual in Marxist-Maoist Tradition

In the sudden demise of R S Rao on June 17, 2011 in a Delhi hospital after a brief illness, the intellectual world that supports people's movements in general and the Naxalbari line in particular lost a highly perceptive and influential spirit. Thanks to the media glare focusing more on sensational events, he recently came to limelight as one of the mediators in the Orissa hostage crisis in late February when Maoists took an IAS officer and a junior engineer into their custody, but his life is much more than that event. In fact, he always used to tell that it is not the events, but the processes one should be looking into. Indeed, the real life process of Regulagadda Someswara Rao, coming from an orthodox Brahmin family of a small town on the margins of Agency forest in Visakhapatnam district transforming himself into a very insightful and inspiring Marxist intellectual, with thousands of admirers, is protracted, momentous and worth recapitulating.

R S Rao's multi-faceted persona has integrated several aspects into one in the best of monist as well as Marxist tradition achieving dialectical unity. A political economist, statistician, dialectician, teacher, writer, public speaker, master storyteller, a person with high sense of humour, a very sharp brain and a consistent friend, guide, sympathiser, and critic of people's movements – all combined into one was R S Rao. Born in 1937 in Chodavaram of Visakhapatnam district he came of age with Nehruvian model of socialist pattern of development (against which

Published in Economic and Political Weekly, Vol XLVI, No. 37, September 10, 2011.

he used his pungent criticism in later years) and did his post graduation in economics from Andhra University in the early years of Independence euphoria.

His career as economist and social science researcher began at Gokhale Institute of Politics and Economics, Pune in 1960-61 and he moved to Indian Statistical Institute, Calcutta in 1967. The city and its intellectual atmosphere in those days are well known for a deep churning giving rise to alternative ideas, theories, and practice. Thus the two-year stint in Calcutta not only brought Rao fame as a fine econometrician, but also transformed him into a committed Naxalite sympathiser and he used to tell how the police repression he witnessed in those days as well as reading volume I of Capital and Theories of Surplus Value brought about the sea change in him. In 1969 he came back to Pune and began his life as an outgoing person that he was for the next forty years. Whether it was Pune or Bombay, Calcutta, Nagpur, Delhi, Hyderabad, Warangal, Visakhapatnam, Sambalpur or remote corners of Dandakaranya, he had flocks of friends, students and admirers discussing his ideas, with or without him.

That impressive stature began to take shape in Pune in the early 1970s when he was instrumental in forming *Sparsh*, a bi-lingual magazine and the group around it. The group and the magazine was the earliest platform for Marxist-Leninist-Maoist oriented debates, discussions, initiations, actions, and work among students and workers. He was so consistent in his ideas and practice that after 40 years also he was doing similar intellectual inspirational activity among students, writers and journalists in Hyderabad, whether it was with *Viplava Rachayitala Sangham* (*Virasam*) or *Veekshanam* monthly journal or revolutionary sympathisers.

In 1974 Rao left Pune to join the Economics Department at Sambalpur University. The university in Burla, an educational township that emerged amidst western Orissa's tribal heartland provided the ground of fertile objective reality to Rao's critical analysis and intellectual application. Based in Sambalpur, he was equally nearer and distant to the revolutionary movement he supported, criticised, corrected and admired. Though Srikakulam struggle suffered setback by then, there was an attempt to regroup which culminated in the upsurge of Karimnagar - Adilabad peasant struggles in the late 1970s. RS Rao's direct intellectual engagement with revolutionary practice dates back to this period, continued through the Maoists' experiments in alternative development model in Dandakaranya and till his participation in negotiations with the government of Orissa, as a mediator on behalf of the Communist Party of India (Maoist).

His residence in Sambalpur, B-1, Jyoti Vihar, came to be known as B1 Collective, was the centre for several socially concerned activities including *Anveshan*, a weekly debate on current topics of students, researchers and employees. "Physically B-1Collective is a staff quarters at Sambalpur University, Burla. That quarters gave shelter to Rao and Bharathi for almost 25 years. It is not a home, not a house, but remained as a shelter evolving over time as a place of intellectual activity. It does not have fixed kitchen, does not have a fixed bedroom, dining room or a drawing room. Depending upon the convenience, its open verandah in the front served as a living place, study place and discussion place," as reminisced by his students. He was in Sambalpur University till his retirement in 1997. During these two decades he not only involved himself in social activities in and around Sambalpur (various fact finding committees, studies, delegations and public lectures, informal Institute for the Study of Society and Culture, besides the debating group), he frequented to Andhra Pradesh and other places to address meetings of writers, students, youth and academics. His sharp analysis of history, social relations, politics, economy and revolutionary movement would enthrall audiences and whoever heard him once would not leave a chance to attend his meeting again.

What was so special about him? Doing incisive research based on facts on any issue, looking differently from others, posing new questions that others do not pose or ignore, provoking to find new answers to these new questions, always bringing back the analysis nearer to reality, making inspiring arguments, providing unquestionable evidence from experience and study and more importantly using and explaining Marxist methodology in lucid terms – these were his characteristic traits.

His major contributions in political economy, Marxist understanding of society and people's movements are several. In 1990, his essay *Abhivruddhi Velugu Needalu* (Development – Light and Shadows) was a thought-provoking event in Telugu society. In that essay he said, "Hirakud dam is next to Sambalpur University where I teach. The dam on the Mahanadi is a multi-purpose project that irrigates

150,000 acres, besides producing a few thousand megawatts of power. However, a number of small villages around this dam do not have electricity. One day I happened to ask a tribal in one of these villages about this and he answered: 'A lamp would throw light around, but it also creates a shadow beneath and there is space in that shadow'. His quick response seemed to me like a philosophical reply. Indeed, the concept of development is complex and simple at the same time. It can be understood simply because of its strong visibility. It is complex since we do not understand the shadow it creates as we do the light it creates."

In the same essay, he tried to define development: "Any development of productive forces is the result of inherent human labour and knowledge. Again that knowledge is born out of a world view. Thus a development project in any form, in the ultimate analysis, takes shape out of a certain world view. Then, the essence of a development project is nothing but the world view that gives rise to the project. In that sense, if one wants to find out whether a dam or a factory or a college is development or not, one has to see whether this development project had brought any change in the world view around it or blended itself with the other world view that is dominant around."

With this understanding on development, he proposed an idea that in popular Indian discourse there is a misconception of treating "development projects" as "development" per se.

However, this sharp questioning and analysis could be traced much earlier when he intervened in the famous mode of production debate in the pages of Economic and Political Weekly. His small piece 'In Search of a Capitalist Farmer' raised at least two important questions then. One was on the use of "per acre value of modern capital equipment" and he said: "the basic idea in taking this as an indicator seems to be to see how far the cultivator has been converting a part of his surplus into capital. If that be so, it is important to note that it is not a necessary indicator, and that it at times it may not be possible for certain farmers (due to either the limitations of scale of production and/or the availability of surplus), to possess modern equipment; but they would still remain in the category of capitalist farmers. Modern is a relative term. An iron plough is more modern than a wooden plough, and a tractor is still more modern; and the three co-exist at a point of time. What connotes the capitalist character is the increasing accumulation of capital, whether old or new."

The second point he mentioned in this piece and further elaborated in 'In Search of a Theory of Agrarian Relations' presented at the second annual conference of the Andhra Pradesh Economic Association, Warangal in 1984 was "what is important in a study of social relations is not 'what is' but 'what is becoming'….to see the dynamics rather than study the statics, and project on the basis of a theory, dynamic implications".

This idea of constant motion was very crucial in all his writings and expositions, irrespective of the theme he was discussing. If there was any other preoccupation that informed his thought, it was the concept of people and labour. Whatever may be the topic he would search for these aspects in it and arrive at startling revelations. A major essay in this regard was History of Ahistoric People, that was commissioned and not surprisingly rejected by the Times of India in 1991.

He was also a keen analyst of literature and his literary criticism was tinged with his political economy and sense of history. Particularly he was enamoured by Gurajada Appa Rao's play *Kanyasulkam* and Kalipatnam Rama Rao's short story *Yajnam* and quoted, analysed, criticised and developed from these two texts. *Kanyasulkam* written in 1892 and revised in 1909 is a social satire that looked critically at the late 19th century orthodoxy, emerging alliance between feudal and colonial ruling classes and tastes and pretensions of modernity while *Yajnam* written in the late 1960s talks about the post-Independent Nehruvian development model of rural development and its disastrous consequences. No wonder these two texts turned out to be sources of diverse analyses for R S Rao.

His not so many writings do not match the innumerable oral discourses and debates he participated in. He left a little over sixty thought provoking essays, both in English and Telugu. His publications include *Abhivruddhi Velugu Needalu* (1990), Towards Understanding Semi Feudal Semi Colonial Society (1995), *Kotthachoopu* (2010) and co-authored On Education (2010) with Mudunuri Bharathi. He was also one of the editors of Fifty Years of Andhra Pradesh 1956-2006 (2007) and supervised a number of M Phil and Ph D theses on themes like handloom industry in western Orissa and agricultural labourers in Orissa.

Remembering R S Rao would be incomplete if his ideas on the Naxalite movement are not taken note of. In a paper presented at a seminar at Indian Statistical Institute, Delhi on the models of the Seventh Five Year Plan in 1984, he said, "the Naxalites may not yet have succeeded but the issues they have raised regarding the centrality of the poor peasant and agricultural labour of the Indian economic scene, the consequent poverty and the market question on the one hand, and the question of depending on foreign technology and aid on the other remain the themes that provide a framework, however loose, for understanding the Indian reality." He not only recognised this fundamental aspect of the Naxalite movement's significance, but also gave his best to strengthen that framework. Adding this with the Marxian understanding of historical motion, he would never openly denounce even the "excesses" of the revolutionary movement, about which middle class was jumping to pronounce judgments. Intervening in the debate on the "private violence" of the revolutionaries, he said, "the sensitive people who think that there is a systematic evolution of punishments and a movement towards civility, should remember that feudal and capitalist ruling classes do not have civic sense at all. These classes use the first opportunity to brutally massacre the people waging struggles against them. Either through draconian legislations or with scant regard for law, the ruling classes indulge in State violence. For that reason, there is no need for the 'autonomous' civil libertarians to preach the people about the 'violence' and 'brutality' of the struggling people who are waging a fight for their lives. The forms of struggle of the oppressed are determined by the repressive acts of the rulers."

That does not mean that he never had any criticism against the revolutionary movement. He certainly had and expressed at the forums he thought proper. But he was very optimistic and would always say, "I believe in practice. Yes, there will be mistakes, but one who is in practice will learn and correct himself. Human being has a potential to make mistakes and correct them and move forward. Revolutions and revolutionaries also follow the same path."

In the second week of March he fell ill with lung problem as well as suspected blocks in heart. Malkangiri hostage crisis began when he was in ICU in a Hyderabad hospital and two days after he was discharged, the Andhra Orissa Border Special Zonal Committee of the CPI (Maoist) had announced that R S Rao would be one of the three mediators. He brushed away the advice of some friends not to undertake this strenuous job in such a health condition. "When the party reposed such a confidence in me, I have to rise to the occasion" he said and went to Bhubaneswar. His piercing comment after the crisis ended was, "we got the IAS officer and the engineer released within a week, but how can I answer Seetanna's wife. The party was only asking the government to tell what happened to that tribal boy, who was picked up by the BSF three months ago. We could not get the government answer. Is the IAS officer's life more equal than that of the tribal?"

That question of an intellectual on behalf of the exploited and oppressed tribal remains unanswered.

❖ ❖ ❖

29

Kishenji: Epitome of Indian Revolution

Biography of Kishenji (Mallojula Koteswara Rao), more than many of his comrades, reads like the complete history of Indian revolution and symbolises its spread, depth and versatility. In his revolutionary life that spanned nearly four decades, he was present in almost all the major battles Indian revolution waged, all the turns and twists it undertook, all the spheres of activity it engaged in and all the sacrifices and steadfast efforts that made the CPI (Maoist) "the biggest internal security threat" in the eyes of the rulers. He sported more than half-a-dozen *noms de guerre* and wrote under many more names to be there in each of these activities at various points of time or at the same time in as many places. Before brutally killed in his 57th year on November 24, 2011, he spent about 40 years in the cause of people and inspired and attracted thousands of people from all walks of life towards Marxism and revolution. He inspired many more people to lend their hand to revolutionary activity, even if not joining the revolution per se. As a sensitive human being, fired with revolutionary zeal, he touched the hearts of thousands of people. Indeed, not only major shifts, but also even minor nuances in his life have something to do with masses in general or mass struggles under the Naxalbari line in particular.

Mallojula Koteswara Rao was born in 1954 into a middle class orthodox Brahmin family of Peddapalli, a small town in Karimnagar district. His father Venkataiah, a priest by profession, had participated

---

Written in 2012, Unpublished.

in anti-Nizam struggle as a Congress man and continued to believe in Congress well into 1970s. However, the father's democratic approach as well as encouragement from mother Madhuramma allowed a pluralist enthusiasm in the family and both Koteswara Rao and his younger brother Venugopal could traverse the troubled paths of revolution.

Besides the favourable atmosphere in the family, earliest influences on Koteswara Rao include Thakur Rajaram Singh, a local advocate, socialist and amateur historian-archeologist, lingering memories of Telangana Peasant Armed Struggle (1946-51) that extended to the Ramagiri hill range in the vicinity of Peddapalli and Separate Telangana movement of 1969. Singh was one of the few initial scholars who discovered the region's historical significance and did extensive research with whatever modest tools available to him. In fact, Peddapalli and surrounding areas on the borders of the Godavari happen to be the earliest known human settlements, with ubiquitous cairns and traces of several important cities of Satavahana era on the banks of the river and many relics of Buddhist predominance in the area during that time. Singh used to inculcate a sense of pride and an exploratory attitude among children and students in the area. As a neighbour, it was natural for Koteswara Rao to come under the influence of Singh. Similar was the influence of Telangana Peasant Armed Struggle. The hill range on the eastern horizon of Peddapalli was the shelter of armed peasant squads in the late 1940s and the struggles led by Gattupalli Muralidhar Rao and Anabheri Prabhakar Rao were still fresh in public memory. Thus brought up with ideals of social service, democracy, pride in one's own people's history and memories of struggle, as a high school student Koteswara Rao naturally jumped into the mass movement that erupted in 1969 demanding creation of a separate state of Telangana. It is reported that he, along with other students, was arrested and spent some time in jail during this time and tasted the brutality of State at a tender age.

That was the time when Naxalbari politics were entering Telangana and the students and youth disillusioned with the failure of separate Telangana movement were looking at the Naxalite alternative with enthusiasm. Exactly in this period Koteswara Rao spent three years in Karimnagar town for his graduation and he not only graduated in Bachelor of Science, but also learnt his Marxism and commitment to people's alternative politics there. That was the time when the first open organisations that propagated the Naxalite politics – Viplava Rachayitala

Sangham (Revolutionary Writers' Association), popularly known as Virasam, and Jana Natya Mandali (People's Cultural Forum) – began their activities in Andhra Pradesh and he was part of the student group that organised the meetings of these organisations in Karimnagar.

While the Communist Party of India (Marxist – Leninist) formed under the leadership of Charu Mazumdar opposed setting up of any mass organisations with the idea that such organisations would lead to economism and revisionism, as vogue in the CPI and CPI (M) tradition, the M-L leadership in Andhra Pradesh thought that there was a need and scope for mass organisations which could break away from the revisionist tradition and take up political work also. With that aim and as an exploratory activity both the literary and cultural organisations were formed and in fact they had to undertake their activity when the actual struggle in Srikakulam was suffering set back. Vempatapu Satyanarayana and Adibhatla Kailasam, both the architects of the struggle were killed by police on July 10, 1970, but the Revolutionary Writers' Association formed a week earlier on July 4 continued to keep the flame alive. Jana Natya Mandali joined the efforts in 1972 and both the organisations together spread the revolutionary message all over Andhra Pradesh and attracted thousands of students and youth into the revolutionary political fold. Thus inspired students from all over the state began forming local units and bodies and engaged both in struggles on student issues as well as propagating revolutionary politics or directly joining the armed struggle. Koteswara Rao was one among hundreds that joined these forces in Karimnagar.

The efforts of revolutionaries in Andhra Pradesh under the leadership of Kondapalli Seetaramaiah for about three years, after the death of Charu Mazumdar and disintegration of the CPI (M-L), culminated in evolving a self-critical document called Road to Revolution, officially released by COC, CPI (M-L) in 1975. The document clearly broke new path in rejecting some of the left deviations of Naxalbari line and at the same time hailing and taking pledge to continue the positive aspects of Naxalbari upsurge. Road to Revolution and its companion Self Critical Report were bases for rural mass work of the party and revolutionary students and youth of Karimnagar, Koteswara Rao being one of them, were putting those ideas in practice.

After finishing graduation, he came to Osmania University, Hyderabad in 1974 to join law but by then he was so much immersed in radical politics that he gave up his studies soon. The first ever attempt to consolidate and coordinate all the radical students into a single structure in October 1974 led to the formation of Progressive Democratic Students Union and some radical students who differed with the manifesto and orientation of the new organisation thought it was also treading the path of previous mass organisations. They broke away from the organisation at its first conference itself. The major bone of contention was whether a students' organisation should confine itself to agitating on students' issues or could also propagate the politics of armed revolution. Taking the radical stance in prolonged serious debates, students supporting CPI (M-L) COC formed Andhra Pradesh Radical Students Union (APRSU).

Koteswara Rao was among the founders of the RSU and his life as a full time revolutionary could have started then. The RSU had its first state level conference in February 1975 in Hyderabad and Koteswara Rao was one of the organisers. However, the RSU could not continue its activity since Emergency was proclaimed in June 1975. But, it was Koteswara Rao and his friends in Karimnagar who held a series of meetings within the respite of three months to inspire students towards the struggle. When Emergency was proclaimed most of the leaders and cadres of the RSU chose to evade arrest and worked clandestinely among students, youth, peasants and agricultural labourers. Suspending fundamental rights and arresting thousands of people from a spectrum of opponents from right-wing reactionary Rashtriya Swayamsevak Sangh to radical Naxalites, Indira Gandhi's government wanted to show itself as progressive and announced a 20-point programme that paid lip service to the amelioration of the deprived sections of the society. The radical students who went to villages began organising people to demand the implementation of the programme and exposed the dubious nature of the ruling classes. In the process, they undertook serious rural studies and came out with wonderful analyses on rural agrarian structure, prevalent feudal practices and the need for agrarian revolution. Emergency was in operation for 19 months and that time was fully used by the radicals to establish themselves among the rural poor.

When the Emergency was lifted and there was a short period of opportunities for over ground work, there was an attempt to consolidate the previous organisational efforts. Peasants and agricultural labourers were mobilised into associations in hundreds of villages against feudal exploitation and oppression. Even as the whole of Karimnagar was at a boiling point at that time, situation was ripe in Jagityal and Sircilla taluqs and on September 9, 1978, a massive public meeting – Jagityal Jaitrayatra (Victory March of Jagityal) was organised. As a simple indication of the credibility of and the hopes people reposed in the radicals, the meeting received hundreds of applications for redressal of grievances ranging from family disputes to change in agrarian relations.

In the post-Emergency period, not only the RSU was revived and held its second conference in February 1978 in Warangal, but also Radical Youth League (RYL) was formed and its first conference took place in June 1978 in Guntur. While the RSU conference called upon students to take up 'Go to Villages' campaign, the RYL conference was a result as well as booster for the campaign. Within a short time units of Rytu Cooli Sangham (RCS) were formed in hundreds of villages and Koteswara Rao was part of the collective that was behind all these efforts.

He became secretary of the district committee of the CPI (M-L) AP State Committee, as the earlier form of the CPI (Maoist) known then. The peasant struggles of Karimnagar and Adilabad were so inspiring to people all over the country that several genuine revolutionaries looked up to this path and as a result CPI (M-L) (Peoples War) was formed in April 1980. As one of the architects of the powerful peasant struggles, naturally Koteswara Rao became the first state secretary of the newly formed revolutionary party. He continued to be there till 1984 in the same position and later on when the functioning of the party became collective he became part of three-member secretariat. One doesn't know exactly what were the positions held by him during the next twenty five years, but at the time of his death, he came to be known as a member of Central Committee and Politbureau in charge of West Bengal. It is also reported that he was also looking after the party's relationship with the nationality movements and international relations.

A person inclined to literature, he was very particular about writing poetry and documenting each and every experience in the mass work. He gave a lot of importance to propaganda work and personally supervised various journals run by the party and mass organisations. He made the activists and local organisers write reports on their struggles and published them concurrently. During his time, Kranti the fortnightly organ of the Peoples War state committee was published regularly and its publication wing had brought out more than 50 books, including translations and reports.

He was also a fine strategist and planner thinking much ahead of many of his companions. It was under his secretaryship, the party had undertaken a daredevil attempt to get KS released from jail. It was during this time not only the earlier organisations like the RSU and the RYL flourished and swelled in numbers, but also new mass oragnisations like Rythu Cooli Sangham and Singareni Karmika Samkhya (Singareni coal miners federation) born and grew both in numbers and militant struggles. Again, it was during this time that a regional bourgeois party, Telugu Desam Party, evolved to challenge the three-decade old entrenched Congress rule and in the process gave a call to Radicals to join him. Of course, Radicals recognised the class nature of the new party and continued their struggle and the TDP rule indulged in most brutal repression during 1985-89.

There were other concurrent developments. While the document Road to Revolution paved the way for this spectacular success after the setbacks of Naxalbari and Srikakulam, there was another document that blazed the trail for the formation of guerilla zones in the favourable terrains. The document prepared by Kondapalli Seetaramaiah came out in 1982, and began to be implemented by the committee led by Koteswara Rao. In fact, the idea of forming guerilla zones was there for quite some time and it was within two years of Karimnagar - Adilabad peasant upsurge that revolutionaries crossed the Godavari to enter Gadchiroli forests of Maharashtra. After three years of work as squads of political education, understanding people, learning their language, working as teachers and paramedics in the forests, the revolutionaries gained confidence of Adivasis and developed a staunch mass base among them. The efforts continued for the next three decades steadfastly and the current scenario of Dandakaranya – alternative model of development under Revolutionary Peoples' Committees (Janatana Sarkar), peoples' militia and guerilla zones – is the culmination of the sacrifices and untiring work of thousands of comrades, of whom Koteswara Rao was one. Not only he guided the movement as part of leadership, but also spent about ten years in Dandakaranya, after he left Andhra Pradesh in the second half of the 1980s.

The revolutionary movement spread to adjoining areas of Orissa, Jharkhand, Bihar and West Bengal and Koteswara Rao was naturally given the responsibilities of this expansion. Thus he came to West Bengal in the mid-1990s and continued there till his death. The Jangalmahal struggles which he led were recognised as the second coming of Naxalbari by many observers. While the people's anger against the revisionist and anti-people autocratic regime of the Left Front led to a number of struggles in West Bengal, it was the Peoples War and later, Maoist party, that stood in the forefront to lead the masses. Koteswara Rao's expertise in mass movements and militancy made the movements formidable and the mainstream media turned him into an icon. Even though this image had its flip side, it also brought the Maoist politics into the main focus and Koteswara Rao's daredevil, sensational attempts played a part in this. The title of a sensational story – 'Hello, this is Kishenji' – in one of the popular dailies speaks volumes about this period.

However, despite anxieties of a lot of friends and well wishers about his safety during this brazen openness, Koteswara Rao survived this period and when he stopped giving interviews and meeting presspersons for well over six months, he was caught and killed in the most brutal way.

❖ ❖ ❖

My association with him is so extensive and intimate that I knew him for over thirty years, used to treat him as my elder brother and he reciprocated. Indeed his own younger brother is my namesake. I might have seen him in Varavara Rao's house in Hanumakonda (part of Warangal), which he used to frequent during 1974-75. Or, else it might be in Hyderabad at the first conference of Radical Students' Union during February 22-23, 1975. But I vividly remember the meetings he organised during the three months between the conference and the proclamation of Emergency on June 26, 1975. The meetings were held at several places in Karimnagar district and I was entrusted to set up a bookshop at the meetings. Koti and I became close in those days and it blossomed during the post-Emergency days. During the early 1980s I had a great opportunity to work with him for a couple of years. Though I was unable to meet him in person after 1986, either through friends or through correspondence we were enquiring about each other.

Though he was never away from my thoughts, he suddenly barged into me sometime in 2009 through a midnight phone call. In fact I was feeling very anxious about his safety for the previous one or two years when he was making news, in the wake of Nandigram, Singur, Lalgarh and Jangalmahal. With a sense of alarm, I was wondering why he was so careless to talk to press and giving his contact numbers. When he called me I poured out all my anxiety and he coolly brushed it aside. He said nobody would be able to touch him as long as he was in Jangalmahal. Though it was twenty five long years since we met each other, the conversation flowed as if we were meeting on a daily basis. The conversation continued for a couple of times more and he started sending me his own poems and articles as well as translations of Bengali writings.

Of course, this sense of intimacy with him is not an individual affair. I have seen him treating thousands of comrades in the same manner. Indeed he had a wonderful skill to turn every acquaintance into friendship, every friendship into intimate affection and turn all relationships into part of revolutionary activity. I joined Osmania University for my MA (Economics) in August 1982 and within a few days he sent a word to me to meet him. At that time he was the secretary of the State Committee of the CPI (ML) (Peoples War) and he used to make use of several people as his messengers or on errands besides his two or three official couriers. He included me in that long list and for the next couple of years he occupied a major portion of my life. The party building and mobilisation and consolidation of the mass organisations were at their peak at that time and hence he had to work with so many hands and meet many people. He had to meet people coming from all the regions in the state as well as the early squads that began implementing the newly released Guerilla Zone Perspective. He also used to coordinate different organs, journals and publications brought out by the party and mass organisations at that time. Undertaking these multifarious activities, he used to take the help of several people for smooth functioning of everything. He made me do so many things at that time, but since he made several other people also to do many things, I think in retrospective that it was not our abilities that counted, but it was his organisational capability to use all kinds of people to get all kinds of things done. While getting things done with others, he never coerced or pushed or bulldozed them. He never acted like a headmaster or taskmaster, but allowed people to realise their latent strengths and asked them to increase their creativity and initiative. In the process many people did those things they never dreamt of.

He used to send a two-line letter to inform the RV – it was usual in those days to shorten every word and this was a short form of rendezvous. Quite often that used to be an Irani hotel, ubiquitous in Hyderabad. We used to meet there, have a cup of tea before coming out and hopping into an auto. Till the auto reaches the next destination, half an hour or a little more, he used to tell what he needed, he used to ask the questions he wanted, seek information, give and take letters, to finally drop me on the road. If I was in a bad mood and met him in melancholy, that would be erased and I would return rejuvenated. Every meeting used to be great and did not leave me without astonishment at his efficiency in doing things. Sometimes the RV would be a bus stop or a friend's house or even a new acquaintance. His knack of turning everything for revolutionary activity was amazing.

His interest in books and literature in general was stupendous. We visited a number of book stores in Hyderabad and generally his eye used to be on the books on weapons, maps, and military affairs. In fact the Indian revolutionary movement at that time did not fully enter the military orientation, besides small squad activities. The first ever ambush from the Naxalites' side would take place five years later, even then he used to read and think a lot about it. He not only read those books, but wanted to introduce them to non-English knowing comrades and got them translated into Telugu. He was not only a voracious reader but also himself a man of letters. He was involved in and fond of publishing, writing, translation, and editing. He was also very particular about documenting everything. He used to say that each and every activity in the mass upsurge has to be recorded, a thorough study of society should be undertaken, and everything should be presented in a systematic way with statistics and facts. More than a dozen books and booklets published between *Nagetichaallalo* on Karimnagar - Adilabad Struggles in 1981 to a number of booklets and interviews on Lalgarh in 2009, he continued that tradition of recording. He wrote quite a few poems and cherished to be recognised as a poet. Even his letters used to be very poetic. He always kept open his windows for learning and learnt so many new things as well as new languages in his life.

Spending time with him always resulted in understanding a number of things from minute personal behaviour to large military and theoretical aspects. Sometimes he used to openly explain and yet other times, one would learn from his example. Be as firm as possible on the issue, but be as caring and accommodative as needed was his dictum in inter personal relationships.

He had a wonderful understanding of how to deal with people, how to explore their creativity and capabilities. I think that's why he became a good organiser, leader, handholder and guide throughout. He stood as an inspiration and guiding force for thousands of people joining revolution or helping revolution in whatever way they could. He revived the optimistic spirit in hundreds of disillusioned comrades on the verge of leaving with his powerful arguments and unfathomable affection.

To sum up, Koteswara Rao's revolutionary political work for about four decades covered almost all sections of people – students, youth, agricultural labourers and small peasants, dalits, adivasis, women, writers, cultural activists, media, propaganda work, party organisation, mass movements, party's financial affairs, military affairs, procurement of arms, nationality movements, international relations, inter-personal relations... in one word, he made his presence felt in almost all the spheres and areas required for Indian revolution. He began his journey in Peddapalli and Jagityal, continued in Karimnagar and Adilabad districts to spread all over Andhra Pradesh. From there he crossed the Godavari, entered Bastar and expanded to Abujmarh. His journey continued to Jharkhand, West Bengal and to North-East. Perhaps there may be very few Indian revolutionaries who walked this thousands of miles of long march on their own feet. The only comparable sojourn may be that of Che Guevara's travels in Latin America. Thus the forty years of his revolutionary life in various spheres, various levels and in various places symbolise the totality and comprehension of the great and complex Indian revolution. He had multi-dimensional expertise. He was a thinker at various levels and a practitioner in multifarious spheres. He was a complete man. He was the new human being created by the Indian revolution.

❖ ❖ ❖